# TEACHING AND LEARNING WITH

by
ALLAN MARTIN
Department of Learning Resources
St. Andrew's College of Education
Glasgow



with contributions from:

MARIE BUCKLAND
MARIANNE HISLOP
ELIZABETH LECKIE
DEREK RADBURN
MARY SCOTT
JANICE STAINES
MARIA SHIELDS
JOAN WILSON

CROOM HELM
London & Sydney

Croom Helm Ltd, Provident House, Burrell Row,
Beckenham, Kent BR3 1AT
Croom Helm Australia Pty Ltd, Suite 4, 6th Floor,
64-76 Kippax Street, Surry Hills, NSW 2010, Australia

British Library Cataloguing in Publication Data
Martin, Allan
Teaching and learning with LOGO.
1. Education – Data processing 2. LOGO
(Computer program language)
I. Title
370'.28'5404 LB1028.43

ISBN 0-7099-3572-2



Printed and bound in Great Britain by
Biddles Ltd, Guildford and King's Lynn

CONTENTS

Contents

Contents

Contents

FIGURES

Figures

# PREFACE

LOGO has long been talked about as an ideal computer language for educational purposes. But so long as LOGO was unavailable for the microcomputers usually encountered in schools, such talk was largely speculation, or descriptions of the work of a few lucky pioneers. The situation is now different, for LOGO is now available for all the micros which are likely to be found in schools of whatever level. With this availability has come an outpouring of LOGO tutorials to satisfy an initial demand to learn LOGO itself.

This volume is aimed at a point beyond this initial level of interest, or perhaps somewhere alongside it. The authors are concerned, as educational practitioners, with examining the ways in which LOGO can be incorporated into the teaching/learning process. To do this effectively, it is clearly necessary to look at the characteristics of LOGO itself. However, this book is not intended as a comprehensive LOGO tutorial. Rather, it is a survey of the opportunities which LOGO can offer, with accounts of how some individuals have taken them up. Aiming a book at an audience whose familiarity with LOGO may vary from complete ignorance to expert programming competence is not an easy task. The tendency here has been towards satisfying the reader whose knowledge of LOGO is scanty, and therefore we crave the indulgence of those whose LOGO expertise makes some passages in the book seem condescending.

The volume has been divided up on the basis of the various facilities which LOGO offers. We have concerned ourselves with the way in which each of the LOGO facilities we look at is being or could be made use of in the classroom. Included among more general considerations are some case studies: accounts of specific applications. These will show how particular individuals have carried out their own programmes of teaching with LOGO, varying the style and the content to their own situations.

At present there is inevitably a concentration upon turtle graphics and the use of floor turtles; this reflects the situation of current classroom practice. However, we have attempted to show the full range of what LOGO can offer at present, including areas of development which are only just beginning to open up (such as control, music and language).

If some readers feel that there are not enough "things to do in your classroom" (with suggested lesson plans), we would answer that any resource for teaching will be used by a teacher in his/her own way, utilising his/her own professional skills. LOGO is a flexible resource for teaching and learning, and its use should be thought about and prepared for in the same way as the use of any other resource. This approach to teaching is, thankfully, built into our educational traditions and is one of the guarantees of the quality of teaching in our schools.

There is a tendency sometimes visible to regard computers in the classroom as "teaching machines" which will take over from the teacher the management of a child's learning. This misconception has arisen from the spread of images of the education of the future which pay little attention to the actualities of the learning process, and ideas that computers will achieve what the "teaching machines" of the 1960s failed to do. Some software producers have been sufficiently taken in by the picture to release programs which only prove that computers, if used as mechanistic presenters of drill-and-practice material, will achieve as litle as those machines of the 1960s. In fact, computers cannot replace teachers, and, like other computer-based facilities, LOGO cannot be used as a teacher-substitute. Like other good educational materials, its success depends on teacher involvement. This does not imply that the teacher need be a LOGO or a computer expert; but it does mean that the teacher should be aware of the benefits which can be derived from effective classroom use of LOGO, and able to plan the use of it accordingly.

Any good book should have solid ends which hold it in place. The bulk of this book looks at the various facilities which LOGO offers the teacher. At the beginning are three chapters of more general discussion about the background of LOGO and about some of the practical directions of thinking which a teacher contemplating LOGO-use might consider. Towards the end, there is some speculation on where LOGO may go in the future, and the implications for education of possible developments. This speculation is not based on fantasy, but on lines of research currently under way on both sides of the Atlantic. There is also a collection of LOGO resources. Some comments are given; I do not however necessarily expect readers to share my opinions, but hope that the details supplied will make obtaining them a more straightforward matter than might otherwise be the case.

Allan Martin

Glasgow, April 1985

ACKNOWLEDGEMENTS

This book has been shaped and nourished by contact with LOGO-users of all ages and persuasions in many places, too numerous to mention. Without this participation in the "LOGO community", it would not have been possible. Particular mention is due to Ken Johnson at Edinburgh University, who gave me my first taste of LOGO, Richard Baggaley at Croom Helm, who kept my nose to the grindstone, Annie Vaz, for help with the graphics, and my wife Vivien, who helped to make it happen in innumerable ways, some very practical, and some more intangible but very very real.

## NOTE

### a] Listings

There are now many LOGOs available, for a wide range of microcomputers. There are LOGO dialects, but these do not differ to the extent that BASICs do, with the result that LOGO procedures in one dialect are translatable without too much difficulty to another. The LOGO implementation used for most procedure listings in this book, unless otherwise stated, is Logotron (LCSI) LOGO for the BBC Microcomputer.

### b] BBC Microcomputer

Any mention of the "BBC Microcomputer" or "BBC Micro" refers to the British Broadcasting Corporation Microcomputer, Model B (32K), manufactured by Acorn Computers.

### c] Upper or Lower Case ?

The subject of this book was originally written as "Logo", and this presentation is still widely used. However, the form "LOGO" has increased in use, particularly in Europe, possibly to avoid confusion with other current meanings of the word "logo" (e.g. in advertising). The latter form is largely adhered to in this book, except in some names of implementations or books. The choice of form should not be seen as an important issue; both forms refer to the same thing, and that is what is important.

Chapter 1

# ABOUT LOGO: SOME BACKGROUND

## WHAT IS LOGO ?

LOGO is one of a number of computer languages to have been developed in the field of Artificial Intelligence. Researchers in Artificial Intelligence (A.I. for short) attempt to understand human thinking processes and behaviour patterns (such as language or vision) by trying to produce computer-based simulations of them. By examining the way in which the simulation works (i.e. the way in which its program is constructed) it is hoped that some understanding of the functioning of the human mind will be gained. The idea behind this is that the mind must go through the same sort of procedures to achieve its goals as the computer program. As one of the major A.I. textbooks puts it,

> Artificial Intelligence is the study of ideas which enable computers to do the things that make people seem intelligent. (1)

Workers in the field of A.I. would not claim that they are creating "computer brains", for they are very much aware of the enormous difference in complexity between the already-complicated programs they use to achieve what may seem to us simple effects, such as recognising shapes, and what would be required to reproduce many "ordinary" human qualities. Language, for instance, we take for granted as an obvious and natural attribute of humans; but attempts to program computers to understand ordinary language as used in our everyday lives have shown just how complex is the intellectual structure underlying the use of even the simplest language.

Researchers in Artificial Intelligence have

had to generate their own computer languages to make the task of simulating the mind as straightforward as possible. The most well-known of these languages is LISP, which was developed in the late 1950's. The name indicates that it is a LISt Processing language; lists of items, enclosed in parentheses, are "evaluated" by a computer running LISP. Processing of lists was an extremely important development brought to computing by LISP; hitherto, computer languages could only deal happily with numeric data. Since lists can be parts of other lists, LISP programs can often be difficult to follow, since they may involve several levels of embedding of lists within lists, indicated by many sets of parentheses. (Some books on Artificial Intelligence and LISP are indicated in Chapter 16, Section A.)

LOGO was developed at the Massachusetts Institute of Technology in the late 1960's as part of a research project to create a language for the teaching of mathematical ideas to children through computer programming. It was intended to be easy to learn, easy to use, easy to read, but also powerful, and therefore able to cope with complex activities. It was soon realised, however, that the implications of LOGO extended far beyond the realms of the mathematical. LOGO was evolved by a team including Wallace Feurzeig (who suggested the name LOGO), Cynthia Solomon and the man who is now the most well-known LOGO figure, Seymour Papert.

Throughout the 1970's research work was carried out with LOGO, mainly in the U.S.A. and Scotland (the latter based at Edinburgh University). Much of this research has been concerned with the use of LOGO in teaching mathematics, but its value in other learning areas has also been indicated. Some of the research will be surveyed later in this chapter.

## HOW DOES LOGO WORK ?

LOGO programs are built up through the use of <u>procedures.</u> Procedures are lists of instructions. A series of LOGO commands (known as "primitives") can be used to form a simple procedure. Simple procedures can themselves be used as single commands in more complex procedures. A computer program in LOGO is just a collection of procedures which achieve a particular objective. The word TO is used when creating ("defining") procedures; this is to emphasise the way we can think of procedures as being like verbs. Thus, when we have defined the procedure ZZZ, our LOGO system knows how to ZZZ, and we can get it to ZZZ just by telling it to. A procedure is "called" merely by using its name: thus the command ZZZ will make the computer carry out the instructions making up the procedure ZZZ.

As an example, here are three procedures, SPACE, WAIT and TITLE.

```
TO SPACE
     CT
     REPEAT 10 [PRINT[]]
     END
```

The procedure SPACE clears the monitor (or TV) screen, using the LOGO primitive CT (short for CLEARTEXT). It then prints 10 empty lines (so that the first words printed appear some way down from the top of the screen). Square brackets are used in LOGO to contain lists. The line

```
REPEAT 10 [PRINT[]]
```

tells the computer to perform ten times the list of instructions following, i.e. PRINT []. PRINT [] tells the computer to print an empty list (there's nothing between the square brackets), and is LOGO's way of producing an empty line. END simply indicates the end of a procedure.

In some LOGOs WAIT is a primitive which produces an apparent pause in the computer's activities. Usually the input units are in 60ths of a second; thus WAIT 60 gives a pause of one second. For LOGOs without a WAIT primitive (or one which does the same job), a WAIT procedure can be writen as follows:

```
TO WAIT  :TIME
     REPEAT :TIME * 1000 []
     END
```

The word :TIME on the top line tells the computer that the procedure WAIT needs an "input". Whatever is supplied as input will be used in the next line

```
REPEAT :TIME * 1000 []
```

which in effect tells the computer to do nothing a very large number of times! Whatever is in the square brackets is to be repeated :TIME multiplied by 1000 times; in this case there is nothing at

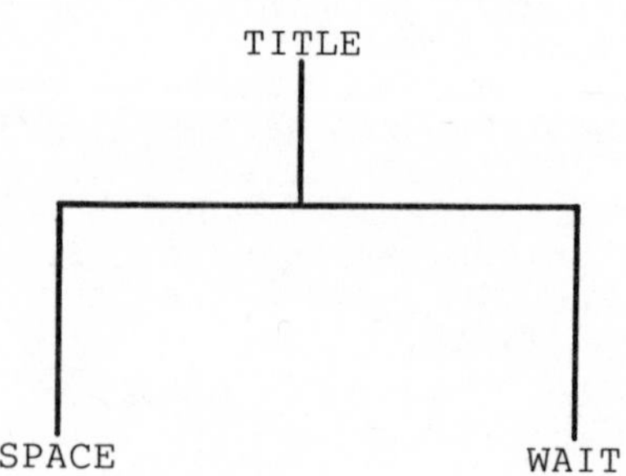


Figure 1.1. Procedure-calls for TITLE

all between the square brackets, but it will take the computer a fraction of a second to discover that. When that fraction is multiplied by a thousand a short pause is produced in the running of the program. The number which is supplied as an input to this procedure determines the length of the pause. WAIT 10 will give a short pause, WAIT 1000 a much longer one.

Having been defined, SPACE and WAIT can now themselves be used as commands in the procedure TITLE.

```
TO TITLE
     SPACE
     PRINT [WELCOME TO LOGO]
     WAIT 120
     END
```

The first line in the procedure TITLE calls the procedure SPACE; this will clear the screen and, by printing 10 empty lines, move the cursor about half way down the screen. The message WELCOME TO LOGO appears on the screen and there is then a pause of 2 seconds.

TITLE may then itself be used as a single command in a larger program. A LOGO program can in fact be thought of as a pyramid of procedures, each one fairly short and thus easy to understand and to modify if necessary. The relationship of the three procedures described above can be shown in a simple structure-diagram. This diagram, shown in Figure 1.1, indicates which procedures are called by others. It shows graphically how procedures can be seen as the building-bricks out of which LOGO programs are made. There is therefore a (rather tenuous) connection between LOGO and LEGO !

LOGO programs can distinguish between two sorts of "data objects". These are words and lists (i.e. collections of words). Either of these types can be accepted by LOGO as a single item.

LOGOTHING
rabbits
Bongo-Drums
28.November.1944

are examples of words ; in fact any set of characters excluding spaces is acceptable as a LOGO word. Numbers are a special sort of word in LOGO; they can be treated just like other characters; or calculations can be performed with them.

381
247.89
0.0638

are examples of numbers; LOGO is not limited to dealing only with whole numbers.

Lists are the most powerful data objects which LOGO deals with. LOGO lists are always surrounded by square brackets. This can create some confusion with microcomputers which do not have a square bracket symbol on the keyboard; a sticker on the relevant keys however overcomes this.

```
[LOGOTHING rabbits Bongo-Drums]
[CANNIBAL CHOCOLATE RUM JUMBO]
[PRINT [Hello LOGO fans !!]]
[[Seymour Papert] [LOGO guru]]
[28 November 1944]
```

are all examples of lists. Notice that lists can contain other lists. LOGO can handle lists containing several layers of such "nested" lists, and has a range of commands which enable the user to examine and process them. The ability to manipulate lists easily is one of LOGO's most powerful features, and makes LOGO useful in many areas beyond the mathematical.

## LOGO AND THINKING

What makes LOGO different from most other computer

languages is that it can be seen as more than just a computer language. Indeed, proponents of LOGO argue that LOGO programming can be seen as a direct analogy of the thinking process itself. Seymour Papert, one of the inventors of LOGO, was deeply influenced by the theories of the Swiss psychologist Jean Piaget (a name familiar to every trainee teacher of the last two decades). For Piaget, the development of the child's mental capacities could be conceived as a process whereby simple "thought-structures" are generated and tested in the course of the child's exploration of his environment; then, later, at the appropriate stage of maturity, these simple thought-structures are combined with other simple structures to form a more complex or more abstract thought-structure, which itself can form a basis for further growth of the intellect. Intellectual growth thus takes place through the combining of progressively more complex ideas.

The similarity between the building up of LOGO programs and the building up of thought-structures is clear. The evolution of a LOGO program by developing and testing simple procedures, then incorporating them in more complicated ones can to some extent parallel the process of thinking. For Papert, this similarity between LOGO-work and "thought-work" is what makes LOGO not just a programming language but a "tool to think with".

The parallelism between LOGO activity and thinking is a crucial element in the case for LOGO's relevance to education. In developing his powers of thinking, the child builds up structures of thought by exploration of the world around him. Faced with a new problem or situation, existing mental structures are combined to produce a new insight, which can then be used on future occasions, and transferred to other situations. Exploration and discovery are thus in the Piagetian view seen as key elements in learning. They also lie at the heart of the LOGO learning experience. The LOGO-user can explore situations and think out problems by developing LOGO programs from procedures constructed by himself.

Learning, at any level, proceeds by a process of trial and error. Inadequately practised or formulated techniques or ideas will not achieve the anticipated results. Teachers must react to such transitional products of learning in a way which will help learning to proceed. Those whose style of teaching focuses upon the rote learning of formulae or exemplars may condemn unexpected or "incorrect" responses as reprehensible evidence of failure to learn, due to laziness, lack of concentration, low intelligence, unsuitability for the subject, or whatever. Production of unexpected responses may result in punishments such as extra homework, withdrawal of privileges, "demotion" to a "lower" group, or public humiliation, in the hope that such measures of "negative reinforcement" will lead ultimately to successful learning. Other teachers adopt a different approach to unexpected responses, seeing them as the results of partial understanding of new ideas or as testing of stuations in which the new ideas are appropriate. In both these cases, the unexpected response is seen as a positive step in the right direction, and the learner is encouraged to think about why the unexpected result occurred. Unexpected results are therefore seen as useful stages in the learning process.

LOGO was designed with the latter style of learning in mind. Inelegantly formed, incomplete, or unintended designs will lead to "debugging", that is, careful examination of each procedure to see what its contribution to the whole design is, and modification of those considered flawed. This debugging process is considered by proponents of LOGO to be an essential part of the learning process, by which conceptual structures are tested and altered until found acceptable. "Bugs" are not seen as "wrong answers" but as unexpected outcomes which should stimulate thinking and lead to the mastery of ideas that comes from an understanding of how to use them successfully.

Exploration of an area of knowledge or technique inevitably involves setting off down tracks which turn out to have dead ends, and using objects and materials whose properties are little known and unpredictable. Seeing where the tracks go, and trying out the materials all add to the explorer's knowledge and understanding. This is how the developers of LOGO hoped that the facilities it offered would be used, and they designed the language accordingly.

## WHAT FACILITIES DOES LOGO OFFER ?

Different sets of LOGO facilities can place the user in different "micro-worlds" which can become environments for exploration and discovery, and thus environments for learning. Some of these micro-worlds are already well-known to LOGO-users, the "turtle world" of plane geometry undoubtedly being the most familiar. Some have been explored, but await fuller development: for instance, the "music world" available on the better implementations of LOGO; the "dynaturtle world" of movement in outer space; database possibilities; robotics and control possibilities; facilities for poetry and creative writing. Many other micro-worlds have yet to be devised.

The most well-known feature which LOGO offers at present is "Turtle Graphics", a system of constructing designs or pictures by giving instructions to a drawing head, the "turtle". The turtle is usually represented on the screen by a small triangle or even a turtle shape, but it is also possible to use a "floor turtle", a robot drawing device which will move around on a large sheet of paper. The drawings produced permit the exploration of shapes and their relationships as well as often being compelling creative works. Turtle graphics are considered in more detail in Chapter 6.

Some LOGO implementations offer a music facility. A number of bars may be constructed; these may then be used in building phrases and melodies, which can then be used in various combinations to make up longer pieces. A wide range of pitches and durations can be chosen, so the possibilities for creating individual bars and then putting them together can be almost limitless. The potentiality for exploring rhythmic, melodic and harmonic patterns in music by the exercise of building it from simple components can be imagined. LOGO music is considered in more detail in chapters 9 and 10.

The same programming structure may be applied to text-handling. LOGO's ability to rearrange and manipulate lists opens many interesting possibilities. For instances, sentences can be created by picking words at random from lists. Because items in lists can be either words or lists of varying length, considerable variation in the sentences produced is possible. Similar techniques can be used to produce poetry or to generate creative writing suggestions. These and further possibilities are discussed in Chapter 12.

Turtle graphics, music and text-processing

are only three of the facilities offered by LOGO; others, such as arithmetic, may be treated in the same way. An area still under development is that of controlling robots and other equipment using LOGO type commands - the floor turtle is one example of this facility. This aspect of LOGO is considered in chapters 4 and 11. Music and graphics facilities are constantly being improved: among the facilities some LOGOs now provide are multiple turtles which may be moved simultaneously, "sprites", which are shapes which can be custom-built then moved as units around the screen, and multi-channel sound under LOGO control.

## LOGO AND SCHOOLS

LOGO is often suggested as "the ideal computer language for children"; and most of the current interest in it comes from educational practitioners. What does LOGO offer schools in particular ?

The main justification for LOGO-use in schools arises from the nature of the LOGO learning experience. Exploration and discovery are generally accepted as essential parts of the experience which schools can offer. LOGO is ideally suited therefore to contribute to the way in which learning happens in schools. It will assist in the development of the child's "thinking skills" by making him actively react mentally to learning situations. LOGO activity can in this way be claimed to have across-the-board educational relevance.

LOGO also offers a ready avenue into familiarisation with and general use of the computer. It is easy to use and to understand, and it makes available a wide range of facilities. In this way the nature of computers and something of their meaning for life in general can be appreciated. In *Mindstorms* and in various addresses since its appearance, Seymour Papert has expressed his particular interest in the way in which computers and computational ideas have become part of Western culture, and the effect this will have on styles of thinking and of learning. For Papert, this "computer culture" has a tremendous liberating potential, and should therefore be diffused as widely as possible. He believes that the use of computers will ultimately make institutionalised educational systems obsolete as learning becomes the prerogative of the individual (with his/her computer). Whilst not all educators would go all the way with Papert in this prediction, what cannot easily be denied is that the computer, and the ideas and techniques surrounding it, have become new and important parts of our day-to-day environment. A familiarity with them has therefore become an essential part of our education.

LOGO offers an introduction to computer programming which is highly structured and encourages "top-down" programming, i.e. the careful construction of programs through the analysis and breakdown of the problem to be solved or goal to be achieved. Learning LOGO thus develops good thinking styles alongside good programming habits. Those who proceed to further computer-use at secondary school or later in life will then be able to bring "good problem-solving practice" to such activity right from the start.

The importance of "debugging" in learning has been mentioned above. One of the great values of LOGO is that it enables unexpected outcomes ("errors" or "mistakes" would not be an appropriate way of referring to them) to be capitalised upon as sources of constructive learning. The question 'Why was this unexpected outcome produced?' is far more positive than 'Why did you make this mistake?'. It enables the analysis of the outcome to become a quest for understanding ('Why was it like this?') rather than a post-mortem on failure ('Where did I go wrong?'). There is a further benefit from LOGO work here, for this sort of activity encourages the pupil to develop a constructive attitude to things that turn out unexpectedly, to seek understanding instead of giving up because "it doesn't work".

It is a common observation of those who have used LOGO in the classroom, that LOGO is enjoyable. The fact that learning is enjoyable is not trivial, for enjoyment in learning is a source of motivation and of concentration. Children with very short concentration spans have been observed to concentrate for noticeably longer periods than normal when using LOGO. It may be that this occurs because children using LOGO feel that they are in control, and in control of something which they understand.

LOGO is most effectively used with groups,

and when so used enables the learning benefits of group activity to be obtained. Discussion and debate is a normal accompaniment of LOGO work as group members contribute ideas and suggestions, and try to understand those of others. Oral fluency and coherence skills are developed as they seek to explain their views or examine those of others. Group members learn from and teach their colleagues, and develop a regard for each other as resources of information and technique, rather than looking always to the teacher. Finally, they gain practice in being part of a team, in co-operating with others to achieve a common goal, in accepting compromise solutions to which more han one have contributed, and in the diverse and complex skills of getting on with other people.

Because of the range of "microworlds" which it can support, LOGO can be used to allow children to explore various and different elements of the curriculum, while maintaining a unity of good thinking practice. Mathematics is an obvious example, however there are also clear possibilities in art, in music, in language and in science. The same LOGO structure of building up simple patterns into more complex ones can be used for instance in drawing pictures, in creating stories, or in making music, all at the computer. Thus through LOGO the use of the computer is fully integrated into the curriculum, and does not remain a freakish extra. It can be used in a style which encourages learning, to approach things worthy to be learned.

It should not be thought that all of these benefits are obtainable solely through LOGO. Many classroom activities can offer some of them. Any good groupwork will gain the benefits of the group situation. Open-ended simulations of the adventure game type will facilitate exploratory learning. Structured programming technique can be taught through most languages available on school microcomputers. To be most effective, LOGO should be used alongside other activities which confer similar benefits, so that as much as possible of a child's educational experience tends towards a creative and constructive learning style.

## RESEARCH ON LOGO

Because early versions of LOGO could only run on fairly large computers, testing its efficacy as a learning medium for children involved bringing small numbers of children into the computer laboratories. It was not until the late 1970's that serious attempts to evaluate LOGO in actual classrooms took place.

The first large-scale LOGO evaluation began in 1977 at Lincoln School in the Brookline, Massachusetts school district, fairly close to M.I.T. itself.(2) The first phase, with 50 children, was based in the computer laboratory; however a second phase took the computers into two of the classrooms. Teaching was nondirective, the idea being to create a pupil-directed LOGO learning environment. Indeed, the teachers themselves were beginners to LOGO; the experts were the children who had taken part in the first phase, and what was claimed as the first "LOGO culture" was observed, with children contributing to and drawing from a pool of LOGO knowledge and ideas. The reports of the Brookline Project contain a wealth of detail, and in particular a series of sensitive case studies of children thinking with LOGO. The researchers were enthusiastic about what was achieved, but the very open-ended learning situations in which LOGO was used made it difficult for any objective measure of success to be taken. A number of useful conclusions were drawn, however. Children enjoyed using LOGO, and all achieved success in it, despite variations of ability in other school activities. There was a high level of pupil interaction, with children discussing problems, exchanging ideas and routines, and teaching each other new techniques. However, this did not mean that the teacher could stand back and observe, for the teacher's role was found to be more demanding than it would have been in more traditonal teaching. The teacher had to act as a discreet observer and monitor of each child's progress, but ready to act as a consultant or stimulator when necessary, to suggest ways out of difficulties, set attainable goals, hint at new developments of existing work, or to demonstrate new commands or skills. At the same time as focusing on individuals, she had also to take in the whole classroom situation. Teaching with LOGO activities involved, that is, the sorts of skills involved in individual- or group-based child-centred learning styles.

An even more intensive experiment began soon afterwards at the Lamplighter School in Dallas,

Texas.(3) The school itself was a private one, with many pupils the children of executives of the Texas Instruments company: support by the company enabled a large number of Texas Instruments microcomputers equipped with a newly written version of LOGO to be placed in the school. Using LOGO proved a great success, since the LOGO learning style fitted in precisely with the type of learning environment already built up in the school. However, the teachers at the school saw LOGO as a particularly good example of the sort of activity which a "progressive" school could offer.

Research on LOGO at Edinburgh University's Department of Artificial Intelligence, with primary and lower secondary school pupils and trainee teachers, began in the early 1970's.(4) The Edinburgh work, by Jim Howe and his colleagues, followed however a more tightly structured pattern, since it was felt that LOGO might be a valuable addition to normal primary and secondary school mathematics curricula. Objective testing to measure learning outcomes has been undertaken, and conclusions presented that LOGO could be useful in learning mathematical concepts. A particularly noticeable finding was that improvements by girls were greater than those by boys.

The attempt to objectively test LOGO in use in schools was also undertaken by researchers (principally Roy Pea and Midian Kurland) from Bank Street College of Education in New York in the early 1980's.(5) They concentrated on looking at whether LOGO experience enhances general thinking skills such as problem-solving or planning. Unfortunately, such skills are easier to talk about than to test, because there is little agreement on what exactly they involve, in cognitive terms, and therefore how they can be measured. The Bank Street researchers chose a number of tasks which seemed to them appropriate, and compared the progress of LOGO-using and non-LOGO-using groups of children. They concluded that there was little conclusive evidence that LOGO particularly enhanced general thinking skills.

The work of Pea and Kurland has aroused a great deal of controversy among LOGO enthusiasts, including much hostility. Some argue that LOGO should not be regarded as generally "good for the brain" until this has been proved, but can still be of value in contributing to specific parts of the mathematics curriculum and possibly some other subject areas. Others claim that the methods used by the Bank Street researchers were not adequate to test the benefits of LOGO: they did not allow the children sufficient time with LOGO to develop general skills, and the almost uninvolved role of the teacher in their LOGO classrooms is neither a typical nor a fair one. In a recent summary of the research into the "transfer problem" (i.e. whether skills learned in LOGO work can be transferred to other areas of activity), Erik de Corte of the University of Leuven, Belgium, remarks:

> At present there is no convincing evidence that learning to program results in the acquisition of generalizable and transferable conceptual knowledge and thinking methods. ... On the other hand the transfer hypothesis can be retained for further study in more systematic and better designed experiments.(6)

The disputes surrounding the Bank Street research are only partly about the extent to which LOGO is beneficial. They are also symptomatic of a deeper division over how the effects of education can be assessed. Seymour Papert and his supporters argue that because "objective" educational researchers seek out what can be measured, so that statistical processes can be applied, they are obliged in doing this to ignore all that cannot easily be measured. And it is in this latter area that the real fruits of education lie. The Brookline and Lamplighter studies therefore concentrate on "interpretive" rather than objective, qualitative rather than quantitative, assessment. They point to happiness, confidence, interactiveness, and the gut feelings of teachers as proof of the power of LOGO for good.

The difference between "objective" and "interpretive" approaches to research is a rift which will continue to haunt LOGO work, just as it haunts all research in education and the social sciences. But the fact that so much LOGO research is now going on, using both styles, is evidence that LOGO is seen as important enough to study in detail. And as the amount of evidence grows, a clear picture may eventually emerge.

There is now a considerable amount of

research into LOGO going on, varying widely in scale and in style, in many parts of the world. In the U.K., probably the most exciting LOGO investigations currently taking place are those under the aegis of the Walsall LOGO Project. A wide variety of work using floor and screen turtles, language and music has been pursued in a number of primary schools. More details of the Walsall LOGO Project are given in the next section. Two research projects which have focused on mathematical aspects of LOGO are the Chiltern LOGO Project, based at The Advisory Centre for Computer-Based Education in Hatfield, and the LOGO Maths Project, based in the Institute of Education at London University.(7) However, many other LOGO evaluations are taking place throughout the country, in both primary and secondary schools. These vary from goverment funded projects, to university- and college-based research, to the careful observations of many individual teachers throughout the country. Some of this work is reflected in the case studies in this volume. Research also goes on in many parts of the world as LOGO gains ground (and LOGOs appear in languages other than English): in most countries of Western Europe, in several South American countries, in Canada, Australia, Israel, and Senegal in Africa. Responses so far are little more than impressions; proving that LOGO is "good to think with" will be very difficult indeed, but the feeling of practising teachers that they have come across what might be a valuable teaching tool is something which should not be ignored. We can look forward to more substantive comments emerging from these evaluations of LOGO over the next two or three years.

## LOGO IN WALSALL

The Walsall LOGO Project was set up early in 1983 by the local education authority in Walsall, which lies in the heart of the urban and industrial sprawl to the north of Birmingham in the English West Midlands.(8) Two teachers, Linda Spear and Julian Pixton, were released from their primary classrooms to co-ordinate the work. From the beginning, the focus of the Project's activity was not upon LOGO as a vehicle of mathematics teaching, but as a stimulus to learning in many areas, of which the most important was that of language experience.

The Project's work has been wherever possible firmly school-based, with the staffs of the six project schools being fully involved in the LOGO activities. The first work was with Bigtrak and floor turtles; soon, however, a turtle graphics chip for the BBC microcomputer, prepared by one of the Project leaders, was introduced. Later, Atari computers with Atari LOGO (one of the best implementatons available) were also supplied to the schools, and when a full LOGO implementation for the BBC microcomputer was at last available, it was issued too. The local Teachers' Centre became the locale for in-service work: regular workshops are held to allow teachers to experience the sort of activities taking place in the project schools. Visits by teachers to other schools were facilitated by the education authority. The production of resource materials has also been an important part of the work; in this way the experiences of teachers are capitalised upon and can become the stimulus for new activities.

The project leaders realised that introducing LOGO is not just a matter of organisation and minor curricular adjustment. According to Linda Spear,

> It was felt that it was insufficient to offer advice solely about classroom management and dissemination of LOGO in school. What needed tackling were the attitudes and mechanisms employed by both teachers and children when faced with a new learning situation. If these were found to be inappropriate then that needed to be acknowledged and we had to be prepared to change to meet such a challenge. We see LOGO as being developed with a clear educational philosophy in mind. For us, it stimulates a climate of trust in the classroom in which the child's curiosity acts as a natural incentive to learn. This allows a participatory mode of decison-making in learning in which children and teachers each have a part. Our computer learning environments try to treat all children as thinking, understanding and contributing individuals.

Beginning with Bigtrak in the infant classes, and moving on to floor turtles, children had, by the time they were using turtle graphics, sprites, and music, gained a sophisticated attitude to discussing and planning their LOGO projects. Some junior children coming to LOGO without the infant experience found it more difficult to get out of the habit of relying on the teacher for direction. However, when encouraged along the road of independent thinking, they were able to achieve this, to the extent of asking for notebooks to log their own progress.

A notable success of the project has been the involvement of parents. LOGO proved to be an area which both parents and children could understand and which both could find interesting. LOGO offered a powerful facility, understandable and attractive to children, without being childish. As a result many parents acquired LOGO for their home computers, or acquired home computers which would run LOGO.

Apart from the value of LOGO, perhaps the most important lesson to be learnt from the Walsall project's work is that educational initiatives will succeed best where all those who have influence in creating the educational experience - local authority, teacher, parent, and child - are committed to and involved in creating that experience together.

NOTES

1. P.H. Winston _Artificial Intelligence_ p.1

2. Reported in: S. Weir et al., _Interim report of the Logo project in the Brookline Public Schools_ MIT Logo Memo 49 June 1978
S. Papert et al., _Final Report of the Brookline Project Part II_ MIT Logo Memo 53 September 1979
D. Watt, _Final report of the Brookline Project Part III_ MIT Logo Memo 54 September 1979
MIT has published a "Bibliography of Logo Memos", obtainable by writing to:
Logo Group, Massachusetts Institute of Technology, NE 43-438, 545 Technology Square, Cambridge, MA 02139, U.S.A.

3. A report, by teachers at the school, is: "Learning with Logo at the Lamplighter School" _Kilobaud Microcomputing_ Vol. 5, No. 9. Sept. 1981

4. Examples of the Edinburgh research are:
J. Howe & P. Ross, "Moving LOGO into a Mathematics Classroom" pp. 89-101 in: J. Howe & P. Ross (ed.) _Microcomputers in Secondary Education_ London

Kogan Page New York Nichols 1981
B. du Boulay, "Re-Learning Mathematics through LOGO: Helping Student Teachers who don't understand Mathematics" pp. 69-81 in Howe & Ross, Microcomputers in Secondary Education
H. Finlayson, "The Development of Mathematical Thinking through LOGO" LOGO Almanack Vol. 1 (1983), 17-21
A summary of the Edinburgh LOGO research, with further references, is:
J. Howe, "Edinburgh LOGO: A Retrospective View" pp. 77-87 in: W.B. Dockrell (ed) An Attitude of Mind Scottish Council for Research in Education Edinburgh 1984
A list of Research and Working Papers available for purchase can be obtained from:
Artificial Intelligence Applications Institute, University of Edinburgh, Hope Park Square, Meadow Lane, Edinburgh EH8 9NW, Scotland.

5. Roy D. Pea & D. Midian Kurland, "On the Cognitive Effects of Learning Computer Programming." Technical Report No. 9, January 1984. Center for Children and Technology, Bank Street College of Education, New York
For details of Technical Reports and papers available, write to:
Center for Children and Technology, Bank Street College of Education, 610 West 112th Street, New York, NY 10025, U.S.A.

6. Erik de Corte, "Logo and Learning to Think" LOGO Almanack Vol. 1 (1983), 10-11. The quotation is from page 10.

7. For information on the Chiltern LOGO Project and details of publications, contact:
Chiltern LOGO Project, A.U.C.B.E., Endymion Road, Hatfield, Hertfordshire AL10 8AU, England
For the LOGO Maths Project, contact:
LOGO Maths Project, Dept. of Mathematics, Statistics and Computing, University of London Institute of Education, 20 Bedford Way, London WC1H 0AL, England.

8. A summary of the Project's work is given in: Linda Spear, "The Walsall LOGO Project" LOGO Almanack Vol. 2 (1984). The quotation is taken from this article. The address to contact for details of the project's publications is:
Walsall LOGO Project, c/o Busill Jones Junior School, Ashley Road, Bloxwich, Walsall, West Midlands, England.

Chapter 2

# USING LOGO IN THE SCHOOL

We have already encountered some of the ideas surrounding the use of LOGO in the classroom. In this chapter we will look at the implications, for the school and for the teacher, which flow from the decisions to think about LOGO as a possible contributor to teaching and learning. Figure 2.1 shows the four major dimensions which require thinking about. Using LOGO involves making decisions in all of these areas. How is LOGO to be incorporated within the curriculum adopted by the school and within the particular curricula of each class? How does it relate to other curricular elements? Deciding on LOGO may mean acquiring new resources, or making decisions about the use of existing ones. Within the classroom, deciding to use LOGO raises questions of organisation of space, resources, and people, and of the style of teaching and learning which is to be adopted. The way in which these implications are worked out in individual schools will of course depend on the particular circumstances; but some general points can usefully be made.

## CURRICULAR IMPLICATIONS

Adopting LOGO will usually be a curricular decision. "Why use LOGO ?" is not just a question about styles of teaching and learning, but about the role of LOGO experience in meeting the school's educational objectives. It involves thinking about two things: the overall experience which the school aims to provide, and the specific requirements of the different groups of pupils for whom the school exists. The two questions are closely linked, for the specific classroom activities occur within the limits set by the

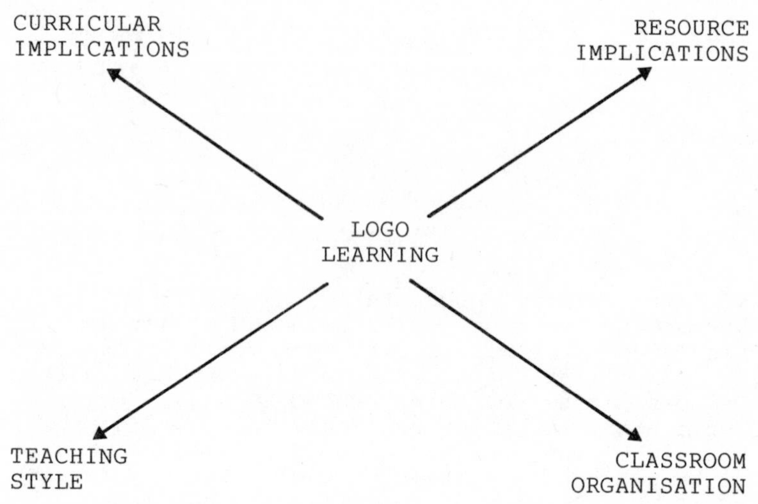


Figure 2.1 Implications of LOGO learning.

general curricular outlines for the school. There is also another level of constraint outwith the school: the general curricular directions encouraged or insisted upon by government, local or national.

All schools operate within limits set from beyond their walls. State schools will experience control from the local education authority or school board, and from central government. Central government may establish general policy outlines, suggesting priorities for the educational system. The policy outlines will be backed up by the activity of inspectors and by financial strategies. An example will show the influence of this level of activity.

In the 1960s "progressive" methods were encouraged in Britain: in Scotland the "Primary Memorandum" of 1965 and in England the Plowden Report (1967) encouraged schools to adopt child-centred and experience-based methods in the primary school:

It is now recognised that learning occurs

> most effectively when the learner is personally involved in purposeful activity which captures his interest or arises from it. Consequently the emphasis in primary education is now more on learning by the pupil than on instruction by the teacher. (1)

New methods were encouraged, the development of new materials funded, and schools built to new designs. But by the middle of the next decade the situation was changing. In the so-called "Great Debate" of 1976-77 voices were raised against what were claimed to be the excesses of progressivism, and the Green Paper Education in Schools: A Consultative Document of 1977 heralded a much more cautious approach to innovation at all levels of the education system. "The Basics" were not to be neglected, and there was to be more emphasis on assessment (of pupils' progress) and accountability (of teachers and schools to their paymasters in local and central government). Innovation would now find it harder to gain the blessing and subsidy of educational authorities. In this climate the adoption of Papert's vision of totally open and unstructured learning environments would soon lead to a school becoming a "centre of interest" (not much of it friendly) for local and central government personnel.

A more recent development at the national level is also of significance. The British government's reaction to the arrival on the educational scene of the microcomputer in the early 1980s was to subsidise the purchase of at least one microcomputer (of British manufacture) for every primary and secondary school in the state sector. The offer was of short duration, and therefore many schools who would have taken some time over acquiring and preparing themselves for the microcomputer suddenly found themselves obliged to get one instantly. There were consequences of this policy at the level of local government too, for local educational authorities and teacher-education institutions were suddenly faced with a huge demand for in-service training and the development of suitable teaching materials. Materials development was assisted by national agencies such as the MEP (Microelectronics Education Programme).

In setting their curricular objectives, then, head teachers must to some extent be guided by the policies and emphases set at local and central government level. They are also guided by their own awareness of what constitutes "good education". In this context, the head teacher must be able to see the value of LOGO in contributing to what he or she considers are good educational experiences.

In most schools, where numerous activities compete for involvement in the learning programme, LOGO needs to be justifiable in terms of relevance to existing curricular objectives if it is to be given time during the school day. This imperative becomes more pressing as one moves up through the age ranges. Many LOGO researchers claim that LOGO has demonstrated its feasibility as a powerful learning medium in different areas of the curriculum and at different age levels.

Indeed, the experience of primary schools so far seems to suggest that LOGO is most successful and productive when developed throughout the age ranges in the school. Thus, a beginning may be made in the infant school with Bigtrak or with one-key entry drawing programs. In later years, progress may then be made to the floor turtle or to the full facilities of turtle graphics. At an appropriate point the creation of procedures can be developed. Work can then branch out into other LOGO facilities, such as music or sprites or control technology. Even in the primary school, groups will emerge who are fascinated (or obsessed) by the act of programming.

In a secondary school, LOGO may be considered in several areas. One use may be in working through certain parts of the mathematics curriculum. A sad and misinformed tendency here is to believe that because LOGO is used in primary schools and with handicapped children, it is therefore suited only to remedial children in the secondary school maths classroom, who can be allowed to play with turtle graphics while the rest of the class get on with "real" mathematics. A glance at Abelson and diSessa's Turtle Geometry will give an idea of the considerable complexity of mathematical investigation possible. LOGO may also be used as a way of examining the nature of music, and creating new music, available to those who do not play musical instruments as much as to those who do. In the English classroom, it may be the vehicle for analysis of and experiment with language, generating poetry and prose or stimulating ceative writing. It may serve as the medium for a course in structured programming in the upper part of the school. Or it may be the way chosen in the lower part of the school to provide enjoyable computer familiarisation to all. In this case LOGO provides familiarity with the equipment (keyboard, monitor, disk drive, etc.), but also with the power of computers to implement human thinking.

Because LOGO can straddle the age ranges from infant to adult, it will be most successful where there is effective liaison between primary and secondary schools. Soon children will pass from primary schools to their local secondary schools with a high level of familiarity with the computer and perhaps with a high level of program planning ability. A computer familiarisation course in the lower secondary school which assumes that children have no background, and moves from "This is a monitor" to simple, or perhaps childish, programming in BASIC will then turn out less than successfully. Children in the maths classroom may ask for LOGO to solve the problems they are presented with.

It is difficult to be specific, and impossible to say "Here is the LOGO curriculum", since LOGO is not an area of content. It is sometimes mistakenly thought that simple turtle graphics is the content of LOGO, and LOGO textbooks and materials for children sometimes convey this idea. In fact, LOGO is a core, a computer facility through which various environments may be offered to the user. As this book will show, turtle graphics is only one of those environments, and the range of areas where LOGO can offer something of value may be limited only by the range of areas in which LOGO-users choose to work.

## RESOURCE IMPLICATIONS

LOGO-use clearly has resource implications. Bigtraks, turtles, computers, LOGO implementations all cost money. However, LOGO is not necessarily a high-cost experience. You don't need a special sort of computer to run LOGO, since there are now full LOGO implementations available for all the computers commonly found in schools (at least in the British Isles and North America). LOGO may come on a chip, a cartridge or a disk, but whichever it is on, it is simple to load. LOGO works best as a group experience, and the computer can be used with one group while the rest prepare or debug programs or carry out related work. So LOGO can be used when there is only one computer available to the class; there is no need for a roomful of computers, in which each child can suffer a lonely and uncreative relationship with a mechanical taskmaster. Similarly, a school doesn't need a large number of Bigtraks or turtles.

What the school should have, however, is a disk drive, a printer and lots of disks. It is essential to be able to save a pupil's LOGO work quickly and without difficulty: this means a disk drive. Fast tape units can sometimes be a reasonable substitute, but reliability has not been shown to be as good as that of disks; they are however much more convenient than ordinary cassette tape units. Hard copy is essential too: beautiful designs should not die when the computer is switched off, and new poems, or programs in development should not have to be copied painstakingly from the screen. Computer printers are no longer the £1000 plus machines they once were; many are now in price ranges where they can be obtained by most schools, with or without help from the PTA. Having plenty of disks available is also most useful. This enables each pupil's work to be retained separately, so that the pupil can feel that something has been preserved which he has created.

## CLASSROOM ORGANISATION

The problems of classroom organisation with LOGO are essentially no different than those with any computer-use. If a class has available to it one computer, or one turtle or one Bigtrak, then some children will be able to use it, whilst the rest do something else. Two factors are particularly important: the teacher's attitude, and the choice of computer-related activity.

In the early stage of the introduction of computers into schools, the "novelty factor" will inevitably make the computer a focus of pupils' attention. However, if the computer is treated as a sort of magical object, which the teacher cannot understand but which will somehow revolutionise education, problems will multiply. The computer may almost become an object of worship, so that all other classroom activities become devalued.

This situation is clearly undesirable. The teacher's attitude is important here: if the computer is treated matter-of-factly, as just another item in the classroom, to be used only when appropriate, the "computer-fetish" phase can be avoided. A subtly dangerous attitude is that the computer must never be inactive, almost as if all learning ceases when the computer is switched off. Seeing the computer in the classroom switched off and inactive is in fact very helpful in developing a proper attitude towards it, i.e. that it is a useful piece of classroom equipment, used whenever it is appropriate, but not otherwise. Even in a situation where a school has a limited number of computers which have to be carefully timetabled so that everyone gets a chance to use them, small periods of inactivity are useful. The computer should be seen as servant, rather than as master, of the learning process.

This attitude can also be reflected in the choice of learning activities. Situations which set the work at the computer apart from other classroom activity should be avoided; work carried out with the computer should wherever possible be closely related to what takes place away from it. This can best be achieved if computer work and non-computer work are both elements of a programme of work or centre of interest. For instance, activities with a floor turtle may be part of a topic on direction and maps, which involves also work on interpreting and making maps, designing and solving mazes, making weather-vanes, measuring or calculating distances. Most of these may not require any computer input; some may require a computer input very different from turtle-use. Continuity is essential to the smooth functioning of classrooms; and activities involving computer-based work should fall into the "classroom tradition" of the sorts of activites which the teacher offers throughout the school year.

LOGO activities are best carried out with groups. Apart from the work they are engaged upon, the interaction between children stimulates valuable experiences: discussion and debate, gaining oral coherence and confidence, working in a team, and getting on with others. The membership of groups is clearly a matter for the teacher's judgement, although many teachers find that mixed-ability grouping is very successful with LOGO activities. While the computer is a novelty, groups who are not currently using it should be made aware that they are going to have a chance to use it, and work away from the computer should be interesting enough to retain concentration. For this reason, the arrival of a computer may sometimes cause a teacher to reassess the work he has been accustomed to offer, a process which can often have very beneficial results.

Distribution of objects within the classroom can be a problem, particularly when using Bigtrak or a floor turtle. Bigtrak needs a lot of space if it is to be used effectively and without total disruption of other classroom activity; a corridor may be the only resort if a large space cannot be cleared in the classroom. Turtles do not need so much space, but they do need an area where users can move around the equipment. Semi-open plan schools are lucky here in having a useful space nearby, but not isolated from the rest of the class activity. For LOGO activities at the computer, the question is where to put it. Having the computer permanently lodged in a room of its own does not seem the best solution, (we are not considering here classrooms designed for teaching "Computer Studies"), since it encourages the attitude that computer activities are somehow special and different from other classroom work (and it also raises problems of supervision). A corner of the room, where the equipment can be discreetly placed, and used when needed without dominating the classroom, is probably the best location.

Using LOGO does not necessarily involve then a massive change in classroom organisation. This can easily be summed up by stating that if you are used to group-work, using LOGO should not present any undue organisational problems.

## TEACHING STYLE

Just as LOGO does not necessarily revolutionise classroom organisation, it does not force teachers to adopt a different style of teaching. But it will be more productive in some contexts than in others. LOGO has very limited value as the basis of a teacher-controlled whole-class didactic teaching style: it can be used to provide quite a good electronic blackboard. It can also be used to produce drill-and-practice, testing, or revision programs to be used by one pupil sitting before the computer. However LOGO only becomes a truly valuable addition to the toolbox of learner and teacher when it used to allow children to explore, to discover, and to construct.

There is an ongoing debate in the educational world about the teacher's role in the process of discovery learning. This can be summed up by the question, How guided should discovery be ? This debate is mirrored in the LOGO community. All would accept that LOGO learning is a process of discovery through the achievement of insight into the nature of a problem or situation. Variations in approach emerge only over the extent to which the process should be guided or channelled.

Seymour Papert argues that placing children in a "computer-rich environment" and allowing them to explore is sufficient for acceptable learning to occur. However, many teachers and researchers who have used or are using LOGO in the classroom would argue that gaining knowledge of a learning area completely by discovering it is a very inefficient and time-consuming process, and that very often the discovery would not take place were it not for the activity of the teacher as a catalyst. Supplying tools for discovery and even hints for the direction of exploration can speed up the process while retaining the insight-gaining experience. Most LOGO learning materials assume that some amount of guidance or challenge-setting is required. In this context, the teacher's role is to set goals and limits where needed, and to advise and if necessary discreetly to guide. The problem is to decide when the level of guidance is such that assimilation of information has supplanted learning by discovery, and to choose materials that do stimulate learning. The prospect of a LOGO syllabus, with LOGO textbooks for pupils to work through and "turtle tests" to work out class placings is one which frightens the inventors of LOGO.

Different ideas about how guided discovery should be, and different school situations have resulted in variations in approach between different LOGO-users. Some LOGO activities thus appear to be more highly organised than others, or are slanted in different curricular directions. These differences will inevitably provoke discussion and can be seen as alternative roads to the creation of learning environments. Teaching activities with LOGO are at present themselves still tentative and exploratory. All LOGO users remain learners.

## NOTES

1. The two key documents are: Primary Education in Scotland Edinburgh HMSO 1965; and Children and their Primary Schools London HMSO 1967. The quotation is from Primary Education in Scotland page 60.

Chapter 3

# CASE STUDY 1: THINKING ABOUT LOGO IN THE CLASSROOM

Derek Radburn

---

Derek Radburn is Head Teacher of Long Clawson Primary School in Leicestershire. He is a founder member and currently Chairperson of BLUG (the British LOGO User Group). As well as using LOGO in the classroom, he has been heavily involved in the development and testing of new LOGO implementations. In this chapter he presents his own views on taking LOGO into the primary classroom.

---

## USING LOGO SUCCESSFULLY

I would suggest, if LOGO is to be used successfully in the classroom, that some thought must have been given to what objectives are hoped to be achieved by its use. Unless this exercise is undertaken, then the teacher/manager of the LOGO learning situation will be "flying blind". In this chapter I seek to identify some of the problems involved in converting this theory into practice.

It is important here to clarify what I mean by "using LOGO successfully in the classroom". There are certain characteristics which one would expect to see in a successfully realised and managed LOGO learning environment. One would relate to the evidence that children were taking initiatives in their own learning in the setting of goals and activities. Another would be the extent to which LOGO knowledge was being transmitted by the teacher. Was the teacher normally regarded as being the only source of answers, or had some trial and error approaches to finding out developed among the children? How much teacher involvement and intervention was there, and what was its quality? Was there evidence of any structure, supplied either by the pupils or by the teacher; or was it a case of a wholly idiosyncratic approach? How much were children communicating with those people around them on the subject of their LOGO activities? What evidence existed to show how easily the LOGO learning environment sits with the rest of the classroom regime? Was there any indication of enhancement in other areas of the curriculum? (There is a distinction between these last two: the first is more concerned with possible conflicts of method, by both pupil and teacher; the second is more knowledge- and skill-based.) Lastly, was it possible to see any tentative attitudes among the longer-term users of LOGO?

I am cautious about appearing too prescriptive, for there is a dearth of reliable empirical evidence on LOGO learning, and this situation is likely to obtain for some foreseeable time. It would therefore be rash to provide definitive answers to the questions above (even assuming this to be possible), apart from which, prescription is hardly in harmony with the philosophy of LOGO learning.

There are two predominant tensions which will

have strong influences on the way in which LOGO gets to be used in the classroom. One is the normal pedagogic practice of seeking to find ways of enhancing and supporting the existing curricular framework. The other is a rather more radical stance, which strongly resonates with discovery learning, which envisages LOGO as a potent learning environment. The danger in education is to argue in absolute terms, whereas the real educational world is singularly bereft of absolutes when it comes to practice. My starting point will lie in the direction of exploiting the potential of the LOGO learning environment, but it will also certainly seek to forge links with other learning activities which children may be engaged in.

## LOGO DEVELOPMENT

I begin with an account of the way LOGO is used in my own school, a small rural primary school with a roll of just under sixty chuldren aged four to ten. I start to use LOGO with children who are four years old. There is no strong reason for beginning with this age, other than that they happen to be the youngest children in the school; if there were three-year-olds there, I would start with them. What do four-year-olds get? They are presented with a sub-set of the LOGO learning environment, taking the form of the following one-key entry commands:

F for Forward
B for Back
R for Right
L for Left

The extent of turtle's motion with each of these keys is determined by me, the programmer. The program is simple to write, and is easily modified and extended. Here it is:

```
TO SETUP
     MAKE "F  [FD 30]
     MAKE "B  [BK 30]
     MAKE "R  [RT 30]
     MAKE "L  [LT 30]
     INSTANT
     END
```

```
TO INSTANT
     MAKE "KEY  RC
     IF  NOT  NAME? :KEY  [INSTANT]
     RUN  THING :KEY
     INSTANT
     END
```

In the first procedure, SETUP, single character words (F, B, R, and L) are given lists (such as [FD 30]) as their values. Once SETUP has been run, it is possible to use INSTANT to run the thing (in this case the instruction list) associated with the key pressed. In the second line of INSTANT, the RC command causes LOGO to wait until a key is pressed - the pressed key is then stored in the variable KEY. That the value of KEY is one of the words defined in SETUP which has a list as its value is tested for in the third line of INSTANT. If the value of KEY is not one of these words, it is ignored, and program flow loops again to the beginning of INSTANT through a recursive call (i.e. the procedure calls itself). If it proves to be a valid key, i.e. one defined in SETUP, then the thing associated with the key pressed is run in the fourth line. Control then loops recursively to the beginning of INSTANT again. Extension of this program would involve defining more keys in SETUP which had as their values valid turtle commands. For example,

```
MAKE "U  [PU]      (i.e. PENUP)
MAKE "D  [PD]      (i.e. PENDOWN)
```

and so on.

Children work in pairs with this program. When they first meet the keyboard, they have difficulties in finding the letters which they want. Not only do they have to discriminate them from the many other non-relevant characters on the keyboard, but they also have to distinguish between the letters B, F, and R which have strong similarities (R and F are also adjacent on the keyboard). I have not found children either unwilling or unable to meet the challenge of this task. They have motivation: when they find the key they want, something will happen. On their first encounter, they do need the help and support of a teacher. This usually takes the form of prompting by drawing letter shapes with a finger and making the sound and saying the word. It is rarely the case that after the first session there is any problem with the keyboard. Notice how here LOGO is in harmony with what we want our youngsters to be doing; they are having to make fine discrimination of shapes, and also exercise an increasing spatial awareness of the keyboard's configuration.

Once they have claimed the four commands as their own, it is largely a case of the teacher being around whilst they begin to use the system for their own purposes. As confidence grows, so too can the sophistication and complexity of the system. The sub-set can be enlarged to include facilities for raising and lowering the pen on the turtle, and clearing the screen. It should be explained that through an accident of history we do not use a physical floor turtle in the school. At the time we had the use of a floor turtle, we were faced with the choice of using the turtle with what I considered an inferior LOGO surrogate, or of using a full LOGO without the turtle. I chose the latter, since I felt that whatever gains would have been made by using the physical turtle would hve been wiped out by the constraints of the software and the confusion that would have come with the re-learning when meeting full LOGO. There is no doubt that the floor turtle brings benefits to young or slow-learning children, but, with older or quicker children, its slowness and occasional inaccuracy can bring frustrations.

The central argument here is concerned with the way in which children can relate their own body geometry to that of the turtle. Both have a heading which can be altered by turning; and both have a position which can be altered by moving. Though the turtle only moves in two dimensions, it is nonetheless a concrete object which exists within the child's own area of spatial awareness. I have found quite young six-year-olds clearly thinking with their bodies when using the screen turtle. When the turtle has been heading down the screen and they have had to decide which way they wish it to turn, I have seen them turn their backs to the screen and play turtle. What I am seeking to do here is not to deny the value that can come with possessing and using a floor turtle, but rather, to suggest that not having one does not preclude worthwhile LOGO learning from taking place.

The next stage is to introduce two-character input, followed by pressing the RETURN key. It is possible to miss this stage and go straight into a full LOGO environment. The only difference is that instead of typing FD and pressing RETURN, a space and a number have also to be typed before RETURN is pressed. I prefer a more gradual development.

Some people feel that children should begin with full LOGO right from the start. They argue that if children are going to learn ultimately to use a particular form of input, they might just as well start with it and avoid the possible confusion which might arise in schema such as the one described here. I can only say that I have not observed any of the confusion alluded to, but have no problem in envisaging the difficulties my four-year-olds would encounter if they were thrown in at the deep end with full LOGO. It is sometimes further argued that sub-sets put constraints on what the children are able to explore. This argument is one with which I have no sympathy: the basis of education is one of selective experiences; one might equally argue that infants ought to start by reading Shakespeare, since eventually that is the type of English many of them will need to be familiar with when they study English Literature.

A flexible structure is used in developing LOGO from these early stages. For example, when I think it appropriate for particular children, I formally introduce the idea of REPEAT loops. The use of REPEAT must be seen as an essential precursor to using procedures. Most children draw squares quite early in their LOGO explorations; they usually do it in a "long-handed" way, by typing in

```
FD 50 RT 90 FD 50 RT 90 FD 50 RT 90 FD 50
```

or something similar. They often do not leave the turtle as they found it. (Finishing as you started is something I encourage them to do, but I leave them to discover its advantages themselves.) I ask children to walk a square, then invite them to tell me what they have done. I ask them what REPEAT means, and then get them to explain what they have repeated in walking a square. Following this session, at first all will go and use the REPEAT command; but after a little while about a third will discard it, and go back to the long-hand method they are comfortable with. This gives a very useful indicator of how children's thinking is developing, since the REPEAT entails some abstract generalisations that some children are intellectually not equipped for. I do not expect children to use REPEATs until they are ready for them. Many, in fact, start using them even before I get a chance to formally introduce them. They pick up the technique by watching the activities of other children. I would not feel very happy about developing the idea of procedures wih children who have not made REPEAT their own. Again though, through the computer culture of the children, this is not a decision which entirely rests with me; the use of procedures gets acquired from other children.

As soon as children are using procedures, they can be shown how to save ther workspace (i.e. the procedures they have accumulated in the computer's memory) to the disk. Without this facility of saving and restoring workspace, there are difficulties of continuity and development for children. It is important to note here that most of this exposition has been about a methodology which enables the child to do things with the computer. There has been no suggestion of the child being presented with pre-determined goals. A noticeable feature is the spread of information among the children themselves. When I started to have children saving their workspaces, at first I used to ask them to erase everything in the computer after they had saved their workspace to the disk. My feeling was that a child's own discoveries might be prejudiced if they "inherited" the workspace of a more sophisticated user. I now believe this to be mistaken. The benefits outweigh the disadvantages. Many children have made advances through playing with procedures which are not their own. This begs the question of whether I should provide some procedures which lie beyond the children's current level of programming expertise, so that they may be led on to further insights by playing and tinkering with these. I think that I should, but am still considering what these should be.

## SOME PRACTICALITIES

One of the first considerations which has to be addressed once it is decided to use LOGO in the classroom is where it is going to happen. The demands on classroom space will clearly reflect whether or not it is intended to use a floor turtle. If a floor turtle is going to be used, then it is not only a question of finding adequate space, but space with suitable attributes. For example, the carpeted surfaces increasingly being used in modern schools are not suitable for the accurate use of turtles. The ideal surface is smooth, firm and flat, but not slippy, one to which paper can be easily and firmly attached. Where classrooms have an informal, open arrangement of furniture, it is essential to be aware of patterns of movement of the people within that space. For example, it is not a good idea for turtling activities to take place in a corner where children rarely move about but in front of a cupboard containing stationery to which teachers might have need of urgent recourse. What is the minimal amount of space needed for turtling? I suggest that an area of at least 1.5m square is needed, plus adjacent space for humans and computer. If the turtle has an umbilical cord connecting it to the computer, then some facility is needed to suspend this out of the way of turtle and humans. This will most probably be a string attached to a hook in the ceiling.

It is possible to try using the turtle on a raised surface, but I see this as presenting two difficulties. One is the ever-present chance of an expensive and precision piece of machinery tumbling onto the floor; such an event would hardly have a very positive outcome for the luckless users who caused the event. The other problem relates to the parallax distortions of perception of space and angle caused by viewing the turtle from a more oblique angle; I see this as sufficient reason to dismiss the notion of raising the turtle from floor level.

Even if a floor turtle is not to be used, there are still certain constraints about location that need to be recognised. Thought needs to be given as to the extent and nature of interaction between computer-users and non-users, assuming that several activities are simultaneously taking place in the same room. In dedicated computer facilities, such as may be found in secondary schools, this is not a problem (but thought needs to be given to the implications and effects of such segregation, particularly with younger or first-time users). The number of users per computer needs to be considered. In formal sessions I would sugest users operate in pairs; solitary usage has the disadvantage of lacking the language interaction which is essential in developing ideas, as well as fostering social skills. I would suggest that user numbers greater than three are not desirable: there is too little opportunity for adequate contact time with the computer, and motivation and attention are likely to be casualties in such circumstances.

Thought needs to be given to the composition of groups of users. For instance, putting one child who is extravert and of high ability with others of average or low ability is a certain way of preventing the active involvement of the latter. What I am asserting here is that it is not enough for the teacher to think in terms of cognitive abilities. Consideration must also be given to the wider issues of personality and attitudes (especially self-attitude). LOGO learning is not simply learning a particular body of facts and assimilating certain concepts; it involves a full humanistic learning process which has as much to do with inter-personal relationships and skills as it does with mathematical or heuristic thinking. It is for this reason that I see the composition of user-groups as being far from trivial. Used in this manner, the computer, far from depersonalising education, actually provides an environment which encourages and emphasises the importance of the human dimension.

## THE TEACHER'S ROLE

Of crucial importance here is the role which the teacher perceives for herself/himself. A completely non-interventionist stance leaves the children in a structureless anarchy in which there is little profit. A strongly didactic approach on the other hand leaves little room for anything other than a narrow, insecure cognitive gain. Three things which are critical are the frequency, timing, and nature of teacher interventions. How often the teacher will come to a group at the computer will depend upon a variety of things: the personalities of the children using the computer, the task which the children are engaged upon, and the other activities and children which the teacher is looking after. The timing of teacher interventions is very important. It is not helpful for children who are trying to solve a problem to receive ill-timed interruptions by the teacher; these can smack all too easily to the children of a lack of teacher confidence in their ability to cope. The teacher's awareness of the children's activities is crucial in assessing timely interventions.

I would see the nature of teacher intervention as being best illustrated by an example. One activity which young children can easily spend a lot of time on is using the WRAP facility in LOGO. This is the situation where, when the screen turtle is moved off the screen, it re-apppears on the opposite edge of the screen. For children, this has the attraction that, by typing very little, they can profoundly affect the appearance of the screen. As a teacher, it is very easy to feel uncomfortable and view such play as "wasting time". Initially it is certainly not time-wasting, but there does come a point with some children where it ceases to be a profitable activity long before they show any inclination to give it up. The way in which a teacher intervenes here could be:

"Right, you've done enough of that, now do something else."

or:

"Try drawing me a square."

or:

"What is the turtle doing here? How could you make use of it?"

I would view the first two interventions as being undesirable because they are teacher-centred and dismissive of the children's activities; they take the initiative for learning away from the children. The third intervention embodies an acceptance of the children's activities and seeks to draw from the children some statement of understanding of the processes involved. It further invites the children to think of some means of developing the use of the WRAP facility, whilst leaving the initiative to do so in their hands.

I do not assert that teachers should never be directive, but that as a general style they should be non-directive. Interventions need to be subtle hints rather than explicit instructions. I do not see telling children about LOGO commands, or giving them LOGO procedures, as being explicitly directive as long as there is no instruction as to what to do with them, for in these circumstances initiative is still in the hands of the learner. The teacher's role is one of enabling and of being a consultant. Of course, even being a consultant has its dangers: appearing to always know the answer can lead to children deferring to the teacher when they could easily have managed without doing so. Teacher sensitivity and perception are critical attributes in creating a LOGO learning environment.

There is plenty of evidence indicating that the use of a variety of teaching styles can be profitable. I would see parallels in LOGO learning. Most of the time the teacher's contribution must be one of increasing the children's control over the computer, by developing and contributing to their knowledge of LOGO. Generally this will be accomplished by extending the range of commands at the children's disposal. When, however, it comes to ideas of programming style and programming concepts, then there are alternative means which I think must be used. In this area there are advantages in giving procedures for children to tinker and play with.

One can see two strands within the LOGO learning environment. The exploratory, open-ended mode, is that in which children will operate most of the time. The other is the heuristic mode, in which targets are set and means have to be constructed to achieve them. Something of the latter, goal-oriented, mode ought to be occurring within the former, exploratory, mode. But the heuristic approach does provide a framework for developing some of the higher order ideas in programming. For example, ideas of top-down programming can be developed by giving an assignment to a group, and through discussion drawing out the ideas of starting from where you want to get to, and thinking about what has to be done to get there. For instance, a group of children aged nine and ten was asked what had to be done to draw a bulldozer. What emerged was:

```
TO BULLDOZER
     TRACK
     ENGINE
     CAB
     DROT
     END
```

(I learned that "drot" was a term for the blade of a bulldoxer from a more knowledgeable nine-year-old.) The group then went on to construct the sub-procedures, which themselves also called further procedures.

Some children can arrive at this sort of

strategy for themselves, but it is my experience that the majority do not. I believe that not only is it necessary for the teacher to be keenly aware of what children are doing, and flexible in approach to them on a day-to-day basis, but that also, in the overall plan of development, there should be a similar flexibility. The teacher ought not to have a detailed plan of development, based on assumptions that at a certain time children ought to be doing certain things, or that children who have mastered item A should proceed to item B before then moving on to item C. Such a route-plan offers no accommodation for the individuality of LOGO learning. Rather, a teacher needs a general idea of development, a knowledge of the possibilities at any particular point.

Getting that knowledge will not be easy. It is unlikely to be gained by simply reading books, though this will help. I think it is only through personal use of LOGO that the teacher will develop it. Such use will take time, but that should not be viewed as a reason for not using LOGO. No teacher would assert that they were a better teacher when they first began teaching than they are now. We all have to start somewhere.

Chapter 4

# TURTLES AND TRUCKS

## ROBOTS TO THINK WITH

For many teachers, the first association they make with LOGO is something crawling around on the classroom floor, studiously avoiding obstacles or purposefully and laboriously drawing shapes with a felt-tip pen. Because of their obvious photogenic qualities, especially when filmed by a cameraman lying on his stomach, turtles and their relatives are often equated with LOGO by the media. This equation is erroneous. And yet turtles do have a special place among LOGO activities, for the turtle is, literally and metaphorically, the vehicle which has brought LOGO out of the laboratory and into the classroom.

In the 1950's the British neurologist Grey Walter demonstrated a "tortoise", a battery-powered robot which could search for and attach itself to a power supply in order to recharge itself. The English "tortoise" became the American "turtle", a robot which moves under direction of the computer, or rather, under direction of the computer-user.

The turtle is for Papert a "transitional object", something which enables the user to make a connection between the knowledge he possesses of himself and his own world and new and powerful ideas existing outside it. It enables the child to explore two worlds which he stands on the edge of: the world of "turtle geometry", where important mathematical ideas may be discovered, and the world of computer control, where machines may be used as tools of exploration and discovery, as extensions of the mind.

There are thus two sets of benefits to be got from turtles. The first derives from the things they can do, the variety of movements and actions which they can perform, and the avenues for conceptual development which they open up. These are firstly mathematical: ideas of distance, of angle, of size and of shape; and ideas of relationships, of one thing to another thing, and of parts to a whole. But building around the activities centred upon the mathematical ideas can be many other sets of skills: among them language skills focusing upon what the turtle has done and will do; creative and aesthetic skills growing out of imaginative placing of the turtle and his/her activities in new contexts; and interaction skills arising out of the need for a team to operate the turtle and its machinery.

The second set of benefits derives from the way in which the turtle does what it does: it is a machine, controlled through a computer. Using it can give a very tangible insight into the facts that technology is controlled by people, that it needs to be controlled with clarity and precision (it will do exactly what you tell it), and that it can be utilised to achieve objectives set by people. That the computer can be an important intermediary in making our control of complex machinery easier is an equally vital lesson.

The floor turtle can be seen as part of a larger set - of programmable robot vehicles. This chapter will therefore also include mention of some vehicles akin to the turtle but with different properties. BIGTRAK is a toy vehicle with a simple range of actions which can be programmed through on-board microchips. "Buggies" can come in a variety of shapes and with a variety of properties. BIGTRAK, turtles and buggies however can all be used in a learning style which gives children an opportunity for creativity, decision-making, and interaction with others in the process of developing skills and concepts.

## BIGTRAK

BIGTRAK is a battery-powered toy vehicle which can be programmed to carry out various manoeuvres through a calculator-style keyboard on its top. The commands used are of a LOGO type, although there is only a very limited number available. The keyboard contains symbols as well as numbers, and the symbols and numbers are combined to make up the individual commands. Forward and backward arrow keys are used to preset forward and backward movement. Thus ↑1 makes BIGTRAK move forward approximately one BIGTRAK-length, whilst ↑12 makes it move forward about twelve times its length. ↓1 makes it go backwards one BIGTRAK-length. Left and right arrow keys (← and .) can be used to program turns to left or right, the arrow key press being followed by a number. The numbers represent minutes on the clock face, so ←15 will make BIGTRAK turn about 90 degrees to the left, →15 will make it turn about 90 degrees to the right. BIGTRAK is also equipped with a flashing light (designated a "laser gun" by the manufacturers) and a hoot, both of which can be incorporated into programmed sequences of actions. Sequences of actions are keyed in, and can then be run repeatedly.

Being pre-programmed, and having its own power supply, BIGTRAK is not limited in terms of the space in which it can operate by the length of a power or control cable. To get the best from it a good area is necessary. A corridor or other open space is often the best place to use it, although a classroom is not an impossible location if enough space can be cleared. If used in a corridor, excessively long trips, which will run down the batteries without adding any learning benefits, should be discouraged.

One attractive aspect of BIGTRAK is the price, which is well below that of floor turtles (although the properties and uses of turtles and BIGTRAK are very different). It may not even be necessary to purchase one, as many pupils may be persuaded to bring their own in (and demonstrate them!).

Use has been made of BIGTRAK at most levels of the primary school. Some teachers prefer to use it with the youngest children in the school (4 to 6 years old); others argue that older children derive more benefit because their conceptual abilities enable them to use it in a more structured way in thinking out and planning manoeuvres. It is often used as the precursor to floor turtle or LOGO activities. Clearly the level at which it is being used will affect the learning outcomes hoped for, the activities set, and the character of preparation necessary. As with many other pieces of educational equipment, when you use it depends on what you hope to gain from it. To derive most benefit from it (as with other teaching/learning aids) work with BIGTRAK should be well prepared.

Most BIGTRAK activities involve manoeuverability and judgement of distance or angle. Typical activities are:

a] Negotiation of a route avoiding a series of obstacles.

b] The converse of avoiding obstacles is hitting them, in games involving knocking over skittles or demolishing pillars.

c] Games involving reaching a target or measuring activities focus on judgement of distance.

d] A more advanced development is laying out a road system along which journeys have to be made, or a driving test circuit on which set manoeuvres have to be performed.

At first these activities may be set by the teacher; soon however groups of children will be keen to develop their own games or street systems. If more than one BIGTRAK is available, there will be a demand from some children for races or other competitive activites. The extent of competitive activity should be considered carefully by the teacher so that learning benefits to all children are not interfered with by the urge to win. Working together to solve a problem is more conducive to good groupwork than the need to beat Group B.

In addition to the judging of distance and angle, and the planning of manoeuvres, many other skill-developing activities may be incorporated into BIGTRAK work. Inventing a game is a complex conceptual task in which rules have to be devised which are both realistic (taking into account the actual setting, equipment and players) and logically consistent . Setting out even a simple street system involves thinking about traffic flow and junctions; adding buildings to make the street more realistic means asking "What sort of buildings do we find on different sorts of streets?"; adding people to the streets and the buildings raises plenty more possibilities.

Some drawbacks should be mentioned. BIGTRAK is not sold as a precision instrument, and perfect accuracy should not always be expected. Accuracy is particularly variable as regards the angle of turn, and is very dependent on the type of floor surface available. Shiny surfaces or carpets with a pronounced lay are likely to produce large distortions. Potential surfaces should be tested for accuracy before use. Changes in surface can create problems, so it is best to choose an area with uniform flooring. BIGTRAK is reasonably robust, but is not designed to be dropped on the ground. Broken BIGTRAKs can be very difficult to mend. Finally, a good supply of batteries should be maintained, as these can be used up at what may seem an alarming rate. Rechargeable batteries can be used, although it is not clear whether results are as good as with new ones.

Two excellent books are available which give a good picture of what can be done with BIGTRAK. Bigtrak Plus is a case study of how BIGTRAK was used in a number of primary schools on the Isle of Wight. It contains descriptions and examples of children's work, transcriptions and photographs of BIGTRAK sessions, and discussions of teaching possibilities.(1) On the right track ... with BIG TRAK is produced by the Walsall LOGO Project. It contains a wealth of good advice and teaching ideas, and is accompanied by a pack of resource sheets which can be photocopied and used by teachers and children. The authors of both books are aware that using BIGTRAK can promote learning in many different ways. The development of attitudes to learning is also seen as important; the authors of On the right track ... with BIG TRAK conclude that:

> using BIG TRAK challenges a fairly strong attitude in school towards always 'getting it right' and promotes a healthy atmosphere of genuine experimentation through trial and error. This can provide children with the means to make sense of their experience through logical reasoning. Working effectively in this way requires good planning strategies, and promotes a higher degree of independence in the child, with all the associated qualities such as motivation and self-confidence.(2)

## TURTLES

Until the recent advent of non-look-alike competitors, the floor turtle familiar to teachers and children in Britain took the form of a perspex dome on wheels supplied with a pen. This is the turtle developed at Edinburgh University's Department of Artificial Intelligence, and is similar to those built at MIT. That the turtle's dome is of perspex is important, as it was essential to the developers at MIT that, like LOGO procedures, the turtle's workings should be as transparent as possible. So even if it is not possible to see how the motors work, at least you see where they are. The turtle is connected to a control box by an umbilical cord supplying both power and control; the control box is linked to the main power supply and to the computer (see Figure 5.1 in the next chapter).

A number of characteristics distinguish the turtle from less expensive devices like BIGTRAK. The turtle can draw lines, using a pen which can be raised and lowered under computer control. It is accurate, so that RIGHT 90 does produce a right-angle turn and regular polygons achieve closure (i.e. don't end up like plans of sheepfolds with one entrance in an enclosing wall). As a mathematical instrument, the turtle in its turning is programmed in degrees, rather than the clock-face units of BIGTRAK (although, strangely, the units of length used by the Edinburgh turtle bear no obvious relation to normally used measures, Imperial or metric). Control is achieved through LOGO-type commands, either in software supplied with the turtle or through links with full LOGO implementations. Thus sets of actions can be built into procedures which can themselves be called as parts of higher level procedures. (A fuller description of this is given in chapter 5.) The accuracy, the computer link, and the more sophisticated control structures make turtles more expensive than programmable toys, and make them suitable for different types of activities.

The most obvious of these is "turtle graphics", the drawing of patterns or pictures using the turtle's built-in pen. Some of the shapes and patterns developed through turtle graphics are discussed in Chapter 6. When drawing is to be done with the floor turtle, the surface needs to be right. Suitable for frequent use, but lacking permanence, is a sheet of plastic-topped board which can be wiped down after use. This has the advantage of offering a large, conveniently-shaped, uniform surface. Large sheets of paper attached to a firm, flat surface (i.e. not a carpet) enable drawings to be preserved. However, repeated changing of the paper can be a nuisance, and it is usually necessary to make do with sheets of paper that are not a convenient size. Wallpaper (not the embossed variety) used upside down, or backing paper are reasonably inexpensive but tend to be too narrow, so that there is always an awkward seam which the pen may snag on. Using paper which is too absorbent may lead to blotching whenever the turtle pauses, as ink from the tip soaks into the paper. Unfortunately, large sheets of good quality paper are expensive, so a decision has to be made on what is preferred.

Floor turtles are not designed with fast travel over long distances in mind, and have until recently been linked to the computer by an umbilical cord of (inevitably) fixed length. This means that the space required to operate a turtle in need not be particularly large. Room is required for the drawing area, the computer and control box, and for movement around these by the operators. If the computer and control box are mounted on a trolley which can be wheeled from room to room, the turtling area can be set up by the teacher's desk or even in the doorway of the classroom (far enough from the door to avoid being hit by it) with very little fuss.

Turtling is essentially a team activity. Setting up is easily achieved if the members of a team of three or four have clear contributory roles. Using the turtle can be efficiently done with three individuals: one to man the keyboard, one to manage the umbilical cord, and one to lift and place the turtle itself. A further individual can be employed noting the results of manoeuvres. Effective turtle-use also depends on good preparation away from the computer, so that groups come to the turtle with programs to key in, ideas to follow through, or procedures already saved on disk which are to be used for further development of an idea or project. Planning and debriefing away from the computer are good habits to develop, for they will educate children out of the notion that you can only deal with computers by sitting at the keyboard. That the activity at the keyboard is only a small part of what using a computr is about is an important element in general computer literacy.

Turtles have recently appeared on the market which lack the umbilical cord. These are controlled either by radio or through an infra-red beam, and powered by batteries. This has led to a debate about the educational value of having the umbilical cord there. It is argued by "pro-cordists" that the cord makes the link between the computer and the turtle tangible rather than requiring it to be deduced from the turtle's behaviour in response to commands typed at the keyboard. "Anti-cordists" argue that the response to keyboard commands is so obvious that the cord is not needed to reinforce the point, and that the cord is in any case an enormous nuisance because it has to be held up all the time, and can still get very tangled whilst drawing a complex figure such as a spiral. Pro-cordists counter this by saying that managing the cord encourages teamwork because somebody has to look after it, and that having the cord has the positive advantage that it discourages long distance travel and therefore focuses attention on the shapes being drawn. Further, the remote turtles need to carry batteries and are therefore very heavy, and also prone to running out of energy during an average session and requiring long recharges. There are in addition communications problems: radio-controlled turtles can be affected by interference; with infra-red turtles, there is the problem of people getting in the way of the beam. There are clearly advantages each way, so individual teachers will use what they have available or, if they have a choice, choose what they prefer.

A related topic is that of "cybernetic feedback". If a turtle and its controlling computer are connected by an umbilical cable, messages can be sent by each to the other. Instructions are sent by the computer, telling the turtle which actions to perform. But the turtle can also send messages to the computer, saying that each instruction has been carried out or, as with turtles equipped with touch-sensors or other devices, reporting back discoveries about the outside world (e.g. that an obstacle has been encountered). Feedback is a powerful element of the link between computer and turtle. It is most easily achieved by provision of a cable between the two. Feedback is difficult to achieve in turtle systems without cable links. Radio control poses problems of signal clarity and interference. An infra-red beam is the simplest way to control remote turtles; however, this communication is only one-way (i.e. from the computer to the turtle), and the feedback possibility is lost. This will restrict the uses of such turtles.

The shape of the turtle is also now an area in which choice is available. The Edinburgh turtle is perfectly dome-shaped, and needs a close look to work out which is the front. More recent turtles have more clearly defined front and back ends; one of them is even shaped like a turtle. This makes it much easier to spot front, back, left and right. But it does mean that you are stuck with a particular shape. This may not be a problem; however some teachers prefer to give their turtles many guises, and the Edinburgh turtle with its uniform shape is easy to disguise. By attaching strips of Velcro to the turtle, various arms, legs, heads, tails, fins, horns and so on can be put on or taken off, to make the turtle a hedgehog, squirrel, fish and so on. The limbs can be made of stuffed fabric or anything considered useful. Another form of disguise is to build new shells for the turtle out of papier mache; these can incorporate limbs, horns, and so on, or they can be glued on afterwards. Simple domed shells which are then brightly painted can transform the turtle into a variety of tortoises, toadstools, ladybirds or other exotic or fantastic creatures.

Floor turtles are being used throughout the primary school age ranges and also in secondary schools. The case studies reported in chapters 5 and 8 give detailed accounts of how they have been utilised in two very different situations, in the upper primary school and in a school for children with learning difficulties. Details of some currently available turtles are given in chapter 17.

## BUGGIES

A rapidly-growing activity is the do-it-yourself construction of computer-controlled vehicles. A "buggy" can be made from whatever materials the builder assembles and have whatever facilities he decides to provide it with. Reg Eyre, of the College of St Paul and St Mary, Cheltenham, has described recently his work with "junk buggies" in a primary school.(3) Groups of 10- to 11-year-olds were given items such as tin cans, old rulers, small chunks of wood, elastic bands, sticky tape, and asked to construct vehicles with these. An inexpensive electric motor and on-off switch was then supplied and the children were asked to install them on their buggies to create vehicles which could be sent across the room or raced. The motivation, teamwork and hard thinking stimulated were enough to make the project very worthwhile for the teacher whose class was involved. The final stage (so far, that is) was to link the buggies to a BBC microcomputer. Buggies with one engine could be turned on and off, however a new generation of buggies with two engines, one for each rear wheel, enabled computer-steerable machines to be developed. With its easily-definable commands, LOGO is a natural language for this activity (more on this in chapter 11). This work, and the inclusion of LOGO command structures, is still going on.

At the moment this is still largely an area for those with some electronic know-how and possibly a soldering-iron, but it will soon be no longer the case. The "BBC Buggy" shows the kind of device which may be constructed from connectable modules and components. It is a computer-controlled vehicle which can, among other things, draw with fair accuracy using an on-board pen, follow a black line using a light-sensor, and read bar-codes. Control of the BBC Buggy through LOGO may now be available.

The distinction between buggies and floor turtles may even now be disappearing, with turtles offering a wide variety of actions, and buggies offering the accuracy of a turtle and full LOGO control structures. An ever larger choice of crawling devices seems to be becoming available, so that teachers will be able to choose a turtle to match their finances and their educational intentions.

NOTES

1. M.D. Meredith & B.I. Briggs, Bigtrak Plus London Council for Educational Technology 1982 ISBN 0 86184 074 7 (P)

2. Walsall LOGO Project, On the right track ... with BIG TRAK Walsall Metropolitan Borough Education Committee 1984. The quotation is from page 10. The book and pack of resource sheets are available from the Walsall LOGO Project, c/o Busill Jones Junior School, Ashley Road, Bloxwich, Walsall, West Midlands.

3. Presentation given to the annual conference of MAPE (Micros and Primary Education) at the College of St Paul and St Mary, Cheltenham, 29-31 March 1985.

Chapter 5

# CASE STUDY 2: A TURTLE ON THE FLOOR

Marianne Hislop

---

Marianne Hislop is a class teacher in a Primary School at Lenzie, just outside Glasgow. She has just moved there from a Primary School in nearby Kirkintilloch, where the work which she outlines in this chapter was carried out. She describes the reactions to the acquisition of a floor turtle of a teacher who had not come across such things before, and the strategies which she adopted to make the most beneficial use of the device, and to integrate it as fully as possible into the school curriculum. The turtle used was the Edinburgh Floor Turtle, with hardware and software developed by Edinburgh University's Department of Artificial Intelligence.

---

## MEETING THE TURTLE

This chapter presents a detailed account of the introduction of a floor turtle to a class of nine- and ten-year-olds, and the subsequent development of their work over a five week period.

I had first met the floor turtle some two months earlier, while attending an in-service course at a college of education. As a result of my enthusiasm there about the possibilities of using a floor turtle, I now, thanks to the college, found myself in the unnerving position of having a turtle in my classroom for a five-week stay. It was bad enough being faced by 27 children at the beginning of September without a turtle also clamouring for my attention! But there was no way out of it: twenty-seven eager minds were desperate to know why we had one apparently mindless turtle in our midst, and to what uses it would be put. They approached it with curiosity, and the turtle responded by humming its signature tune, the first few bars of "Scotland the Brave".

The turtle itself is a dome-shaped perspex object with a wheel at either side and a pen in the middle. The pen may be lowered to leave a trail as the turtle moves across the floor. If no trail is required, the pen may be raised by using the appropriate command. The length and direction of movements taken by the turtle depend on the command typed onto the computer keyboard. The measuring capabilities of the floor turtle are precise: in fact, it can be a very accurate mathematical instrument.

The turtle is connected by a cable from the top of its dome through an interface box to the microcomputer (in this case an Apple II, lent to us by the college along with the turtle.). The computer is linked to a monitor screen and disk drive. (see Figure 5.1)

The software used to make the turtle understand commands given to it is called OKLOGO, and comes on disk. The O.K. stands for <u>One Key</u> as the children only have to press one key for each command. In each case the key pressed is the one with the initial letter of the command you want. To make it completely clear, the monitor screen displays the whole of the command word. Thus if you type F the screen displays the word FORWARD.

The commands are very simple. One is F for FORWARD. When F is followed by a number, the

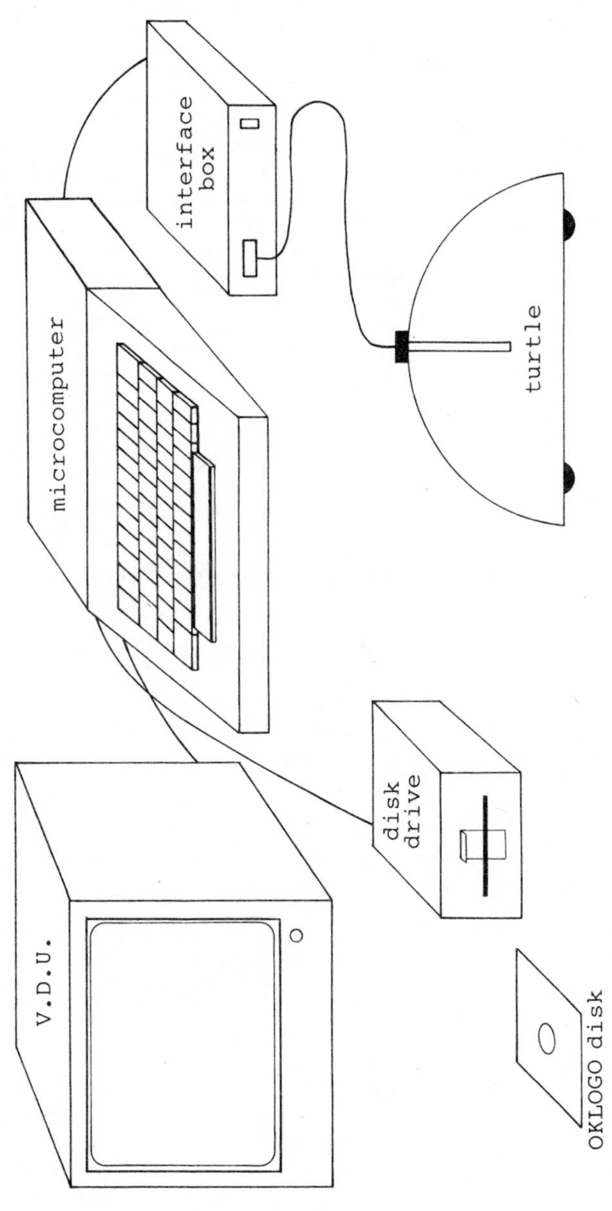


Figure 5.1 Hardware for running the turtle.

floor turtle will move forward the specified number of units.

So if you type F5

the screen will show FORWARD 5

and the turtle will move forward by 5 units. One unit is slightly less than one centimetre (it would be very convenient if it were exactly a centimetre). Typing B for BACKWARD will make the turtle move backwards, so B4 will make it go back four units. The turtle's direction can be changed using R for RIGHT and L for LEFT. These commands make the turtle rotate in the appropriate direction by the number of degrees specified. So if you type R60 the screen will show RIGHT 60, and the turtle will turn 60 degrees to the right, without changing its position. The next FORWARD or BACKWARD command will send it off in a new direction. The command U makes the turtle lift its pen up, and D makes it lower the pen. In this way you can choose whether or not the turtle leaves a line behind it as it moves. The turtle I was using is known as an Edinburgh turtle, because it was first developed at Edinburgh University. When the system is switched on, it plays a few bars from "Scotland the Brave". It will also produce this music when the command H for HOOT is given.

Commands can be repeated easily by using the command T (for TIMES). Thus

T 3 H (displayed as TIMES 3 HOOT)

will make the turtle play its tune three times over, and

T 4 R 90 (displayed as TIMES 4 RIGHT 90)

will make the turtle turn through four right angles in rapid succession, ending at its original heading.

Single commands can be combined into procedures. Procedure names become extra commands available to the user. In OKLOGO the command given to create a procedure is M (for MAKE) followed by the name to be given to the procedure.

So if you type M SQUARE

the screen will show MAKE SQUARE

The user will now be invited to PLEASE ENTER PROCEDURE; the commands making up the procedure are then typed in in the order in which they are to be executed, finishing with E (for END). If all is well, the message PROCEDURE ACCEPTED will appear. The command P (for PROCEDURE) can then be used with the procedure name to execute the procedure. Procedures can be incorporated within other procedures to make simple but powerful programs.

This example demonstrates the use of procedures in programs to control the turtle.

| | |
|---|---|
| SIDE<br>F 100<br>R 90<br>E | This procedure makes the turtle go forward 100 units then turn right 90 degrees. |
| SQUARE<br>T 4 P SIDE<br>E | The procedure SIDE is repeated four times to draw a square. |
| SPIN<br>P SQUARE<br>R 45<br>E | After drawing a square, the turtle will turn 45 degrees to the right. |
| SQUARES<br>T 6 P SPIN<br>E | A pattern of six squares rotating by 45 degrees each time is created. |

Complex patterns can be built up in this way using very short procedures.

I was fascinated by the possibilities which the floor turtle might offer in helping the children to form mathematical concepts, and to see whether the children's understanding of angles and shape work would benefit through their work with the turtle. I also wanted to find out just how easily the children would manage simple programming in LOGO.

## PLANS AND PREPARATIONS

Although the school had had a microcomputer (a PET) for some eighteen months prior to the arrival of the turtle, the children had had no previous experience of programming, that is, giving the computer sets of instructions to carry out. The children were however familiar with the keyboard, monitor, disk drives, and a certain amount of computer jargon. But the turtle was a completely new experience in logical thinking and programming. So my class and I set out to learn as much as we could about LOGO in the following five weeks.

The school is built on a semi-open plan pattern. The basic "design shape" is one of three classrooms opening onto a project area. The project area is floored with vinyl, which provides an ideal surface for the turtle to move across.

The project area was used to carry out the practical LOGO sessions. Tables and cupboards were positioned so that a large LOGO bay was formed. A table against the wall was used to hold the microcomputer, monitor, disk drive and turtle interface box. On the wall behind the table I fixed two large charts, one showing how to run LOGO and the other presenting the LOGO commands. The children could thus easily glance up from the keyboard to check on how to operate the system. On another wall I displayed LOGO work which the children had made and the programs used to produce each item. Written work, paintings and related mathematical work were also displayed on the walls. A small table held all that the children would need while using the floor turtle: large rolls of paper, sellotape, scissors and pens. Beside this was a display of books about computers and electronics at the children's reading level, which they could use as reference material or read for interest.

The turtle itself used the floor space in front of the computer. It ran on top of strips of paper 46 cm wide and about 3 metres long taken from a large roll and sellotaped together on the floor. This provided a fairly large paper area for the turtle to move about and draw on. The project area and the displays provided what seemed a suitably stimulating environment in which the children could work with LOGO and the turtle. A plan of this area is shown in Figure 5.2.

While planning the LOGO project for the class, I thought about other areas of the curriculum which would form natural links with "turtle geometry". Using these links, the class's work with LOGO could be integrated with the other elements of their curriculum.

The most obvious area was mathematics. As

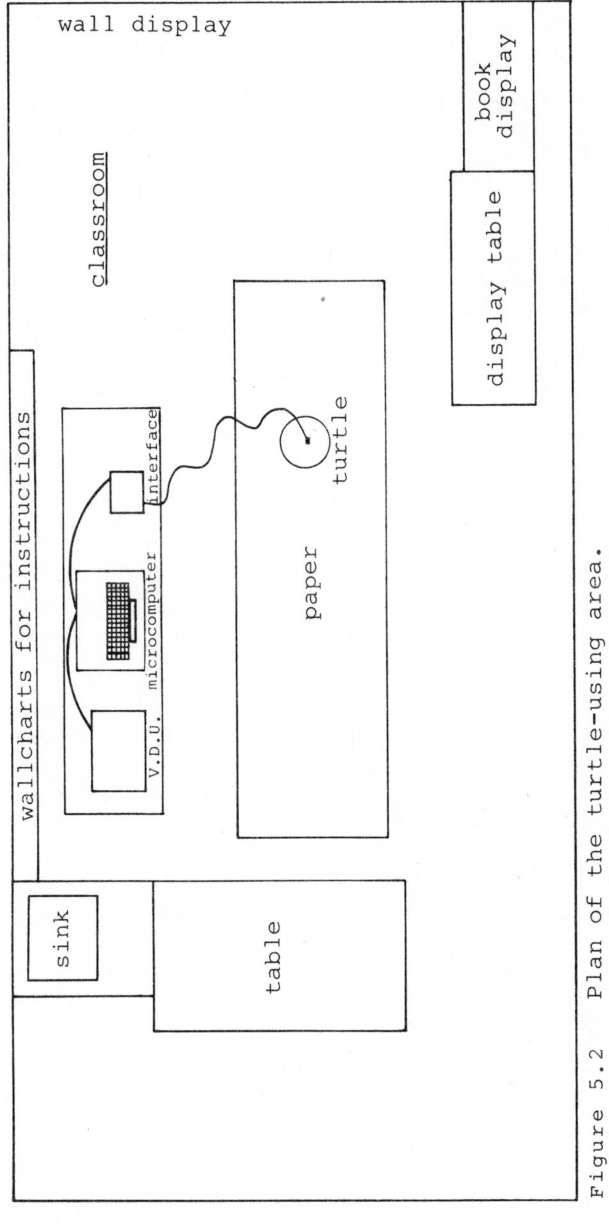


Figure 5.2 Plan of the turtle-using area.

the school uses Primary Mathematics from the Scottish Primary Mathematics Group (SPMG) as the basis for mathematical development, this became the focus for exploration of other parts of the mathematics curriculum which would fit in well with turtle geometry.

The shape work outlined for the Primary Six class (P6, i.e. ages 10-11) includes the following topics:

Recognition of certain flat shapes and discussion of their properties.
Tilings.
Curved stitching.
The introduction of degrees and measurement of angles.
Revision of acute and obtuse angles.

This could fit in well with possible work on the floor turtle: it therefore became the core of our LOGO project.

Firstly, I thought, the children could be told to make the turtle draw straight lines, then to turn corners of varying degrees. This would help them become familiar with the turtle commands. Once they had gained confidence in this, they could be asked to make the turtle draw certain simple mathematical shapes. These shapes and their properties could be discussed. From this we would go on to planning and drawing more complex shapes, such as the pentagon and octagon; then on to circles. Obviously a lot of work and discussion about angles would take place at this time. The children should be able to explain quite clearly why they were making the turtle turn a certain number of degrees.

When planning the development of work for the 5-week period, I tried to incorporate as many areas of the curriculum as possible. The links with language work were many and varied. There would be a lot of opportunity for discussion and the development of logical thinking. Through discussion the children could discover how they had produced unexpected outcomes in writing their procedures, and could then "debug" their programs. There could also be much discussion about the workings of the computer. Less able children could derive considerable benefit from the talk surrounding the turtle and its activities. There were many possibilities for written work within this topic. Opportunities would also arise for

| | |
|---|---|
| Language | Discussion - oral language skills<br>Vocabulary build up - list building<br>Dictionary work<br>Alphabetical order<br>Reference work<br>Instructional writing<br>Creative writing<br>Poetry |
| Science | Basic principles of the computer<br>Examining microchips with microscope |
| Geography | Compass rose and directions<br>Taking bearings |
| Art | Designs<br>Drawings<br>Paintings |
| Mathematics | Flat shapes<br>Tiling<br>Curved stitching<br>Angles<br>Rotations |
| Physical Education | Body movement |

Fig. 5.3 Activities developed through turtle work

different types of written work - instructional writing, creative writing and poetry. I also hoped to develop vocabulary and spelling through the specialised words associated with computer technology (many of them now entering our everyday language). Other reading skills such as dictionary work and ordering procedures could be practised, as well as reference skills, for which the books about computers and microtechnology would be available.

Other curricular areas could be incorporated in the work too. There would be opportunities for science. I hoped to explain the basic principles of a computer to the class; show them the inside of the computer (the easily removable lid of the Apple would make this possible); and look at microchips under the microscope. Geography and P.E. could both be incorporated through directional work. In P.E. the themes of movement and direction could be explored too. Children could do activities where they had to change directions, follow paths and make up a sequence of movements to travel along a certain route. For links with geography, I intended to revise compass points and bearings; the children could use compass bearings to work out routes and a lot of directional activities could be incorporated into their mapwork. Art work could be used as a medium for communication and display. As well as projected designs or patterns, the children could paint or draw pictures suggested by turtle trails produced through the computer. The activities developed through our work with the turtle are listed in Figure 5.3.

## USING THE TURTLE

After having decided on the areas of the curriculum to be integrated, the next stage was to show the children how to operate the computer equipment. The computer and the peripherals had been labelled so that the children would learn the correct names for each part. The function of each element was explained to the class.

When I introduced the Apple computer to the class, we had a discussion about the basic principles involved in the working of a microcomputer, and the extra interface card which had been added to make the turtle run.(1) Each child was given a packet of microchips which could be examined under the microscope. The children were also shown the inside of the computer.

I first used the turtle to demonstrate the various commands. The simplicity of the commands, and the fact that the monitor screen showed the full word of each command was helpful. The children also found the wall charts showing the operating instructions and turtle commands useful. By consulting them, both the children and myself could easily check what to do! The children were then invited to make the turtle do various things such as drawing straight lines, turning various angles to right and left and raising and lowering the pen.

The class was roughly divided into ability groups. This was done because I felt that when working with procedures (small programs to make the turtle carry out sets of instructions), some children would become left behind if more able members came to dominate each group. There were three children in each group, and nine groups in the class. Certain ground rules had to be laid down for all the groups. Only one pupil at a time was allowed to use the keyboard; another member of the group was needed to hold the turtle cable, otherwise it could become caught underneath the turtle. The third member of each group discussed, advised and wrote down any programs. Jobs were rotated within the groups, so that each child got a chance to do each job. A wall chart was drawn up to record the frequency with which the various groups used the turtle. When I started this work, we also had access to the school's BBC Microcomputer and Commodore PET. The usage of these machines was also incorporated in this chart. The children themselves kept a close eye on the chart to make sure that the groups worked with the turtle in the correct order!

When the children were in the early stages of using the turtle, they needed quite a lot of guidance. I had planned that each group should work for a period of one hour; this time was integrated into their normal class and groupwork timetable. This worked well when the children were making simple shapes such as squares and rectangles. But when they progressed to making procedures I found that they required more time, in order to be able to discuss their project satisfactorily, and to do any debugging necessary. As there was no editing facility with OKLOGO (i.e. a procedure had to be re-entered completely if a change needed to be made in it), debugging took rather a long time. I also had to allow for mistakes, syntax errors, and procedures being accidentally wiped out. Because of this, each group usually had only two LOGO sessions a week.

The first task for each group was to be able to load and run the disk, and thus operate the OKLOGO system. Once this had been accomplished, the group then tried simple commands in order to control the turtle, commands such as FORWARD, RIGHT, PEN DOWN, etc. The next stage was to build a simple shape. The group was allowed to choose its own shape, but most chose something easy to begin with, usually a square or a rectangle. At this stage, the children had not learned how to use procedures, and so the instructions for a square would be:

```
F 50
R 90
F 50
R 90
F 50
R 90
F 50
R 90
```

After this, the group was left to experiment with the turtle and make their own shapes. In this way they were able to familiarise themselves with the equipment and the OKLOGO commands.

When the children were confident that they could operate the system and make simple shapes, they became desperate to move onto more ambitious shapes. The universal cry was "How do you make the turtle draw a circle ?"

Well, I wasn't very sure of the answer myself. So we decided to try to find out. In order to do that, there was a lot of discussion about angles and degrees. The children knew that there were 360 degrees in a circle, but they had to work out the relationship between the angle being turned, the total number of degrees in a circle and the number of repeats necessary to complete the circle. Making a circle therefore required combining two elements:
a] The distance forward and angle being turned.
b] The number of repeats needed to make a circle.
Our first circle was very large, using 1 degree turns. The program consisted of two procedures, ARC and CIRCLE.

```
ARC                   CIRCLE
  F  10                 T 360  P ARC
  R  1                  E
  E
```

ARC moves the turtle forward 10 units, then turns it right 1 degree. CIRCLE repeats the procedure ARC 360 times. The children watched with fascination as the turtle obeyed the commands and repeated ARC 360 times. A wave of pleasure and relief filled the room as the turtle completed the circle and stopped exactly on his starting point. Circles took the turtle a long time to draw, as the ARC procedure had to be repeated so many times; one pattern of repeated circles took 20 minutes to draw.(2)

The children now realised that they had to

use procedures to make certain shapes. Each procedure had to be given a name. Procedures can be combined to make more complex shapes; thus the procedure CIRCLE made use of the procedure ARC. The more able children in the class picked this up quite quickly but some others required a lot of guidance in order to develop the concept.

When they first started to use procedures, the children were fascinated to discover that they could give their procedure any name at all and the computer would accept it. Lots of wierd and wonderful names were invented! After several very frustrating bugs in one program, one group took great pleasure in naming their procedure KILL!

While some groups were able to concentrate on programming procedures, others preferred to use the turtle to draw pictures. The favourites were men, houses and faces (using the newly discovered circle technique). This work was very time-consuming, as the children frequently made mistakes in programming which had to be unscrambled. A lot of time was spent in debugging programs: much thinking was done, and much was learned about the necessity for logical thinking and planning in making programs.

The work was recorded in several ways. Each pupil had a jotter in which they noted all computer-related work. This ranged from maths to poetry and included programs, the anticipated result, and the actual shape drawn by the turtle. A wall display of pictures, patterns and designs was put up in the project area. The programs for each were put alongside. This meant that children could if they wished use part of someone else's program to put into their own shape. It also helped the less able children, as they could use this reference source to consolidate their understanding of programs and procedures. A class book was made to display smaller pieces of work. Instructional and creative writing was incorporated in the wall displays, booklets and personal jotter work. Throughout the project, group discussions were tape recorded, and children's thinking patterns could be noted. A transcription of one such discussion is presented at the end of this chapter, along with examples of some of the children's writing.

When the class first started using the turtle, the discussion was mainly centred around the operation of the keyboard. By referring to the wallchart, children could easily work out which keys to press. In the initial stages, the most common error was forgetting to press the RETURN key. However, since they were working in groups of three, there was always someone who spotted the error! Later, when using procedures, forgetting to put the command END at the end of a procedure was a common error.

Part of the philosophy behind LOGO is that children can correct their own mistakes by working out at what point in their program they have gone wrong and then amending the program accordingly. When the children were using simple commands only to program the turtle, it was often easy for them to work out the correct commands required before touching the keyboard. While observing different groups, I noticed that there was usually someone who had positioned his body to face the same way as the turtle. In this way they could work out whether to turn right or left and by how many degrees.

As the class developed their programming skills to include making procedures, the bugs were not however always spotted before the program was executed. Usually the children started with a sketch of what they thought their finished shape would look like, and worked out their procedure from the sketch. The most common mistakes involved the angle being turned. When a program went wrong, there was a lot of discussion about exactly where was the elusive bug. Sometimes there were differences of opinion about where the turn should occur, and by how many degrees the turtle should turn. However, if the "bugged" part of the program were worked through on its own, it was possible to discover the angle required.

There was also a lot of discussion about the properties of certain shapes. Questions arose such as:

"How many right angles will there be in that design ?"

"Is that an acute angle or an obtuse angle ?"

"If we turn 5 degrees in each part of the circle, how many repeats will we need ?"

Such questions provided very valuable discussion within and between groups about the properties of shapes, designs and pictures, made by themselves and other groups. To take one example, making a circle required a lot of thought and planning. It also took a much longer time to draw a circle than a straight-sided shape. One child was heard to ask "Does a large circle need a small number of degrees or a large number ?"; and another asked "Will the size of the circle depend on the amount you make it go forward ?"

When the class were nearing the end of the project, we decided to explain our work to a small group of children from a Primary 7 class (i.e. aged 11-12). The older pupils were invited into our class, and two of our children, Kirsty and David, were asked to describe and explain the hardware, software and peripherals. Kirsty and David had no warning of this, and yet they explained very clearly the functions of each part of the computer system. Other members of the class then taught the Primary 7 pupils how to write a simple program in OKLOGO and instruct the turtle to carry it out and produce a drawing. The explanations were very clear and precise, and the inexperienced visitors were able to follow the instructions quite easily. They were impressed to find the turtle obeying instructions, and my class were even more pleased to find that they could not only do something which the older class knew nothing about, but that they had taught some LOGO to them as well!

## EVALUATION

At the end of the five-week period, I decided to evaluate the work undertaken. Firstly, mathematical concepts had clearly derived benefit from the work. When I observed groups working with the turtle, it was clear that they were using their bodies to work out the routes that the turtle would take. I certainly felt that they had gained a greater understanding of angles and shapes than could have been achieved without the turtle. There was also a development in what one might call the children's "general thinking skills"; when working with them, I noticed that it became easier for them to pinpoint a specific difficulty and work out a logical solution. Technical vocabulary over the period also developed noticeably.

Programming with OKLOGO was easy for the children. Even the poorest readers in the class found no problems. They didn't need to have to remember particular spellings, which might have discouraged them. All they had to do was type the initial letter of the word, and the whole word could be seen on the screen as a reinforcement. The turtle, acting like a robot to their instructions, gave the children confidence in controlling the computer.

The discussion which arose within each group showed clearly that the children were engrossed in problem-solving situations, and were usually able to succeed with the minimum of interference on my part. This was particularly noticeable when children were trying to debug a program by studying the turtle trail:

> Lorna: It should have been RIGHT 90 instead of RIGHT 135.
>
> Louise: That's it ! Otherwise it won't join onto that line.

All the children could set up the system without help. Much to my surprise, the turtle turned out to be very robust. We used it every day for five weeks, turning it on initially about 9.30 a.m., with the final close down usually about 3.30 p.m. Throughout this period we had no technical difficulties whatsoever. The only part of the setup procedure that required my help occasionally was positioning the pen inside the turtle. This had to be very accurate so that it went up and down at the precise height required.

The fact that the Edinburgh turtle can store only ten procedures put quite a limit on the children's work, as often good procedures had to be deleted to make room for others. As there was no editing facility, procedures with bugs had to be retyped in toto. Several children suggested that, if using the turtle again, a printer would be a great benefit, to maintain a "hard copy" version of programs. The children were keen to find out if there were other types of turtle available. A lot of them showed an interest in transferring the work of the floor turtle to a screen version of LOGO or a turtle graphics package.

My workplans for the period had included the development of related work in non-mathematical areas. I was not sure how successful this would be, and was pleasantly surprised by the results. Clearly, language was the main area of development. The discussion which took place within the groups was of a high standard and seemed to show a development of logical thinking processes. As their experience with the turtle grew, they became more confident in their own ability to solve problems and to debug programs. Their dependence on myself as the teacher to solve problems when they arose became less.

I had taught the class a certain amount of technical vocabulary throughout the period of work. The children understood it and used it confidently in their everyday talking and writing. They became very interested in books about microelectronics and computers. It had been intended that these be used as reference material, but many children wanted to take them home at night to read and digest. I therefore arranged with the local library service for extra copies of some of the books. This was the first time that the children had come across books at their own level on the new technology, and they were very eager to read them. This provided excellent motivation for their further development of reference skills and higher order reading skills through contact with these sources. Using the turtle and reading about computers provided a basis for creative writing. Poems as well as passages of descriptive writing were produced about the turtle, as well as stories about life in the future. Some of the children's writing is presented at the end of this chapter.

Something which hadn't been planned for, but which arose throughout the project, was contact with television programmes about computers. We watched a few programmes showing the potential of the computer as an everyday tool and how computers could overcome problems which existed today. The children just took it for granted that computers would become part of their everyday life, and showed none of the fears which are apparent in some adults. They had grown up with microtechnology and could not conceive a world without the "chip".

I had managed to obtain several packets of microchips, which the children examined under the microscope. They were fascinated to see the circuitry on these, and pleased to be able to keep their own packets of microchips and take them home to show their parents.

The mathematical work on angles transferred very well to the compass bearing work planned for geography. Previously we had been using 360 degree protractors to measure angles, and this proved a great help when we came to take compass bearings. The children used Silva compasses, and after a little help they were able to master simple bearings and directional work. A short orienteering course was set up in the playground, first with six points, then with ten. The children had to work in pairs and take bearings to find their way around the course. Had there been more time available, we could have gone on to more complex orienteering outside the school grounds.

In Physical Education, the children were again split into groups. To begin with, we played simple following type games, to get the idea of movement and turning. Then we moved on to more complex sequences of movement involving rolls, jumps, balance and running, all of which included directional change to make a pattern within the sequence. Throughout this work, changes of speed, body shape and direction were emphasised. Members of the class were then able to make up a sequence with a partner. These sequences involved sometimes mirroring and sometimes following their partner's movements.

The artwork achieved was mostly patterns and drawings suggested by the OKLOGO programs. Some children painted or drew others at work in the project area, while two groups of children made a large class frieze to ilustrate the way they thought we would be living in 1999. This frieze was stimulated by a story from one of the computer books, and the stories written by the class presenting their ideas of life in 1999.

The children got a lot of enjoyment from their work with the turtle, and it certainly made them think more carefully about mathematical concepts. My class are now quite confident in using LOGO as a programming language and are looking forward to using a screen version of LOGO. The turtle certainly proved itself a valuable learning tool. It also became a friend to the children, who nicknamed him Tommy. As the time approached for him to leave our school, the children said farewell to him by writing poems and limericks telling of the many enjoyable experiences they had shared.

NOTES

1. This card is not necessary when running the turtle from a BBC Microcomputer.

2. Faster approximations of circles can be produced by making the angle of turn bigger in the ARC procedure, e.g.

```
ARC                      CIRCLE
  F  10                    T 36   P ARC
  R  10                    E
  E
```

## APPENDIX 5A: CHILDREN'S WRITING

Here is a selection of some of the work produced during our time with the turtle. Each number indicates the start of a separate piece of writing.

### Inside a Computer

1] The computer has a lot of chips inside to make it work. The Apple has extra memory added and now has 48K. The Pet only has 32K.
Rom stands for Read Only Memory. Information in this part is put in when the micro is manufactured. Commands like RUN LIST RETURN are stored here. The ROM memory cannot be rubbed out.
Ram stands for Random Access Memory. Anything you program in is stored here. The Ram memory can be changed if you want.
Other information for the computer memory can be stored on tape, floppy disk or hard disk.

### Programming the Turtle

2] After you have plugged in everything, you switch on. Then you put in the disk and you type in LOAD OKLOGO2. Then you type in your name and program it to do something. Then you put the pen in and put it down and make sure the paper is straight. Now you can tell him to do something like F10 R90 B20 L45 or something.

3] First you must take out and set up the equipment and switch on. Put the disk in the disk drive and close the shutter. Type LOAD OKLOGO2.

Then type your name. Make sure the paper is down and the pen is down on the paper. Now you can put in your program:

```
F 100
R 90
F 100
R 90
F 100
R 90
F 100
```

4] To make a square, you have to give it a title but you have to type in the commands as well. Here are the instructions that you need to make a square:

```
SQUARE
  F 100
  L 90
  F 100
  L 90
  F 100
  L 90
  F 100
```

Then you type END.

5] First make a procedure which you can call SQU then type in F 100, R 90 and press E for END. Then make another procedure and call it SQUA then type in T 4 P SQU and then END.

```
SQU
  F 100
  R 90
  E
```

```
SQUA
  T 4  P SQU
  E
```

6] To make a triangle you decide what size you want the sides. Then type in F 100 if you want the side 100 then R 120 then F 100, R 120, F 100, END. Now you have a triangle.

```
TRIANGLE
  F 100
  R 120
  F 100
  R 120
  F 100
```

Things I like about the Turtle

7] On our second shot on the turtle we all tried to make a sort of star. We got a sort of one.

A Turtle on the Floor

The turtle is good because it does just what you tell it to do. It will draw anything you program it for. Its good because it gets you off your work. I like it. Its good fun.

8] On Tuesday the Primary Sevens came through to our area to have a shot on the Apple computer. Lorraine told Karen how to make a shape for a roof top. It worked out in the right shape. There were four primary sevens having a shot of the Apple computer. I like the turtle because when you make a procedure you can times it lots of times and make bigger and better shapes. Three people go to the computer in groups about once a week.

9] I liked the turtle a lot and it was good fun being on it. I would like it to come back again. the procedures are good and the turtle is good. I think the turtle is better than the BBC Buggy because it is nicer to look at.

10] Sarah and Adrian are in my group. I have worked on the turtle for three times. We have made lots of different shapes like squares, rectangles, circles and houses. The turtle is good to work with. One time we drew a house with windows and a door. It had a roof with a chimney on the top. The roof was pointed. Other groups have been making shapes too and we sometimes try to copy them. . . . I like doing circles and once we did a teddy bear on stage. He was a good teddy bear to make. He was made of circles, which I like doing best, and he had a nice hat to wear on top of his head. He had a walking stick too. He had two eyes and a nose. He had a mouth as well and it was smiling.

Poetry

11]
There was a young turtle called Tim
Whose classmates were incredibly dim.
They played all day long
Without the pupils going wrong.
Their shapes are all right
And now they are bright
Thanks to Logo and our turtle Tim.

12]
We now have a turtle called Tommy
He draws and makes lots of shapes.
And if we carefully hold his wire up
He won't make any mistakes.

13]
A turtle called Tommy was on the floor
When all the children came rushing through the door.
The shapes were good
So they should
Be thankful to Tommy the turtle.

## APPENDIX 5B: TURTLE USERS TALKING

These transcripts of group discussions around the turtle will give a flavour of some of the talk which was stimulated.

### 1. Drawing pictures in immediate mode

This was taped very early on in the LOGO work. The children were still experimenting with line lengths and the various angles necessary to turn in certain directions. This period of free play and drawing was very necessary as it enabled the children to gain full familiarity with the LOGO commands and therefore to use them successfully when they learned to work with procedures.

Peter: Wait there ! Leave it !
Jane: Make a wee boat. If we know how to do a circle then we'll do one.
No. We'll move it up. Press U !
Peter: We're doing a boat. Let's do a destroyer.
Jane: We're not doing one of them !
Ann: Forward 100.
Peter: Forward 100 again.
Jane: No. That's too much. Delete it !
Peter: Forward 100 now.
Jane: Right. That's 100.
Peter: Look. It's going to be a destroyer.
Jane: It needs to go round. Right 90.
Peter: No ! It's just R 45.
Ann: Then turn left.
Peter: No ! It's 70. That's perfect !
Jane: It's going to be a wee sailing boat we're doing.
Peter: I know. Try Forward 30.

A Turtle on the Floor

Jane: I hope you're writing all this down, Ann.
Peter: Forward 10. That'll do.
Jane: Forward a bit more.
Peter: No. Wait there !
Jane: Left 90, left ... left 16.
Peter: Right.
Jane: Left 80.
Ann: What have you done, Jane !
No, it's left.
When it's turning that way it's left !
Peter: It's right.
Ann: 35 and what ?
Peter: Right 90 ... another bit.
Ann: What do you put after 35 ?
Jane: Another 90. No, another 45.
Peter: Right ! That's it perfect.
Jane: Forward 200.
Peter: No. It needs to be a bit more.
Forward ... forward 100.
Jane: A wee bit more. About 15.
Peter: Forward, forward about 14.
That'll do anyway.
No ! Wait there Jane !
No ! Just do 10 ! Do 10 !
Jane: No ! ... no, 5 more.
That's it.
Ann: Forward 5.
Jane: That's it ! Now turn right 90 ...
No, right 45.
Peter: If it's turning right, it's going to go that way.
Jane: It's going to go left now.
Peter: No ! Turn right 100.
How's that for skill !
Jane: Forward.
Peter: Right. That was ...
Jane: 35, 40.
Ann: Forward ?
Peter: Try 20 and we'll see. That'll be on the safe side. ... Another 5.
Jane: We've done the degrees wrong.
Peter: It's supposed to be like that.
Jane: Another 3.
Peter: No, that's right !
That's all right just now !
Ann: Now right 1.
Jane: Forward.
Ann: Forward 1. Then right 35 ... then another little bit right.
Forward 10. No, right 10.
Jane: No! Right 5. Just to see where we get to.

Peter: That's it !
Jane: No, it isn't! Remember it's got to be in a straight line.
Ann: Forward about 10.
Peter: Another 1.
Jane: Another 2.
Peter: Go forward 2.
Jane: That's it !
Peter: It's finished ! It's finished at last !

## 2. Using Procedures

This was recorded just after the children had begun to use procedures. The procedures referred to are:

PEN: a straight line.
PENT: one side of a pentagon with a turn at the end.
PENTAG: one complete pentagon.
SLOOP: a repeated pattern of 10 pentagons with a right turn of 30 degrees between each pentagon.

Sally: How many times ?
Morag: Five. Five would make a pentagon. Type T 5 P PENT. Make PENTAG.
Sally: How many times do you want it ?
John: Ten times.
Morag: No. Because that would be the same as SLOOP.
John: Make it 15 then.
Morag: 15 should do. Type T 15 P PENTAG.
Sally: Is it not procedure PEN ?
John: No, it's PENT because PEN doesn't have an angle in it.
Morag: We don't need PEN to have an angle in it.

## 3. Explaining LOGO to P7

Here are two of my Primary 6 class explaining the system to two of the members of the Primary 7 class who came to see what we were doing.

Alison: The F key is for forward, the B key is for backward, the R key is for right, the L key for left. You only press one key.
James: You can't do more than 999 forward or backward, or else it will just say

SYNTAX ERROR and it won't work.

Alison: If you don't want it to go left for a right angle, you just press 45 or any number, not 90 after pressing L, and you always press RETURN after it.

James: You can make programs by pressing M and then you put in the name. Then put the procedure in. If you want the name of the procedures you press N and if you want to wipe out the procedures you press W. If you want the pen to go up you put U and if you want the pen down you press D. When you have finished your procedure you put E for END and then you press RETURN. If you want it to hoot press H. All the commands are on the wall if you get stuck.

That's the screen, that's the computer and that's the interface. That's the disk drive and then you put in the disk and put it down. Then you type in LOAD OKLOGO2 then make it RUN. It says PLEASE TYPE A COMMAND. If you want to times the procedure you put T (times) procedure, like REC; then it will make 5 RECs if you put T 5 P REC. If you want to see the quick reference guide, it's got all the names you might forget, just press Q.

# Chapter 6

# TURTLE GRAPHICS

## WHAT ARE TURTLE GRAPHICS ?

The most well-known feature which LOGO offers at present is "Turtle Graphics", a system of constructing designs or pictures by giving instructions to a drawing head, the "turtle". The turtle is usually represented on the screen by a small triangle. It is also possible to use a "floor turtle", a robot drawing device which will move around on a large sheet of paper; the possibilities with floor turtles are discussed in chapters 4, 5, and 8.

The principal guiding the control of the screen turtle is the same as that underlying the floor turtle: to direct it, you must take the turtle's point of view. To children already used to a floor turtle or BIGTRAK, this is no problem; for others, it is a change of orientation which they take to remarkably quickly.

However, the microworld they now move in is no longer the real one of the classroom floor, but the notional one of the monitor screen. This world is not so tangible and walkable as the classroom floor, and real people can't mix with turtles in it. It is a world not bound by the restrictions of the solid world outside the screen, and the possibilities are therefore different. Things happen much faster, and they can happen in different colours. Turtles can multiply, and can be rapidly transported from one location to another. Shapes can mysteriously overlap as the turtle leaps off one edge of its world to reappear at the opposite edge. It is even possible to create splendid shapes in a huge invisible universe of which the screen can only show a small corner. And as quickly as you want it, this world can be declared utterly empty, and ready for new creation.

In the transition from using a floor turtle to turtle graphics on the screen, the most apparent difference is in speed. The laborious ambulation of the floor turtle is replaced by the swift sketching onto the screen of the figure requested. This speed of execution makes experimentation easier and more tempting, since results of experiments can be delivered in a moment, and without the consumption of large amounts of paper. It is possible to move on from the relatively simple manipulations of shapes which tend to characterise floor turtle use, and to investigate more complex shapes. In particular, the principals underlying the manipulation of shapes can be examined by experimenting with shape-making procedures that require inputs.

## SHAPE MAKING

The following procedures show how complex patterns and ideas may be developed from simple ones.

```
TO TRIANGLE
    REPEAT 3 [FORWARD 150 RIGHT 120]
    END
```

This procedure, TRIANGLE, will draw a triangle with equal sides of length 150 units, as shown in Figure 6.1. Something similar can be drawn easily with a floor turtle.

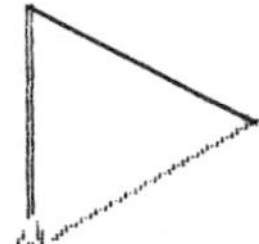

NOTE: In this, as in other figures in this chapter, the screen turtle is shown in its final position.

Figure 6.1 TRIANGLE

```
TO TRI :LENGTH
    REPEAT 3 [FORWARD :LENGTH RIGHT 120]
    END
```

The procedure TRI also draws an equilateral triangle, but it draws it whatever size it is told. TRI 50 will draw a very small triangle, TRI 150 a bigger triangle, and TRI 300 a big one (see Figure 6.2). This procedure makes possible a distinction between the <u>shape</u> and the <u>size</u> of the figure. The procedure name TRI tells us what shape we want, and the input figure 50 (or 100, 200, etc.) how big we want it to be. By looking at the procedure itself, the question can then be asked, what part of the shape is being varied to make it bigger or smaller?

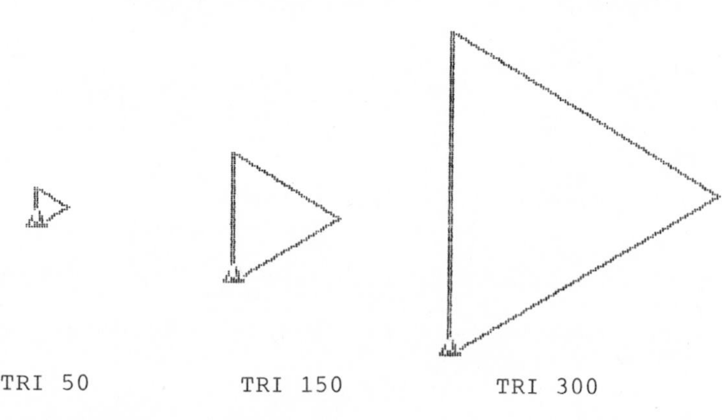


Figure 6.2 Triangles with TRI

Combining simple shapes to make more complex ones can be achieved through short and straightforward procedures.

```
TO SPINTRI
    REPEAT 12 [RIGHT 30 TRIANGLE]
    END
```

SPINTRI is a procedure which combines twelve 150-unit triangles into a wheel-shaped pattern (see Figure 6.3). The size and the number of triangles used is fixed.

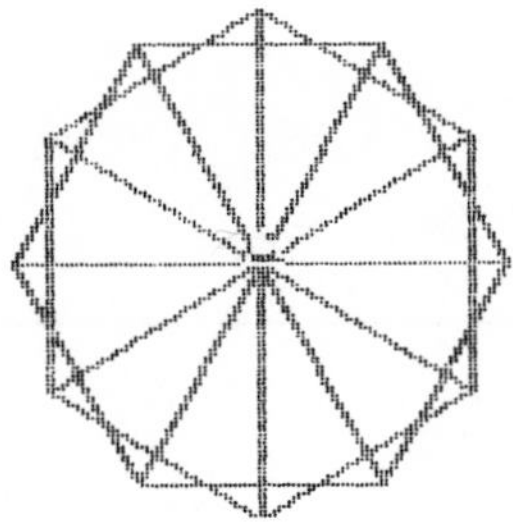

Figure 6.3 SPINTRI

```
TO TRIWHEEL :NUM
    REPEAT :NUM [RIGHT 360/:NUM TRIANGLE]
    END
```

However, TRIWHEEL enables the user to decide the number of triangles to be combined into a wheel-pattern. The number of triangles to be used is supplied as the input :NUM. Thus TRIWHEEL 5 forms a wheel-pattern with five triangles, while TRIWHEEL 20 does the same with twenty triangles. Experimentation with varying inputs will throw up patterns which can provoke a lot of discussion and posing of further questions (to be answered by further experimentation) about the effects of combining shapes. Figure 6.4 shows some TRIWHEEL products.

```
TO POLYGON :SIDES
    REPEAT :SIDES [RIGHT 360/:SIDES
                FORWARD 150]
    END
```

POLYGON shows that there is a connection between closed shapes no matter how many sides they have. By changing the input value, triangles, squares, and figures with any number of sides can be generated. Some products of POLYGON are shown in Figure 6.5. Because figures drawn with POLYGON soon get too big for the screen if they have lots of sides, it is useful to build a POLYGON procedure that has a variable size property:

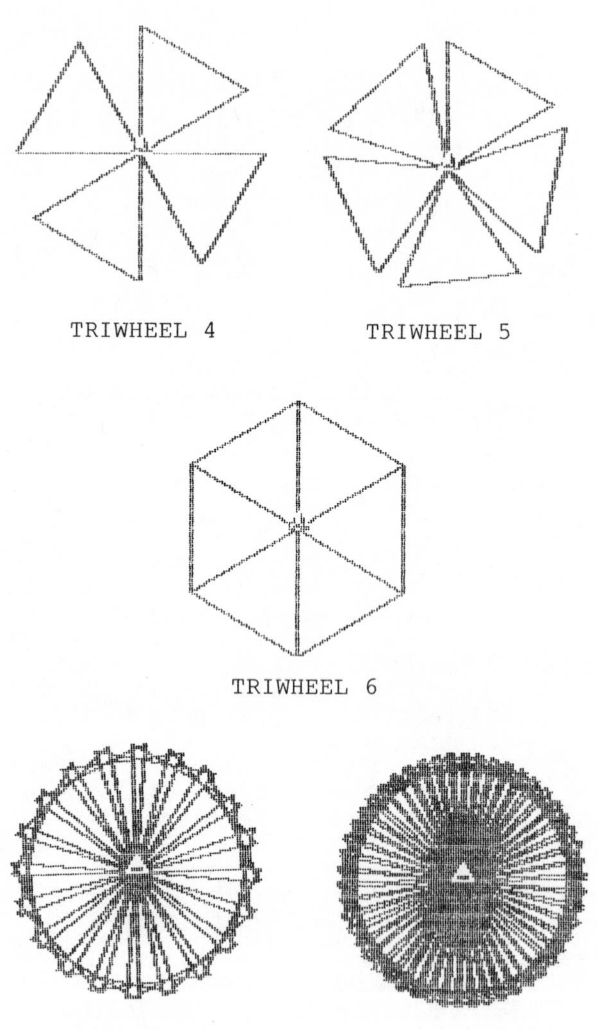


Figure 6.4  Shapes with TRIWHEEL

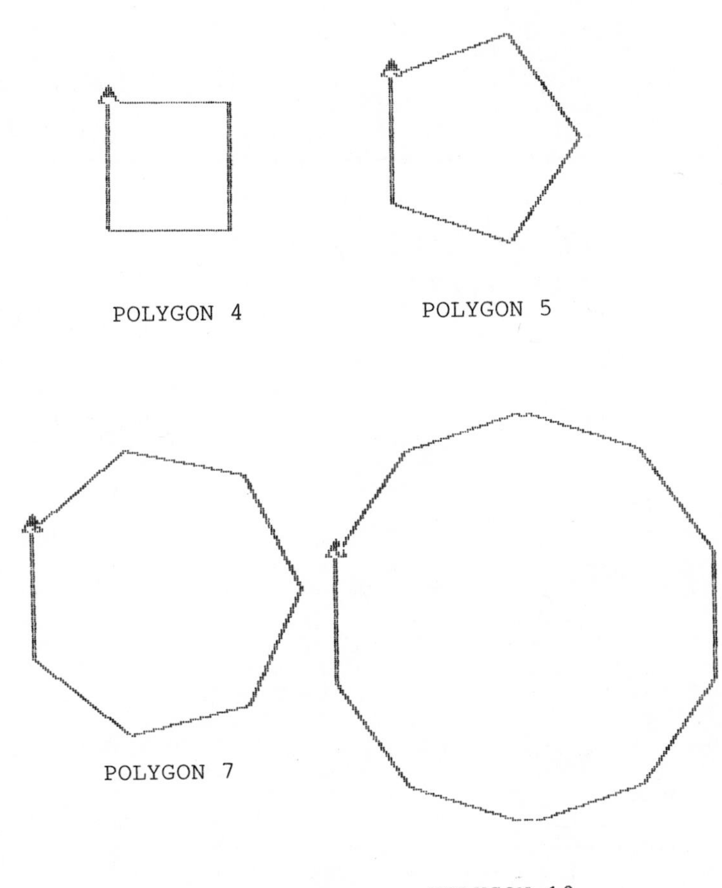


Figure 6.5 Shapes with POLYGON

NOTE: The turtle was placed at a suitable point on the screen to avoid running off it by a procedure MOVE:

```
     TO MOVE
          PU LT 90 FD 250 RT 90 FD 80 PD
          END
```

```
TO POLY :SIDES :LENGTH
     REPEAT :SIDES [RIGHT 360/:SIDES
                FORWARD :LENGTH]
     END
```

Using POLY, figures with many sides can be viewed. One question which can be raised here is: when does a polygon become a circle?

Using recursion, the ability of a procedure to call itself, makes possible another level of complexity.

```
TO SPIRAL  :LENGTH :ANGLE
     FORWARD :LENGTH
     RIGHT :ANGLE
     SPIRAL  (:LENGTH + 5) :ANGLE
     END
```

This basic spiral procedure will generate, through manipulation of the length and angle, an enormous range of interesting designs.(see Figure 6.6)

## USING TURTLE GRAPHICS

In the examples above, some questions about the characteristics of shapes have been raised. Much work by teachers with turtle graphics has concentrated on mathematical elements of the curriculum, and in particular work on shape, angle and distance. A great deal of mathematical development is possible through work with turtle graphics; consider for example the ideas involved in the creation and understanding of spiral designs.

Of course, turtle graphics are not only used for the exploration of the properties of shapes. They are also available for drawing pictures or diagrams, and for creating attractive and aesthetically pleasing designs. Creating pictures can involve much structured thinking if encouragement is given to consider carefully what the intended picture should consist of. This should not be thought of as reducing "creativity"; art history shows that paintings and sculpture which seem full of movement and life are usually the product of careful planning and preparation, including the calculation of proportions and perspectives. Indeed, it is the structure upon which they are built which gives them much of the power and three-dimensionality which they possess.

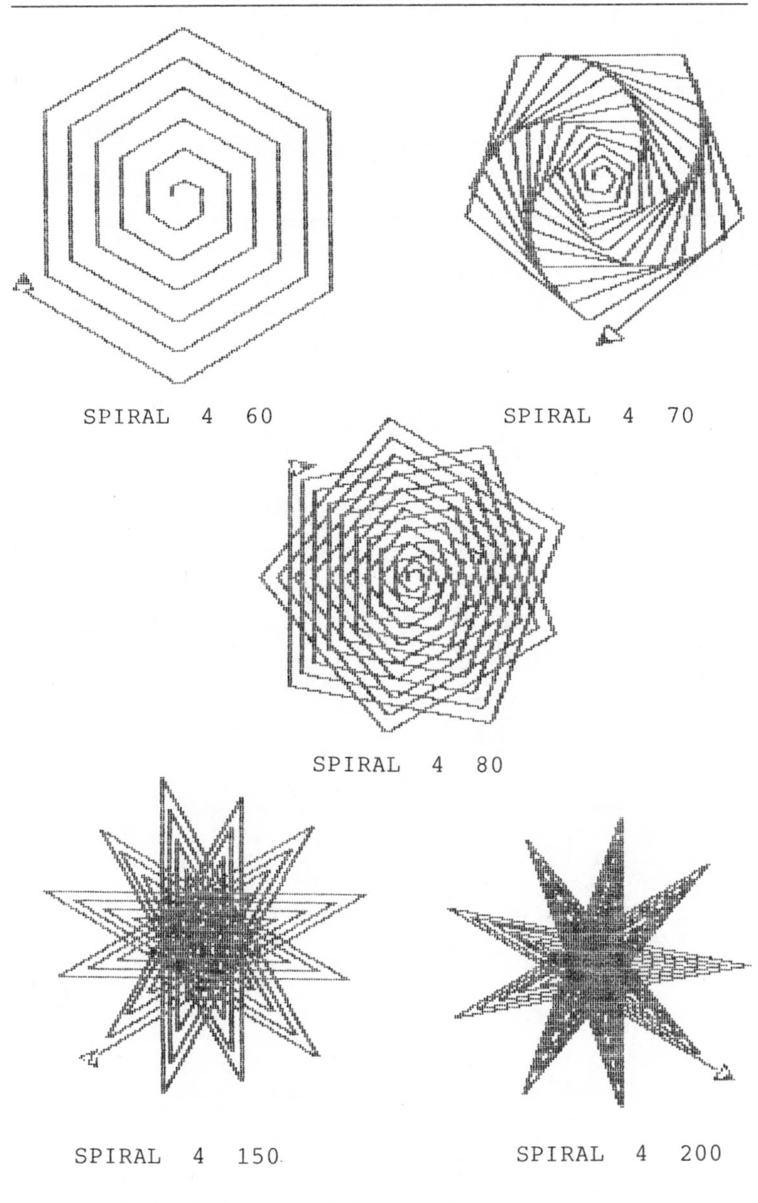


Figure 6.6 Spirals with SPIRAL

Creating pictures will not always follow the road of careful planning. It is an oft-encountered feature of LOGO use in classrooms that some children who set out with every intention of creating object A, when their program, due to some bug does not produce the expected likeness, suddenly decide that they really wanted to make object B, which the bugged program for object A conveniently produces. Planning involves hard work, and therefore teachers should ask themselves what is being achieved when conversion of bugged designs occurs. It may be that the conversion is a sign of realisation that the original objective was too complex to be realistically attained by those attempting it; or it may lead to a new phase of planning as the new objective is developed and refined. But it may also be a sign of avoidance of intellectual labour, and lead to little positive result. The teacher, with her expert knowledge of the children involved, must be the judge.

A feature which is becoming available with most LOGOs now is the capacity to support "sprites". These are graphic objects which can be moved around the screen as single units. They can be given an order of viewing priority so that they can move in front of or behind each other. Using sprites makes effective animation possible within LOGO; thus pictures in which the elements can be moved at will can be created, as well as exciting games.

It is only possible in this book (which aims to look at the full range of LOGO's features) to give a brief indication of what turtle graphics offers. However, there are many good LOGO books which demonstrate well the tremendous variety of possibilities available when using turtle graphics. Some of these are listed in Chapter 17. Much of the material in LOGO magazines, or computing magazines with a LOGO section, is also focused on turtle graphics. And every teacher who has used turtle graphics has examples of impressive or surprising materials produced.

## TURTLE GRAPHICS WITHOUT LOGO

Turtle graphics are just one of the features which LOGO offers. It is however possible to obtain programs which only offer turtle graphics, without all the other features of LOGO. Some of these, such as Tandy Color LOGO or Acornsoft Turtle Graphics are fast machine code programs which genuinely offer a sub-set of LOGO commands, and support such features as multiple turtles, full recursion, a full screen editor, and maintenance of a good number of user-defined procedures in the computer's memory.

Others can fairly be described as simulations of part of LOGO's turtle graphics facility. These are usually written in BASIC and, compared to LOGO itself, are slow, and limited in what they offer. Sometimes features alien to LOGO have been introduced, such as line numbers (1), or using the equals sign to give variables their values.(2) Turtle graphics simulators were produced in Britain mainly because of delays in full LOGO implementations appearing for the Sinclair Spectrum and, particularly, the BBC Micro, when many teachers, aware of the claims made for LOGO and wishing to try it out, looked for something which would offer at least part of what LOGO could do, especially its most well-known facility. Some of these programs, such as DART (3), are faithful attempts to reproduce, albeit in limited form, the characteristics and actual commands of LOGO. Others are less faithful to LOGO but claim to support LOGO-type learning situations. Others are little more than BASIC programming exercises which reproduce the commands FORWARD, LEFT and RIGHT, and not much more.

Now that full LOGO implementations are available for school computers, there is less need for these programs. Indeed, the handbook to DART advises the user to put it aside when a full LOGO is available. However, many teachers were and are able, using the better turtle graphics simulators, to offer genuinely exploratory learning environments and a good introduction to LOGO-type experiences. Some teachers prefer to use, say, DART, as an intermediate stage between work with Bigtrak and use of a full LOGO implementation. Much of what is said about turtle graphics in this book can in fact be applied to good quality turtle graphics simulators. There is an unfortunate tendency for such programs to be sneered at by some LOGO enthusiasts, and over-generalised talk of "true" versus "pseudo" LOGOs can obscure the useful work that can be achieved in classrooms through the thoughtful use of good turtle graphics simulators.

Unfortunately, the situation has become confused because some turtle graphics simulations are claimed by their inventors to have all the essential features of LOGO itself. Confusion is further increased when the word LOGO is used in the names of such programs. Be suspicious if you see a "LOGO" which is offered on cassette (the exception being Sinclair LOGO for the Spectrum) or which does not offer list processing. For example, a publisher's catalogue for 1984/5 describes one turtle graphics program as "omitting only list-handling from standard Logo" and "allowing programs with line numbers as well as procedures." Turtle graphics programs are (or should be) much cheaper than full LOGOs (if one is not, there seems very little point in buying it); but before buying one, make sure it has a good reputation, and check exactly the features which it offers. Match these with the price and the sort of learning situation which is to be supported. Consider that, although it is more expensive, a full LOGO implementation offers much more power and flexibility and many more facilities than a turtle graphics simulation.

It is a telling tribute to the attraction of LOGO that so many cheap imitations have been produced. It is now a favourite exercise of writers of BASIC textbooks to include a program which attempts to simulate turtle graphics. Such simulations are usually however only a pale reflection of the powerful graphics facility which real LOGO offers.

## NOTES

1. In the computer language BASIC the "flow of control" of a program runs sequentially, following the order of the line numbers, except when directed otherwise by GOTOs and GOSUBs, which themselves use line numbers to fix destinations. Structured BASICs have introduced control structures which do not employ line numbers as destination markers, especially procedures. In LOGO the flow of control is directed by procedure calls. This makes the structure of the program very clear, and line numbers unnecessary (or even confusing).

2. In BASIC the equals sign is used to give values to variables. This was originally

associated with the command LET. Thus

```
LET  NUMBER = 26
```

assigned the value 26 to the variable NUMBER. However, in most BASICs the LET can now be dispensed with, so that the command

```
NUMBER = 26
```

is sufficient to assign 26 to the variable NUMBER. Assignment commands set or change the values of variables. Thus

```
LET  NUMBER = NUMBER + 3
```

makes the new value of NUMBER the old value plus 3 (i.e. in this example 29). Without the LET, this statement reads

```
NUMBER = NUMBER + 3
```

Learning that "=" means "the same as" is a fundamental element of school mathematics, and in that context

```
NUMBER = NUMBER + 3
```

is self-contradictory or meaningless. The use of the equals sign in a completely different way in computer programs can therefore lead to confusion not only in programming but also in wider mathematical understanding.

LOGO avoids this problem by using the command MAKE to give values to variables. Thus in LOGO

```
MAKE "NUMBER  26
```

gives the value 26 to the variable NUMBER, and

```
MAKE "NUMBER  :NUMBER + 3
```

increases the value of NUMBER by 3.

The inverted commas and colon are used in LOGO to avoid another source of confusion, the distinction between the _name_ and the _value_ of a variable. The inverted commas always refer to the name of a variable, the colon to its value. Thus the command

```
PRINT  "NUMBER
```

will produce

```
NUMBER
```

while the command

```
PRINT  :NUMBER
```

will produce

```
29
```

assuming this to be the current value of NUMBER.

3. DART is available for the BBC Micro; as well as screen graphics, it can be used to control an Edinburgh turtle. It can be obtained from: Advisory Unit for Computer-Based Education, Endymion Road, Hatfield, Herts AL10 8AU, England.

# Chapter 7

# CASE STUDY 3: TURTLE LEARNING IN THE HOME

Elizabeth Leckie

---

Elizabeth Leckie is a parent and, like most parents, she takes a keen interest in her children's learning. The home is a much more powerful environment for learning than any educational institution and, with the current influx of microcomputers into homes, another area with great potentialities is opening up. It is sometimes easy for teachers to forget that much of children's computer awareness comes from their experience at home. As this chapter shows, the home can be as much an environment for learning through LOGO as the school, particularly when a parent is sensitive to the needs of her child and to the potentiality of LOGO.

---

## ENCOUNTERS WITH LOGO

News of LOGO crystallised a vague and resigned feeling that I ought to acquire a micro for my two daughters. A BBC B arrived and we waited ... and waited ... and waited for LOGO; and then gave up and bought a turtle graphics pseudo-LOGO. This has been used in three short bursts of interest with longer periods of neglect in between, mostly by my six-year-old and myself. Although my three-year-old enjoys playing at the computer, with or without her sister, I feel her introduction to LOGO can be postponed at least until the arrival of a full implementation. The learning environment is therefore very different from that of a classroom. If my role is an ambiguous one, somewhere between learning partner and teacher, it is also a very fluid one; especially as I don't have to render account with a palpable educational credit.

I haven't pursued an unswerving strategy of "structure" or "non-intervention". Useful though such terms may be in putting over an argument in the space of an article, LOGO is a very flexible medium, allowing for fine adjustments to personality and the circumstances of a rather informal home environment. It is counter-productive to tell a six-year-old, who has no official experience of measurement of turn in degrees and who is playing LOGO voluntarily, in her own free time, to draw a hexagon today because she did a triangle yesterday; especially if the parent is stood there, answer book in hand and not sharing the secret. If she needs a hexagon for something, doing battle with the fine degree of accuracy of turn required is another matter. So, for us, motive is the measure. The obvious danger of this is that an unrestricted and arbitrary flow of incoming data and experience will swamp the formation of a 'gestalt' and dissolve confidence. Having made a house, then a row of houses, she decided to make a scene with a street, a park, a ... . I blenched inwardly, but throughout she has been able to adjust the vision to her assessment of her capabilities. When she designed some fields, she wanted to put rows of cabbages in them. She said that she didn't feel ready to do curves or circles and settled on hexagons as she had done one before when making a Doctor Who control console. When she had made a row of suitably sized hexagons, she said "Your go. Could

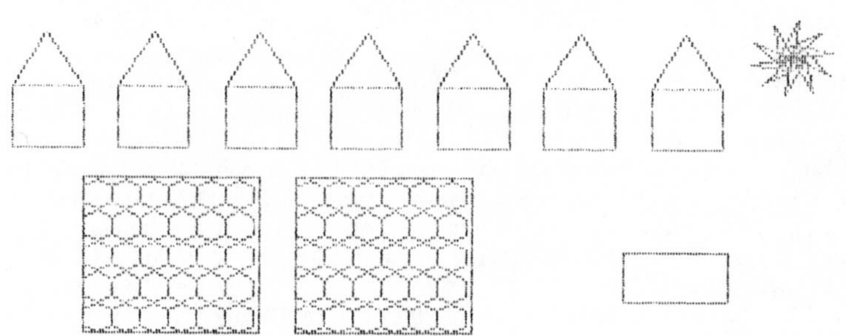

Figure 7.1 SCENE

This was never finished. The filled squares were fields of cabbages and the oblong a swimmng pool. She intended to add flowers and climbing frames in a park area.

you fill my field with them?" I'm quite happy to share like this sometimes. (See Figure 7.1)

Sometimes we work/play alongside each other. Even when apparently engrossed in some other activity, she'll interject, "Pen up, Mum" or query a new command. I have used both HOME and SETY, SETX out of laziness when I thought she wasn't looking. She used HOME the next time she was at the keyboard. She has bumped up against negative numbers from time to time and likened their use in SETY, SETX to Minusland in Roald Dahl's <u>Charlie and the Glass Elevator.</u> She has since suggested that I use them, but hasn't yet ventured to use them herself. I put up a SETY, SETX chart next to our large lettered list of abbreviations for commands. When a command to LIST wiped off some lengthy exploratory work of her own, she countered with a list of our stored programs and stuck it up alongside.

She does play at the computer alone and unprompted sometimes, especially when she's doodling. After making the hexagon her doodles centred round turns of approximately sixty degrees. But she is far less likely to go off on her own to play with the computer than she is to generate other intellectual and imaginative

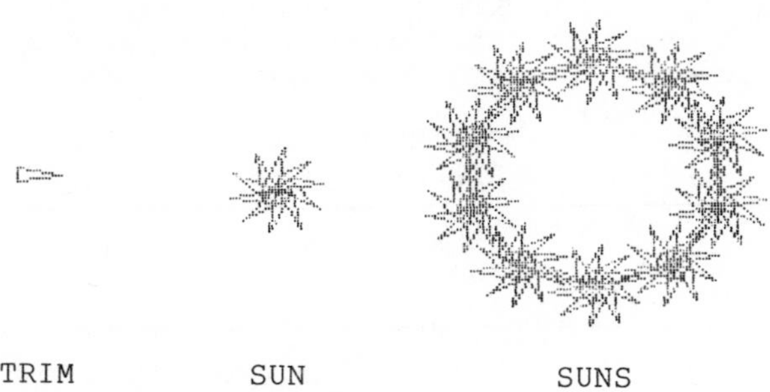


Figure 7.2 Creation of SUNS

TRIM was intended originally as a carrot to fill a field in SCENE, but was used to make SUN, which forms part of SCENE, and then SUNS.

---

occupations for herself. She "experiments" and "invents" machines and games both of the board game and imaginative type, and even sets me the occasional puzzle. I don't think she will ever become computer crazy but perhaps with time she will want to go off and play with it. It can't be picked up just anywhere; it means making a decision to go off into a separate room and breaching the code of the keyboard. She picked up letters, capitals included, very easily, but she is not comfortable with QWERTY. I think she in particular might be helped by an explanation of the historical reasons for the QWERTY layout next time I get an opening, but I am considering a concept keyboard.(1) I do occasionally type in to her dictation if she's already put in a lot of slog and it's way past bedtime.

When she wants to share, I think there is a lot to be gained, both in retaining enthusiasm and in generating "Mathsland" conversation. Such conversation can be carried on away from the computer room, into the garden or the bathroom, as can playing turtle. She doesn't walk it out as a turtle; she's never seen a floor turtle and when we were reading about the Cheshire Cat in Alice in Wonderland her screen turtle became a rabbit called Primrose who only shows her ears and sometimes disappears altogether. Primrose features in stories to which the younger daughter also contributes, with other imaginary characters and several battered puppets. Primrose performs magical feats by LOGO, and her ultimate weapon is SIZE 0. Humphrey the school guinea pig inspired a nonsense program which went something like:

```
DEFINE HUMPHREY
REPEAT 1,000,000
DANDELION
CHEW
AGAIN
END
```

I try not to give help of the type which makes for dependence; to draw out rather than tell. I am also well aware of the inhibiting effect of flaunted parental accomplishment in any sphere, albeit only comparative. Response to a request for help is quite different to unrequested exposition. If the latter is unwelcome, her expression closes and any continuance is met with a ceremonious stuffing of the fingers into the ears. She can say "let me do it myself" without compunction.

The occasional unconditional gift of information can be very rewarding. On one occasion an irritating interruption nipped a nascent curve in the bud. When the curve didn't revive at the following session, I produced two different sized circles. She then took over and made a nest of circles. She cleared this off accidentally by calling LIST to find an old program to use as a treasure box at the centre. The renewed effort incorporating rotation also foundered during an attempt to delete the final circle in the nest because it impinged on the edge of the screen. By then, it was getting very late and so I introduced the SIZE option without any exposition of variables, etc., and the nest was saved as TOT (Tunnel of Treasure - the treasure box never did get in) and rotated as TROT. (See Figure 7.3) She then asked if she could use a geostrip contraption I had made to illustrate turn measured from a continuing straight path. When I returned to the room she had made a set of four spoked fans in each geostrip size. These she insisted on taking up to bed along with paper and pencil, and she proceeded to work out her four times table from them. The following day she made a nest of triangles using the SIZE option. And,

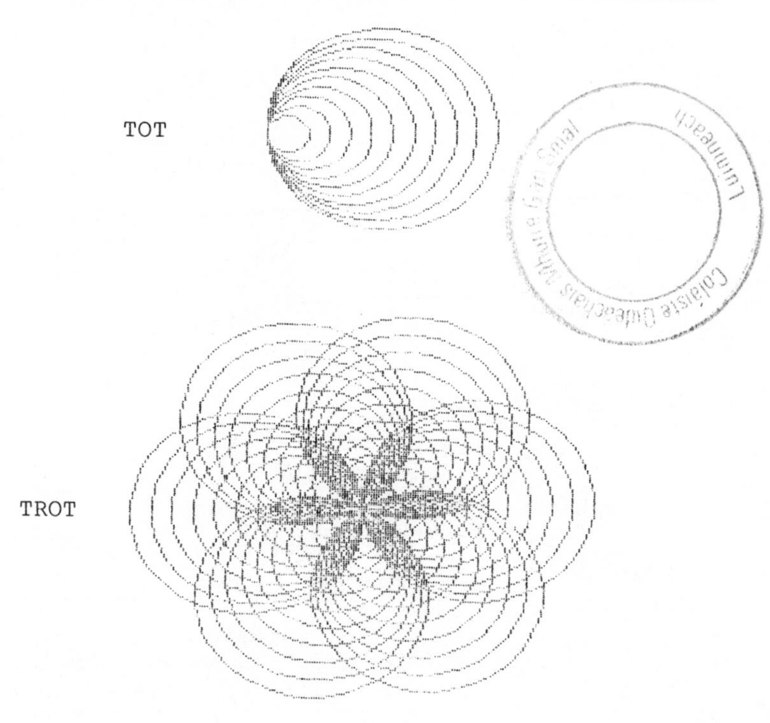


Figure 7.3 TOT and TROT

if she was momentarily disappointed to get a striped triangle, she didn't show it, but suggested it would make a good cobweb if rotated and left me to get on with it. (See Figure 7.4) Whether she could now produce a curve is another matter.

Apart from the inbuilt formality of the hardware, LOGO adapts easily to our personal styles of play. And though it can't rival drill programs for tidiness, it creates a lot less maternal back-bending than, say, the much-favoured dressing-up activities. Though they go unstated, the educational purposes which LOGO fulfills are also very varied. Whilst I don't feel I have to justify the use of LOGO by some measurable end

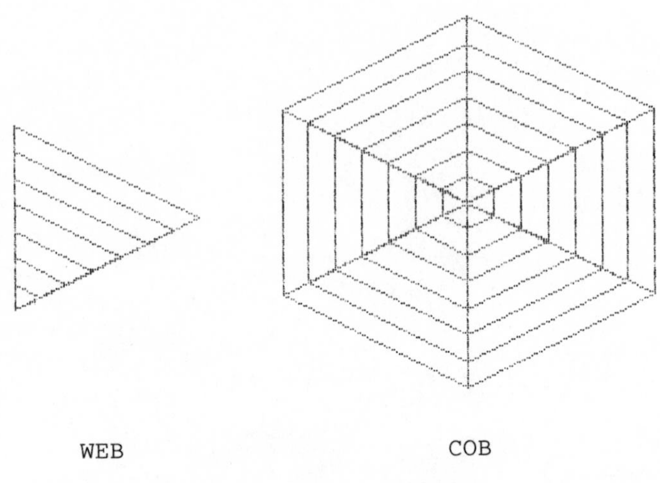


Figure 7.4 WEB and COB

product, I do have one rule, that it should be enjoyable. There are days when she scowls and says "No", and long stretches of disuse. This is perhaps a pity, as it's not like a project subject, but, like a language or maths, it needs to grow and to be used to keep it in working order.

## THE BENEFITS: ABSTRACT AND PRACTICAL

So what has she gained from her encounters with LOGO and what would I expect her to gain from future use of it? It is so easy for children, particularly the academically assured, to emerge from the educational process with their personal initiative deeply buried, if not extinguished, and their capacity for applying their considerable knowledge in practice very undernourished. The reasons for this are, no doubt, complex sociological and psychological ones, and I am not laying the blame on secondary, still less primary education. But any process which can circumvent it should be encouraged. The practice of LOGO has a contribution to make in developing "problem-solving" skills. But it requires sensitive adjustment to indivdual needs if it is to extend initiative and self-reliance and preserve that exciting but vulnerable freshness of mind which most young children possess.

What LOGO certainly does provide is a valuable dialogue between the abstract and the practical, not only providing a pathway to abstract understanding through practical work, but also providing for the testing and application of the child's abstract theories. The latter possibility is particularly valuable for a rather cerebral child. She has taken easily to the planning, conciseness and clarity of thought called for in the top-down analysis mould, but finds it more difficult to muster the perseverance to, say, pinpoint an exact amount of turn required. She is less likely than I to forget instructions like PEN UP or SHOW, and wasn't going to be caught twice by the wipe-off effect of LIST; she's even inclined to put her experimenting in Define Mode.

Whether LOGO encourages habits of careful planning to be carried across into other areas is another matter - I still find myself ordering furniture without calculating for radiators impeding access to the back of the drawers. But the debugging exercises which crop up in LOGO use do help one to look at mistakes in a constructive light. The child can assess her efforts on the screen without relying on the measure of someone else's judgement, slowly learning to take a pride in patient self-correction.

I feel that alternative approaches to problem-solving should also be aired. I can't claim to be very energetic in this respect, though opportunities arise in the home frequently. The girls each had a bunch of four balloons (from a wedding), filled with hydrogen or another gas lighter than air. These kept clustering on the ceiling, and the children couldn't reach the string. The elder tied something to her string and the balloons waved, flower-like, from the floor. The younger one wound a handy string with three beads round hers, and they floated attractively with just the tip of the highest balloon touching the ceiling. The elder asked for some beads. "O.K.", I said, "If you get into the bath, I'll fetch some." She complied, but I cheated and plonked down to read the T.E.S. Computer Extra. After washing her doll for a while she said "Tell me about EDIT". I took up the LOGO use first, but the book aspect got drowned in doll-washing chatter. A pause, then "Have you finished with any of that paper?" "Well ... what do you want it for?" "To tie on my balloons." I tore off a very small piece and tied it on kite-fashion. It wasn't sufficient. "Try scrumpling it up, Mum." [Last year's gliders, etc. play?] Perfect. She returned to washing her doll's hair.

LOGO has certainly given her a means of communicating with the computer. She likes most to build everything into procedures, as it enables her to keep her work; it might be otherwise with a turtle. She loves to build up a scramble of sub-procedures into a new whole. She delights in choosing her own whimsical names for programs. These opportunities for verbal fun and the absence of preconditions for simulating violence may make LOGO particularly suitable for encouraging girls to take to the computer, if the widespread rumours of reluctance are to be believed.

Use of LOGO has also contributed to her understanding of various mathematical concepts, although this is difficult to pinpoint exactly as against other activities. I have had pangs of anxiety. Measurement of turn by degrees doesn't appear in most maths schemes until 9-10 year old level, but she has grasped 360 degrees, 180 degrees, and 90 degrees because they are useful to her. Her understanding of left and right is much clearer near the times when she's using LOGO. Occasionally LOGO gives rise to the use of a calculator or a paper and pencil vertical sum. One such must be worth several pages in an exercise book because she needs the answer. She also gets a use for her acquaintance with three-figure numbers.

The effects of LOGO on her art have been marked. She produces quite complex symmetrical patterns. When she first did repeats with rotation she went off and drew round templates in rotated positions. Her drawings are often hastily produced but she takes quite a lot of care to match up her patterns. I would be concerned if she didn't also produce plenty of freer work. I feel it would be fruitful to consider whether her own hand needs elaborate commands to get to an approximate point on paper and draw, but no opening has yet appeared. As with problem-solving skills, I feel different ways of composing, whether it be a picture, a story or an argument should be given conscious attention. LOGO might foster conciseness and a renaissance of good paragraphing, but it might also predispose to a static vision stunting the development of ideas by their own dynamic. In the main, books on LOGO have been an honourable exception, but the average computer manual is no advertisement for clarity of exposition, let alone eloquence.

LOGO has enjoyed wide and enthusiastic media coverage and this is well merited, but sometimes this zeal has fanatical overtones of the elect rooting out heresy from within. Although I do think certain approaches preferable to others, too inflexible an attitude will only cause anxiety and inhibit on-the-spot response. The flexibility of LOGO is one of its major strengths; it has room for many varying approaches and goals.

## NOTES

1. Perhaps the keyboard puts girls in mind of the controls of domestic appliances which have to be operated in set ways to effect particular results and which they are probably either forbidden to touch or taught to treat with caution (quite rightly too). Boys are more likely to have toys with plenty of buttons and knobs which do nothing; no wonder they're delighted to use some which do! I now provide open access to my old portable typewriter.

2. Beware the remarks of friends and relatives who may be used to lush arcade graphics or defensive about computers. It is very annoying to see a child who has gone to the effort and risk of working something out for herself being deflated by a thoughtless remark.

Chapter 8

# CASE STUDY 4: TURTLES FOR SPECIAL CHILDREN

Marie Buckland

---

Marie Buckland is a class teacher at Glevum Special School, near Bristol. In this chapter she describes how, making use of the "Concept Keyboard" and a floor turtle, she has been able to provide stimulating and challenging educational experiences for children with learning difficulties. The Concept Keyboard is a membrane-type keyboard (it looks like a flat plastic pad) which can be programmed to recognise input from any specified area on its surface. Paper or plastic overlays can be used to show pupils the current layout. The potential of the Concept Keyboard and similar devices, particularly in areas where the normal typewriter keyboard layout is too complicated or distracting, is enormous.

---

## Turtles for Special Children

The use of computers in Special Education is proving to be successful. Obviously the computer can be an emancipatory tool for many handicapped pupils; it also has endless patience when used in an instructional mode, and many children are highly motivated to use games and simulation programs. However, the conjectural mode, in this instance LOGO, appears to offer a child an open-ended experience whereby he can explore his environment using a powerful computer as his tool.

I teach in a school which caters for the needs of boys and girls with moderate learning difficulties. The reasons for a child's placement in this type of education are usually a combination of the following: a low basic ability; a slow rate of learning; lack of progress; anxiety or emotional problems; poor concentration; perceptual difficulties; poor language development; behavioural difficulties; poor attitude; and/or minor physical handicaps.

### THE FIRST TRIAL

In 1982 our school already had a BBC micro and a Sinclair ZX81, and we had acquired a few educational programs. At this stage the most important benefit was the computer awareness skills that the children (and also the staff) were gaining. This was a vitally important period when we gradually started to understand the potential of using micros in schools.

Towards the end of that year, Bristol SEMERC (Special Education Microelectronics Resource Centre) asked me if I would like to use an RML380Z and a floor turtle with my class of 13- and 14-year-olds. This was to be for a trial period, at the end of which I was to assess its suitability for use in Special Education. Before introducing the equipment to the class, I became fully familiar with the software - OKLOGO (described in more detail in Chapter 5) - and with the movements of the turtle, and I also spent a good deal of time planning and organising the classroom so that the turtling area would be screened off from the rest of the class group.

The initial interest was high and the novelty aspect made whole class demonstrations necessary. After two such sessions, the majority of the children understood the techniques of giving simple commands to the turtle, and groups of two or three children were able to work in the turtle area without causing too much distraction to the rest of the class.

The children who showed an interest and understanding straight away were those who had good spatial awareness, and had the confidence to think ahead and talk through their proposed actions with their partners. At each step they had to consider the position of the turtle and decide how the next movement would affect this position. The majority of older children, who had a good understanding of number, were able to use the turtle in direct drive, and four children out of my class of fifteen developed an interest in building up simple procedures. These were the more able members of the group. Another group of four children were unable to use the equipment in a meaningful manner, as they did not possess the necessary understanding of number, or were unable to use the QWERTY keyboard. Many of the children had no real knowledge of angles of rotation, and for those who possessed an appreciation of large numbers, turtling offered a most worthwhile concrete introduction to this form of measuring.

During the two terms of the trial, one of the most interesting developments was the linking of younger and older pupils. For these sessions a 13- or 14-year-old was paired with a 6- or 7-year-old pupil, so that the older child could use his or her computing skills and mathematical understanding to interpret the wishes of the younger pupil. This type of exercise was most valuable in promoting good social links between children of different ages and it also helped the older child to adopt a more mature, caring attitude towards younger pupils. Many of the older pupils wanted to show off their expertise in turtling and were very willing to work in younger classes or to bring young children up to their class. The pairing of the groups was important, and I usually asked the children to choose their partners. Each older pupil was also taught to direct the turtle session in such a way that the younger pupil was encouraged to talk about the activity. These linking sessions lasted for about one term, and with a few of the older pupils there appeared to be a marked improvement in their confidence and self-image. This improvement was noticed by many members of the school staff. There also appeared to be a more positive approach and attitude to other subjects. This was not a long enough trial; however, it was an interesting outcome of this first turtle experience.

In Special Education, much emphasis is placed on improving a child's self-image. Prior to entering this form of education, a child has often experienced a good deal of failure and has little confidence in himself. One of our most important tasks is to help build up the child's opinion of himself, so that he becomes more confident in his own abilities and is able to make real progress.

We made several general observations during the trial period:

a] The children found the sessions enjoyable and were motivated to use the equipment.
b] The "on task" concentration appeared to be longer than with other activities.
c] It provided a good opportunity for interaction between pupils.
d] The experience offered problem-solving situations, often set by children themselves, and gave them the opportunity to exercise their logical thinking and reasoning skills.
e] The equipment was quite robust and suitable for school use.
f] The turtling sessions appeared to highlight a child's strengths and weaknesses.
g] The content of their work, i.e. the spatiality aspect and estimation of number, appeared to show an improvement after several sessions.
h] The turtle allowed those who used it to succeed according to their own ability.
i] By controlling their environment, many pupils improved their self-image and self-confidence. This had an effect on other areas of activity.
j] The main disadvantage of the system was that the majority of children in the school would be unable to use the equipment in a meaningful manner, as they did not possess the necessary mathematical undestanding or the manipulative skills to use the computer's QWERTY keyboard.

## WIDENING THE EXPERIENCE

At this particular stage, I felt that a turtle experience should be available to all the children in the school, regardless of ability. As the school policy was to purchase BBC microcomputers, any future development should be designed to run on these machines. However, we wished to make use of an alternative input device to the normal keyboard; and one which looked most promising was the concept keyboard.

The turtle development I envisaged would take the form of a series of carefully structured programs which would suit the needs of children who had little understanding of numbers up to ten. Not being a programmer myself, I needed the use of a skeleton LOGO program that would enable me to configure my designs onto a concept keyboard. Through contacts made at the first BLUG (British LOGO Users Group) conference in September 1983, I obtained such a configuration program, written by Paul Chung of the Department of Artificial Intelligence at Edinburgh University. Bristol SEMERC supported my research by lending the hardware, and by giving me helpful and constructive advice whenever I needed it.

I adopted an action research approach suggested in Kemmis' Action Research Planner by:

i. developing a plan of action to improve what was already happening.
ii. taking action to implement the plan.
iii. observing the effects of my action in the context in which it occurred.
iv. reflecting on these effects as a basis for further planning and subsequent action.

Many teachers adopt this approach to teaching, but the main point of action research is to plan, act, observe, and reflect more thoroughly, and whenever possible to co-operate with other teachers. In fact a co-operative action research exercise evolved as many class teachers became involved in the development through discussions and interviews.

For children with learning difficulties, a learning experience has to be broken down into very small stages so that success can be achieved at each step of the way. As stated earlier, the programs were to suit the needs of children with little real understanding of number. One of the major difficulties in the first turtle trials was the confusion between right and left. To resolve this problem I decided to adapt the turtle dome by sticking on an attractive, colourful face to indicate the forward movement, and also by attaching large ears made of card and sticky-backed paper. These cosmetic, but useful modifications are shown in Figure 8.1. The ears are colour-coded, with the turtle's right ear red and its left ear blue. As the initial sounds for "red" and "right" are the same, it was thought

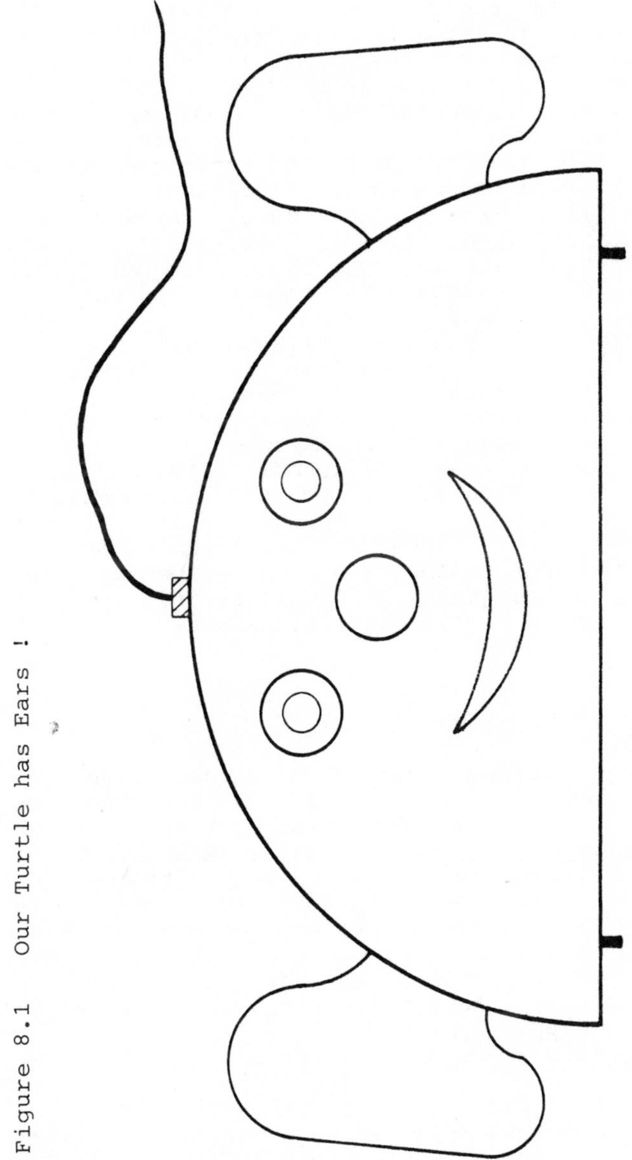

Figure 8.1 Our Turtle has Ears !

that the children might begin to use the correct terms for directions during later turtle sessions. To turn the turtle right is a very abstract concept for a child. But if you ask a child to turn the turtle towards its red ear, you can demonstrate the movement, and it is much easier for the child to perceive.

The other area of difficulty was the degree of turning. The children for whom this work was developed would most probably never need to use angles of rotation in adult life. Depending upon their ability, later in the school they would use a more conventional form of LOGO, but this would only be suitable for the more able older children.

An understanding of number happens very naturally with many children. But with the vast majority of our younger children with special needs, the concept of number is difficult to acquire. The ordinality of number and one-to-one correspondence need to be experienced in a variety of ways. Even when a child is able to count up to ten, he may be unable to associate the word with the numerical figure, or to the set of objects within the number set. Another difficulty may arise when he is asked to name a number between two limits, for example, any number between five and ten. All of these difficulties indicate that a child hasn't really internalised the concept of number.

## OBJECTIVES AND DESIGN

The concept keyboard is a touch-sensitive pad linked through a flat ribbon cable to the User Port of the BBC microcomputer. There are at present seven programs available, each associated with a different overlay which is positioned over the concept keyboard. A movement of the turtle is caused by a sequence of two key (or pad) presses, the first being the movement key, which might for example turn the turtle towards its red ear, and the second being the command key, which causes the movement to happen.

The programs are as follows:

Program DATA1 [overlay shown as Figure 8.2]:
This program has one forward movement, large enough for a young child to notice, a 90 degree right and a 90 degree left turn, and a hoot. Objectives are:

Figure 8.2 Overlay for DATA1

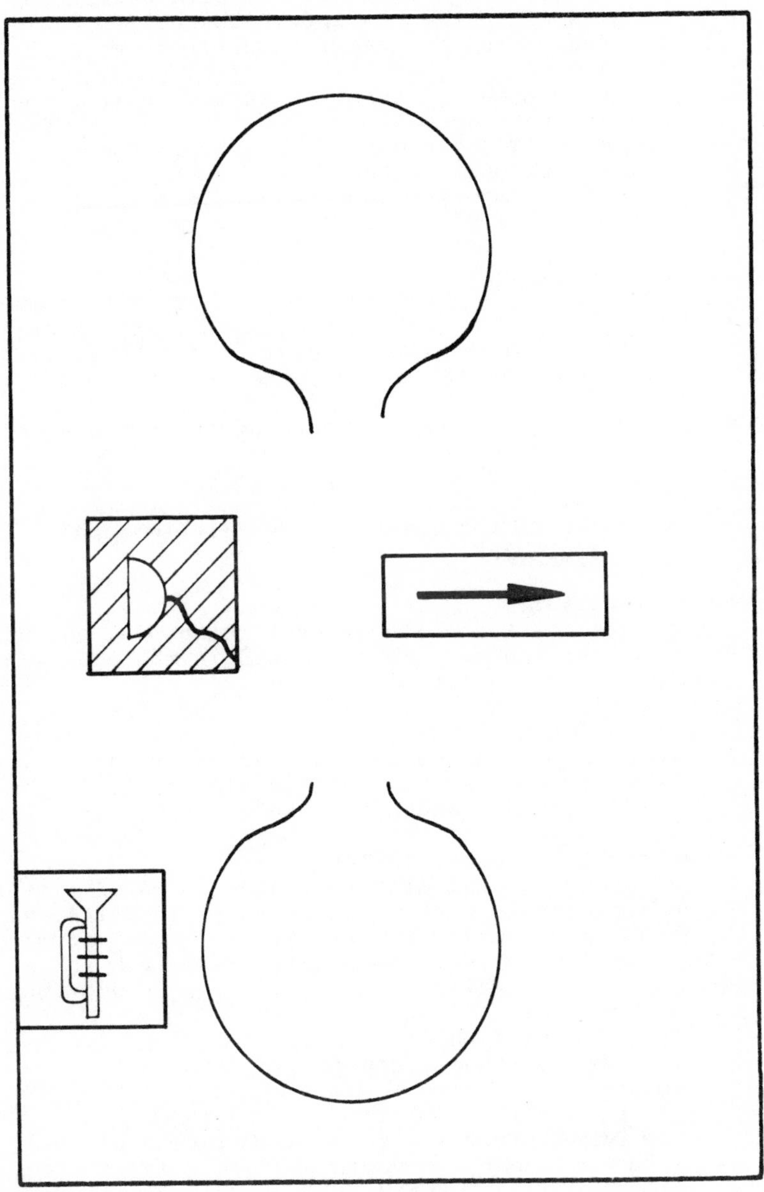

1] To cause a change in the turtle's situation by learning the order of the two-part sequences of presses on the concept keyboard.
2] To predict and program the turtle to move forward.
3] To predict and to turn the turtle towards the red or the blue ear.
4] To understand the difference in turning towards the red or the blue ear.
5] To predict and program the turtle to hoot.
6] To learn the right way to press the keyboard.

Program DATA2:
Two stages of turning are introduced, a 45 and 90 degree right and left turn, but there is still only one forward movement available. Objectives, in addition to those for the previous program, are:
1] To understand the movements of the two stages of turning.
2] To predict, choose and program the stages of turning.
3] To refer to the rotations as "little turn" and "big turn".

Program DATA3:
There are now three stages of turning, 30, 60, and 90 degrees; these are also used in the following four programs. Additional objectives are:
1] To understand the movements of the three stages of turning.
2] To predict, choose and program the rotations.
3] To refer to the turns as "little turn", "middle turn", and "big turn".

Programs DATA4, DATA5, DATA6:
These programs gradually introduce units of linear movement, three forward movements in DATA4, six forward movements in DATA5, and ten forward movements in DATA6. At this stage each forward unit is equivalent to 10 cms. Additional objectives are:
1] To understand the linear movements.
2] To predict, choose and program these movements.

Program DATA7 [overlay shown as Figure 8.3]:
Backward linear movements are introduced. Additional objectives are:
1] To understand the backward linear movements 1 to 5.

Figure 8.3 Overlay for DATA7

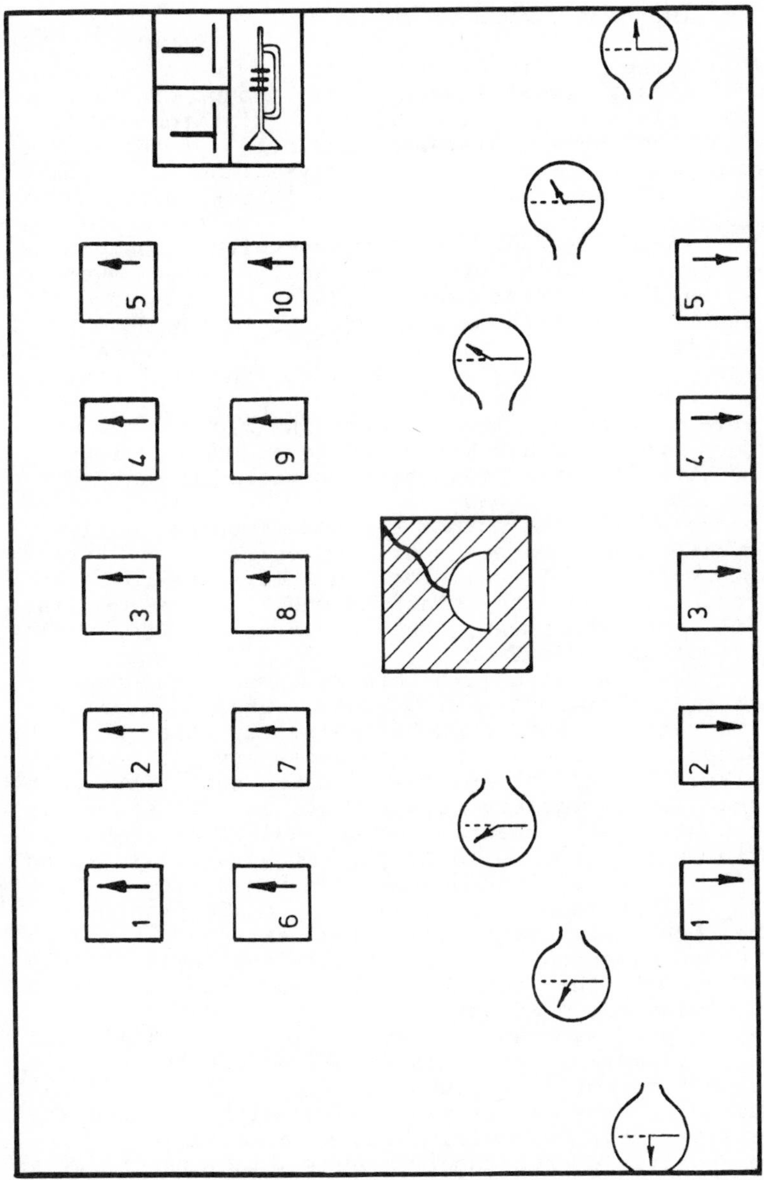

2] To predict, choose and program these movements.

## TURTLING AS A CLASSROOM ACTIVITY

Once the first program designs were working, preliminary trials with small groups of children took place in isolation from the classroom groups. Prior to this I discussed the needs of the groups with their teachers and analysed the functioning level of the children who were to take part in the project.

For four sessions I worked with three groups of two children within the age range of seven to ten years. After each session I analysed the results and often made amendments to the designs. The trials were taking place during the autumn term, and due to illness among the children, it was not always possible for me to work with certain groups. The children who made up the work group were highly motivated to use the equipment, and this interest caused their peers to want to be included. It was at this stage that other teachers in the school started to become actively involved in the project, and so I started working with groups of children in their classrooms and gradually, as the class teachers became familiar with the equipment, they began to use the turtle without any help from me.

When working with this equipment, the teacher is still extremely important, and his or her observation and understanding of the child's educational needs is most necessary, so that the correct level of program can be used. It can be used in a variety of ways, and can therefore fit the style of teaching of an individual teacher. With our young children, structured learning experiences are necessary where boundaries are set and rules laid down, and as a child progresses, the boundaries are gradually extended and more freedom granted until eventually the child is able to accept the responsibility and freedom offered by a wide range of options.

Expressive and receptive language skills are very important at this level, as are the child's perception of his own spatiality and that of the turtle. Many activities linked with learning are passive (for example, sitting at a table, trying to write a sentence). But using the turtle presents an opportunity for young children with learning difficulties to cause a change in their own environment. It appears that they are highly motivated to use the equipment, because they nearly always remember the sequence of presses necessary to bring about a movement or a hoot, even with children as young as three and a half.

The overlay programs start at a very low level, and in most cases it is necessary for children to start at the first level and, as they gain confidence and understanding, gradually progress to the next overlay. Record sheets accompany the turtle equipment, so that a child's progress and comments about his performance can be noted.

The children use their estimating ability during the drawing sessions with the turtle, and I have also designed some large mazes which incorporate most of the moves on DATA7. Using the PEN UP facility, the children take turns at driving the turtle around the maze. Games using specific words, such as "in front of", "behind", or "by the side of", can be introduced, and also a large turtle-sized grid for playing games like Noughts-and-Crosses or Five-in-a-Row.

In fact the joy of using the turtle is that it can be used in so many ways. This versatility means that different approaches and teaching styles can be adopted to meet children's individual needs.

Imagination plays a very important part in turtling, and many of our children need a set starting point, as they often find the initial idea difficult to achieve, and so, when drawing with the turtle, they often use a set of simple outline pictures to get started. Even when mistakes in drawing occur, the children are usually quite happy to turn the picture into something else; this happens particularly with younger children.

## STREETS AND HOUSES

Obviously the turtle can be used to draw shapes, but at the early level only squares or rectangular shapes can be achieved. This did not limit one young class, as their teacher decided to follow up a project on roads and houses by turtle drawing a road and houses on a large sheet of paper. Every child took part in the work.

The session was started by laying out large

pieces of paper and getting the children to put building blocks on top of the paper. These blocks represented houses, and the children were asked to drive the turtle around the houses so that it didn't knock any down. One or two of them found it rather difficult, and they did bump into things, but on the whole they worked very carefully and enjoyed the idea of the turtle being like a car or a truck; this really captured their imagination.

The children worked in pairs, in friendship groups, and the sessions lasted for about ten minutes, or about fifteen minutes for the slower groups. Everyone had the opportunity of using the turtle that morning, and as soon as they had driven it around the houses and had made their roadway, they then .wanted to go and finish doing their plan. They did this freehand with felt pens by drawing buildings and trucks around their buildings. During these turtle sessions the other children were happy to wait their turn, or they were already involved in the detail on their roadways. Only one boy found it hard to wait, however this was a reflection of his normal behaviour pattern.

The children were very interested in seeing what others had done, and a lot of positive comments were made; this experience motivated everyone to finish their pictures. When a few had finished, they compared their results quite spontaneously, without any direction. Once the pictures were finished it was suggested that perhaps other people would not know how they had been made, and that perhaps they could explain.

The class teacher received some very interesting writing showing that the children had remembered up to four sequences of actions that had happened during their turtle work. Their writing also highlighted the particular part they enjoyed most of all; only one child mentioned the building bricks. Because they had all experienced the same activity in a controlled situation, everyone had something to contribute, and the language they used was good. Their written accounts were better than normal, and the class teacher compared the results with those received when the children have been on a visit or perhaps when a guest speaker has visited them.

As the teacher pointed out, because the children were using the first basic program, it was necessary to spur their imagination by turning the turtle into a truck or car. She thought it could be turned into an android next time and driven across space. These children were nine and ten years old, but their ability level was much lower than their maturity level, and basic work must be approached in a different manner.

## TURTLING WITH CONFIDENCE

In my class of 14-year-olds, about six out of the fifteen children are at a stage of designing fairly complicated straight line pictures prior to using the turtle. Even at this age, all but two of them would prefer to use DATA7 rather than the OKLOGO available on another machine. These two children are more mathematically able and have a good understanding of spatiality and logical reasoning, and they have just started to produce simple procedures, again by initially designing simple straight line drawings, and by adding a listing beside the design.

One interesting observation of children of varying ages using the concept keyboard overlays is that they seldom look at the monitor. With the concept keyboard, it is possible to have the touch-sensitive bleep switched on or off; the children like to hear this bleep as it signifies that the pad has been pressed correctly. If the turtle doesn't move when they have pressed a sequence of pads, they rarely look at the monitor to see if the instruction has been displayed, but instead just press the keyboard again. Older children, those who are fairly proficient at using the DATA7 overlay, start to watch what is happening on the monitor; this appears to coincide with the time when they are ready to start using the conventional form of LOGO in a meaningful manner.

I am far happier for children to use the facility of a micro without having to sit down at the keyboard and continually look at the monitor. The main advantage of floor turtling is that it is an active, sociable experience, and to my mind social skills and the art of co-operation and communication are areas of prime importance in the education of all children, not only those with learning difficulties.

In the earlier trials I felt sure that there would be difficulties with the lead that links the turtle and the micro. However, over the past two years I have come to the conclusion that this lead is a major factor in encouraging interaction and co-operation between children. When children work in groups, one child has the responsibility for holding the lead, making sure that it doesn't tangle or become too stretched, and must concentrate fully on the turtle's activity. The lead also determines the boundaries of the turtle activity; this again is important when the turtle session is viewed as part of the normal activities in a classroom.

Turtling is timetabled for use throughout the lower and middle school, catering for children up to 14 years old. One conclusion that is difficult to prove but has been observed by many of the school's teachers is that, by closely watching a child solving a problem using a turtle, you are in fact seeing how a child thinks and are possibly seeing his true potential. In this way it may be possible to view turtling as a diagnostic tool. This is especially apparent when working with a child for the first time. Perhaps it is because the child comes to this new activity without any "hangups" about failure.

At present we have one set of equipment on a trolley which is wheeled into various classrooms during the week. This causes just a few problems, as it is school policy that an adult must take charge of the transportation; however over the last two years we have had no major accidents. The children usually behave in a very controlled way when they are near or using computer equipment, and the serial turtle I have today is the same one I used two years ago. I have found that thick felt pens fit into the penholder with a little bit of adjustment, and for young children the thicker pen line produced is more acceptable than a thin one.

I have taught the older, more technically able children the correct way of setting up the equipment and various ways of loading the programs. When I am unable to leave a class and there is a problem in another part of the school, I often send one or two of my "experts" to investigate the situation and either make the necessary adjustment or report back with a full explanation of what is wrong. They are surprisingly astute, and very quick to learn. They have gained good computer awareness skills, and these tasks help to improve their confidence and self-image; it is also surprising how often they have the right answer to a problem. In schools of our size there is no technical assistance, and it can be most frustrating to have problems with equipment and nowhere to go to solve them.

## OUR TURTLE'S FUTURE

The turtle is now being used throughout the school, with children from three and a half to sixteen years old, and it is being viewed, by teachers and pupils, as a part of the normal timetable. The programs developed so far will, no doubt, be reviewed, evaluated and amended to suit the varying needs of our children.

We have programs that will allow the children to key in procedures via the concept keyboard, and this gradually introduces the need to use a QWERTY keyboard. One of the main advantages of using the floor turtle and a concept keyboard is the truly active, concrete experience it offers to children. However, eventually we hope that many of our children wil be able to use a screen turtle with the full facility of LOGO.

NOTE: For support and encouragement during the project, I would like to thank the following:
The Headteacher, staff and children of Glevum School.
The staff at Bristol SEMERC and Bristol Polytechnic.
County of Avon advisers.
and last but not least, my husband and son.

Chapter 9

# MAKING MUSIC WITH LOGO

## DECOMPOSING

Some LOGO implementations offer a music facility. Using the same process of building up complex procedures from simple ones, the LOGO music facility can be used to explore some aspects of music itself.

To look at this, we can first see how a piece of music can be broken down into smaller units. When listening to a tune, like the verse of a pop song or a hymn, it is often noticeable that it is made up of sections, some of which seem to appear more than once. For instance, a hymn tune of four lines may be made up of only two musical "phrases", each as long as one line of the verse. Sometimes these alternate, as in the pattern A B A B (where A represents one phrase, B the other); sometimes the pattern may be A A B A, with phrase B appearing only once. A common pattern is A A B C; Figure 9.1 shows an example of a tune of this type, "Good King Wenceslas".

Figure 9.1 Tune of "Good King Wenceslas"

If we wanted to write a procedure in LOGO to play this tune, we could list the phrases making up the tune:

```
TO GOOD.KING.WENCESLAS
    PHRASE.A
    PHRASE.A
    PHRASE.B
    PHRASE.C
    END
```

The title is rather long, and cumbersome to type in, so that can conveniently be shortened to the initials GKW. PHRASE.A is repeated, so using LOGO's REPEAT expression, the procedure can be shortened to:

```
TO GKW
    REPEAT 2 [PHRASE.A]
    PHRASE.B
    PHRASE.C
    END
```

Figure 9.2 shows the structure of procedure calls for the tune as analysed so far. The four phrases

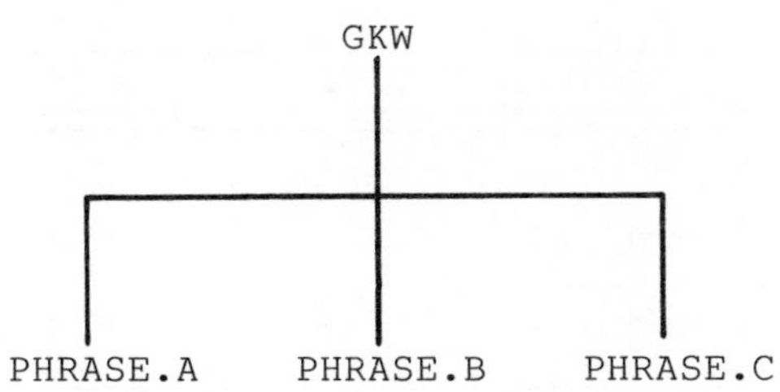


Figure 9.2 Procedure Calls for GKW

making up the tune are shown separately in Figure 9.3. The music is divided into bars. PHRASE.A and PHRASE.B each contain four bars, and PHRASE.C five. Each bar is of equal length (i.e. the time value of the notes adds up to the same), with the "time signature" at the beginning of the tune indicating the size of each bar. Thus 4/4 (sometimes written as "c" for "common") means that each bar is the length of four crotchets. Phrases

Line 1 

PHRASE.A

Line 2 

PHRASE.A (repeated)

Line 3 

PHRASE.B

Line 4 

PHRASE.C

Figure 9.3 Phrases in "Good King Wenceslas"

can therefore be taken apart into the bars making them up. So PHRASE.A (lines 1 and 2 in Figure 9.3) can be written:

```
TO PHRASE.A
     BAR1  BAR2  BAR3  BAR4
     END
```

PHRASE.B (line 3 in Figure 9.3) can be written as:

```
TO PHRASE.B
     BAR5  BAR6  BAR7  BAR4
     END
```

PHRASE.C (line 4 in Figure 9.3) can be written as:

```
TO PHRASE.C
    BAR8  BAR9  BAR5  BAR10  BAR11
    END
```

Notice that just as phrases can be repeated in a tune, so bars can reappear and be repeated.

Bars are made up of individual notes or rests. The rests (or silent notes) are just as important as the notes that are heard. Procedures for each bar can therefore represent the individual notes or rests. BAR1 can be written:

```
TO BAR1
    C
    C
    C
    D
    END
```

C is played three times, so BAR1 can be rewritten:

```
TO BAR1
    REPEAT 3 [C]
    D
    END
```

A complicating factor, however, is that a piece of music may well extend over more than one octave. The procedure will have to show which octave each note belongs to. One way of doing this is to use the octave numbers given in the table on page 181 of the BBC User Guide. Octave 4 gives a sound not too high or too low. We can rewrite BAR1:

```
TO BAR1
    REPEAT 3 [C4]
    D4
    END
```

Another problem now comes up. We have specified the notes, but we haven't indicated how long they will last. We must therefore add to each note an indication of its duration. Taking the crotchet (♩) as 1, our procedure for BAR1 now becomes:

```
TO BAR1
    REPEAT 3 [C4 1]
    D4 1
    END
```

Here are the procedures for the rest of the bars. Since in LOGO it is not necessary to put every command on a new line (only a space need separate commands), for compactness, these have been reduced to one or two lines.

```
TO BAR2
    REPEAT 2 [C4 1]
    G3 2
    END

TO BAR3
    A3 1  G3 1  A3 1  B3 1
    END

TO BAR4
    REPEAT 2 [C4 2]
    END

TO BAR5
    G4 1  F4 1  EE4 1  D4 1
    END

TO BAR6
    EE4 1  D4 1  C4 2
    END

TO BAR7
    A3 1.5  G3 0.5  A3 1  B3 1
    END

TO BAR8
    REPEAT 2 [G3 1]
    A3 1  B3 1
    END

TO BAR9
    REPEAT 2 [C4 1]
    D4 2
    END

TO BAR10
    C4 2  F4 2
    END

TO BAR11
    C4 4
    END
```

Instead of listing each bar as a separate procedure, we could of course merely put all the notes making up the tune together. This would be shorter to write out, but much more difficult to understand, since the patterns into which the music falls would be less clear.

We can see from this examination that a tune can be gradually broken down into very small pieces. At each level, the relationship of the pieces can be considered, so that, for instance, patterns of repetitions or alternations can be spotted. Breaking down melodies step by step into their component parts, and representing these as LOGO procedures enables the constituent elements of music to be familiarised, one level at a time. It also shows us that the ideas underlying LOGO can be applied to almost any set of circumstances; that LOGO is about effective thinking as much as, if not more than, about computer programming.

## RECOMPOSING

Having "decomposed" a melody, it is now possible to reconstruct it, using the building bricks of music, so that the computer can play it. Children can thus gain an understanding of how music is constructed as well as how it works. What they can get out of music themselves is thereby so much the greater.

We must now turn to the production of notes themselves. Different computers have different sound facilities, ranging from nothing to four "voices" (that is, four sounds can be played simultaneously). Because of this disparity, music is one of the areas where there is the widest variation between LOGO implementations for different computers. With some LOGOs there is no music facility at all. Terrapin LOGO for the Apple has the primitive PLAY, requiring inputs for pitch and duration, and using one voice only. Atari LOGO has a primitive TOOT, requiring four inputs, for voice, pitch, volume and duration; two voices are available. BBC LOGOs have the primitive SOUND (similar to that in BBC BASIC), requiring the same four inputs, although here there are four voices available. There is also an ENVELOPE primitive which enables detailed specification of the type of sound required.

We will assume to start with that one voice only will be used, and that notes will have two characteristics, pitch (how high or low the note

| | |
|---|---|
| semibreve | 4 |
| minim | 2 |
| crotchet | 1 |
| quaver | 0.5 |
| semiquaver | 0.25 |

Figure 9.4 Durations for note procedures.

is) and duration (how long it is). Thus, using Logotron LOGO for the BBC, the note C in octave number 4 can be expressed as this procedure:

```
TO C4 :DUR
    SOUND 1 -12 101 (:DUR * 10) - 1
    SILENCE
    END
```

The input required (:DUR) represents the duration of the note. Durations, in terms of conventional musical notes, are shown in Figure 9.4. The SOUND primitive takes four inputs. The first, channel number, is set here at 1, since we are at present using only one voice. The second, volume, is set at -12, but could be set at any preferred level. The third, pitch, is the appropriate number read from the table on page 181 of the BBC Micro User Guide. The fourth, duration, requires the input number to be multiplied by ten to bring it in line with the larger input numbers for duration needed by the SOUND primitive. One unit is deducted from this number; this one unit of duration represents a tiny silent period stuck on the end of every note procedure, and called SILENCE. Here is the procedure for SILENCE:

```
TO SILENCE
    SOUND 1 0 53 1
    END
```

SILENCE plays a very short note with no volume, i.e. a tiny silence. This is needed in every note procedure so that when two identical notes come one after the other (as in BAR1) they do not become joined together into one long note. With SILENCE incorporated, each note sounds distinct.

The only other note required for BAR1 is D in octave 4. Here is the procedure:

```
TO D4 :DUR
    SOUND 1 -12 109 (:DUR * 10) - 1
    SILENCE
    END
```

Procedures for all the other notes required can be written by substituting the name and octave number of the note in the title, and the correct frequency number (as on page 181 of the User Guide). Any suitable symbol can be chosen for sharps and flats. Thus sharps can be represented by the hash (#), flats by lower case 'b'. Here is the procedure for C sharp in octave 4:

```
TO C#4 :DUR
    SOUND 1 -12 105 (:DUR * 10) - 1
    SILENCE
    END
```

The note E must be written EE (for instance, in BAR6), since a single E followed by a number will be interpreted by the computer as "scientific notation" for a very large or very small number. Using EE solves this problem.

A rest procedure is not required in Good King Wenceslas, but can be simply provided when needed:

```
TO R :DUR
    SOUND 1 0 53 (:DUR * 10)
    END
```

In a bar of music, the letter R can now be used, along with a number for its duration, just like any other note.

Using these procedures, the tune of Good King Wenceslas can now be created as a LOGO program. The structure of the program is shown in Figure 9.5. The development of this program is a good example of "Top-Down" programming, in which a task is broken down, level by level, into its constituents until the lowest level is reached at which component elements can be programmed. Any tune can be broken down, examined, and then reconstituted in the same way as Good King Wenceslas.

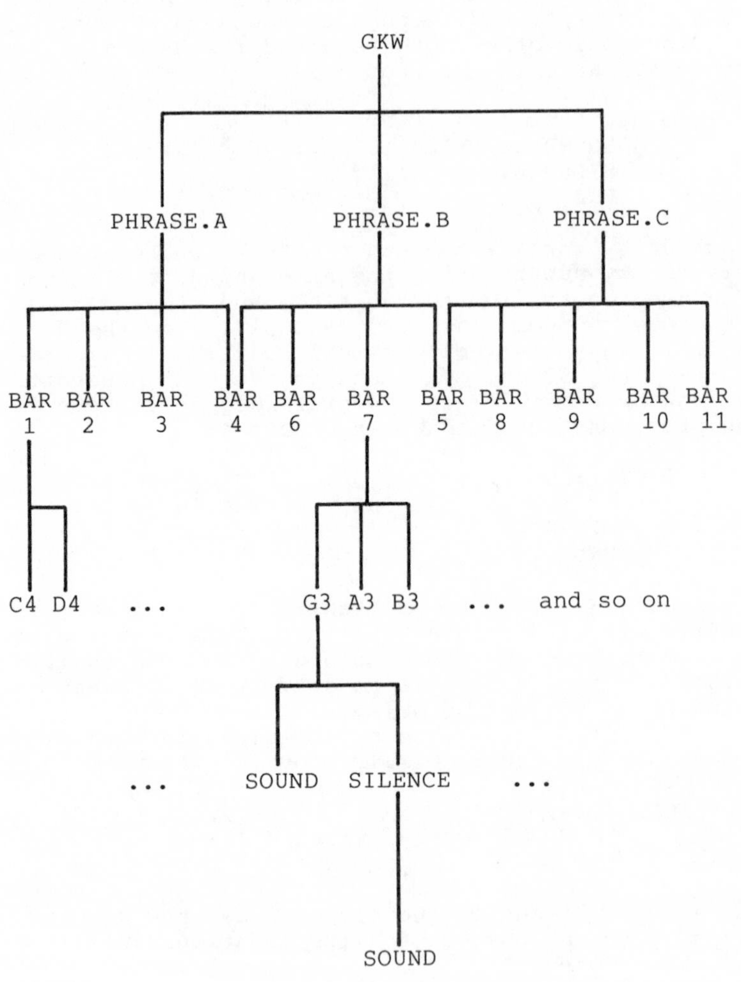


Fig. 9.5 Procedure calls for GKW (final version)

At the fourth level (individual note procedures, specimens only are given to avoid overcrowding on the diagram. The SOUND primitive and SILENCE procedure apply to all the note procedures.

## INVENTING NEW MUSIC

Using the components of existing tunes, new melodies can be created. Bars of GKW can for instance be played in a different order. Here is one possibility:

```
TO NEWTUNE
    REPEAT 2 [PART.A  PART.B]
    END

TO PART.A
    REPEAT 3 [BAR5]
    BAR6
    END

TO PART.B
    REPEAT 2 [BAR8]
    BAR5
    BAR4
    END
```

Sometimes this exercise will produce passable melodies, sometimes not. Asking why some of these new tunes are acceptable and others not stimulates some interesting critical thinking on the part of children. It makes them think about what it is that makes a piece of music satisfactory as music, and further, what makes it enjoyable.

New bars can also be created, then tried out in different combinations. Initially restricting the range of notes available, for instance to pentatonic scales, may lead to the production of immediately acceptable music.

The effect of rhythm can be explored at this point. Bars demonstrating different time signatures can be developed, like this one:

```
TO COMMON.TIME
    C4 1
    REPEAT 3 [C3 1]
    END
```

For eight bars of this we just need the command REPEAT 8 [COMMON.TIME]. A simple all-purpose rhythm demonstrator can be made use of:

```
TO TIME.SIG :TOP :BOTTOM
    C4  4/:BOTTOM
    REPEAT :TOP - 1 [C3  4/:BOTTOM]
    END
```

In this procedure :TOP represents the top figure in a time signature, :BOTTOM the bottom figure. Thus, for a time signature of 3/4, the procedure call would be TIME.SIG 3 4; for 7/8 it would be TIME.SIG 7 8; for 3/2 it would be TIME.SIG 3 2.

Building up notes into bars, bars into phrases, and phrases into tunes, can lead to the creation of impressive and original pieces of music.

## IN HARMONY

Of course, most music we hear is not played in just one voice; two or more suitable notes played simultaneously produces a harmony which enhances the staisfactoriness of the sound of the music. When tunes have been produced using LOGO, simple harmony can be added to them. This stimulates work on chords, so that children can become aware of which notes "go with" which.

To produce harmony, new note procedures are needed which include the channel number as an input. Here are two examples:

```
TO C3 :DUR :CH
    SOUND  :CH  -12  53  (:DUR * 10) - 1
    SILENCE :CH
    END

TO C#3 :DUR :CH
    SOUND  :CH  -12  57  (:DUR * 10) - 1
    SILENCE :CH
    END
```

A list of the frequency numbers is shown in Appendix 9A. The SILENCE procedure has to be amended to:

```
TO SILENCE :CH
    SOUND  :CH  0  53  1
    END
```

and the rest procedure to:

```
TO R :CH :DUR
    SOUND  :CH  0  53  (:DUR * 10)
    END
```

Using these procedures, chords can be created, such as:

```
TO C.CHORD
    C3 2 1
    EE3 2 2
    G3 2 3
    END
```

```
TO F.CHORD
    F3 2 1
    A3 2 2
    C4 2 3
    END
```

```
TO G.CHORD
    G3 2 1
    B3 2 2
    D4 2 3
    END
```

Earlier tunes can now be modified to add simple harmony to them. Here, for instance, is a very basic rendition of the first phrase of Good King Wenceslas:

```
TO BAR1
    C3 2 2  C4 1 1  C4 1 1
    EE3 2 2 C4 1 1  D4 1 1
    END

TO BAR2
    G3 2 2  C4 1 1  C4 1 1
    C4 2 2  G3 2 1
    END

TO BAR3
    F3 2 2  A3 1 1  G3 1 1
    F3 2 2  A3 1 1  B3 1 1
    END

TO BAR4
    REPEAT 2 [G3 2 2  C4 2 1]
    END
```

Notice that writing the bar procedures becomes more complicated, in order to get the computer to play the notes in both channels at more or less the same time. Music with more than two voices would get more complex, but would still be a relatively straightforward mattter to program.

A problem which may arise, especially when long tunes with harmony are being played, is that inexplicable pauses may suddenly interrupt the music. These are due to "garbage collections": these take place whenever the computer is running short of memory to run a program, and involve a reorganisation of items in the computer's memory in order to make as much memory as possible available to run the program. Automatic garbage collections are part of all LISP and LOGO systems. They are essential, since these systems tend to use up a lot of memory whilst running programs;

and garbage collections maximise the amount of memory available. But they do produce a short pause in the program run, and can occur at inconvenient moments. To avoid trouble in musical pieces, the easiest path is to include a command which will cause a garbage collection to take place (this is known as "forcing a garbage collection") in the program. This should be done at the beginning and, if it's a long piece, at further convenient points, such as the beginnings and ends of phrases, where a very short pause will seem natural. The primitive reqiuired to force a garbage collection in Logotron LOGO is RECYCLE (TIDY in Acornsoft LOGO). So the GKW procedure becomes:

```
TO GKW
    RECYCLE
    REPEAT 2 [PHRASE.A]
    PHRASE.B
    PHRASE.C
    END
```

Appendix 9B contains the program for a rendition in two parts of a Bouree (a dance of the 17th century) by Handel.

## LEARNING ABOUT MUSIC

LOGO programming is a vehicle for channelling thinking. When LOGO is used to investigate music, the thinking must be focused as much on the music as on the LOGO. To make the programs work (i.e. play music), it is necessary to examine music itself. This means that in using LOGO as a means for the exploration of music, the teacher must be prepared for the exploration of music as well as of LOGO programming.

Teaching strategy will be a matter of choice. One decision which needs to be made is whether the LOGO work will come after the learning about music, or alongside and amonst it. If it comes afterwards, the LOGO work can be a culmination and recapitulation of what has been studied already, giving children an opportunity to put into practice the concepts previously encountered. If it comes alongside, concepts can be explored on the computer as they are encountered in other music work.

Another decision requiring to be made is that

of structure: how structured should the investigation of music using LOGO be? For Janice Staines, who describes her experiences in the next chapter, it was very much a matter of a joint journey of exploration, herself and her class moving together into the worlds of music and LOGO. Some teachers may prefer however to offer a more structured introduction to relevant musical ideas. In this chapter, for instance, we began by looking at the way in which pieces of music could be broken down into smaller and smaller units, and then rebuilt them using LOGO procedures. Other approaches might be to develop other basic musical ideas first, and build up on them, introducing LOGO music construction at appropriate points.

Computer-based music offers a practical experience of music which many children will not find elsewhere. A sizeable minority of schoolchildren learn to play a musical instrument; for many of these, however, this practical experience is limited to simple recorder lessons at primary school, or the first lessons on another instrument before they (or their parents) decide to give it up. The majority of children do not learn any musical instrument. Children who do play an instrument will derive a lot of benefit from transferring their practical musical skill to a computer. But for those who do not know an instrument, the computer offers a route through which practical experience can be gained; and LOGO's music facility enables that practical experience to take place without the discouraging intervention of arcane programming techniques. With LOGO the child can use the computer; he does not have to fight it.

# APPENDIX 9A. NOTE FREQUENCIES AND DURATIONS

Note frequencies and durations are given here for LOGOs for the BBC, Atari, Apple and Commodore microcomputers. Octave numbers follow those in the BBC User Guide. Figure 9.6 shows how the octaves are distributed on the stave.

Figure 9.6 Stave showing octaves 3 to 5

Making Music with LOGO

BBC LOGOs

Frequencies

| | | | | | |
|---|---|---|---|---|---|
| C3 | 53 | C4 | 101 | C5 | 149 |
| C#3 | 57 | C#4 | 105 | C#5 | 153 |
| D3 | 61 | D4 | 109 | D5 | 157 |
| D#3 | 65 | D#4 | 113 | D#5 | 161 |
| EE3 | 69 | EE4 | 117 | EE5 | 165 |
| F3 | 73 | F4 | 121 | F5 | 169 |
| F#3 | 77 | F#4 | 125 | F#5 | 173 |
| G3 | 81 | G4 | 129 | G5 | 177 |
| G#3 | 85 | G#4 | 133 | G#5 | 181 |
| A3 | 89 | A4 | 137 | A5 | 185 |
| A#3 | 93 | A#4 | 141 | A#5 | 189 |
| B3 | 97 | B4 | 145 | B5 | 193 |
| | | | | C6 | 197 |

Durations (as available to the SOUND command)

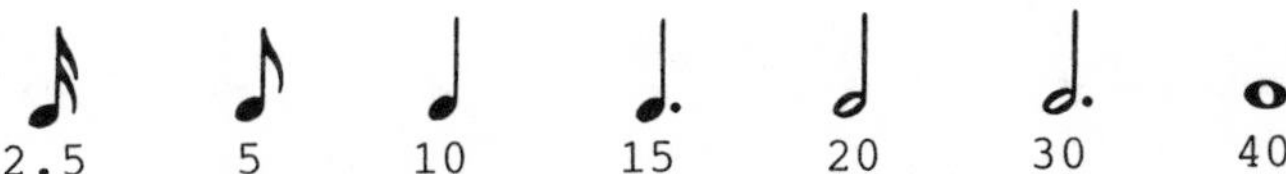


This table has been compiled from information in the BBC Microcomputer User Manual, page 181.

Making Music with LOGO

ATARI LOGO

Frequencies

| | | | | | |
|---|---|---|---|---|---|
| C3 | 132 | C4 | 264 | C5 | 528 |
| C#3 | 140.25 | C#4 | 280.5 | C#5 | 561 |
| D3 | 148.5 | D4 | 297 | D5 | 594 |
| D#3 | 156.75 | D#4 | 313.5 | D#5 | 627 |
| EE3 | 165 | EE4 | 330 | EE5 | 660 |
| F3 | 176 | F4 | 352 | F5 | 714 |
| F#3 | 187 | F#4 | 374 | F#5 | 748 |
| G3 | 198 | G4 | 396 | G5 | 792 |
| G#3 | 209 | G#4 | 418 | G#5 | 836 |
| A3 | 220 | A4 | 440 | A5 | 880 |
| A#3 | 233.75 | A#4 | 467.5 | A#5 | 935 |
| B3 | 247.5 | B4 | 495 | B5 | 990 |
| | | | | C6 | 1056 |

Durations (as available to the TOOT command)

5 10 20 30 40 60 80

This table has been compiled from information in Chapter 10 of this book.

Making Music with LOGO

TERRAPIN LOGO for the Apple II and Commodore 64

Frequencies

| | | | | | |
|---|---|---|---|---|---|
| C3 | 8- | C4 | 8 | C5 | 8+ |
| C#3 | 9- | C#4 | 9 | C#5 | 9+ |
| D3 | 10- | D4 | 10 | D5 | 10+ |
| D#3 | 11- | D#4 | 11 | D#5 | 11+ |
| EE3 | 12- | EE4 | 12 | EE5 | 12+ |
| F3 | 1 | F4 | 1+ | F5 | 13+ |
| F#3 | 2 | F#4 | 2+ | F#5 | 14+ |
| G3 | 3 | G4 | 3+ | G5 | 15+ |
| G#3 | 4 | G#4 | 4+ | G#5 | 16+ |
| A3 | 5 | A4 | 5+ | A5 | 17+ |
| A#3 | 6 | A#4 | 6+ | A#5 | 18+ |
| B3 | 7 | B4 | 7+ | B5 | 19+ |
| | | | | C6 | 20+ |

Durations (as available to the PLAY command)

This table has been compiled from information in the manuals for Terrapin LOGO for the Apple II and the Commodore 64.

NOTE PROCEDURES FOR ATARI LOGO

```
TO C4 :DUR :CH
    TOOT :CH  264  12  (:DUR * 20) - 1
    SILENCE
    END
```

For other notes, substitute the number from the frequency table as the second input to TOOT.

```
TO SILENCE :CH
    TOOT :CH  3000  10  1
    END

TO R :DUR  :CH
    TOOT :CH  3000  10  (:DUR * 20)
    END
```

To achieve the silent parts of music, a note with inaudibly high frequency is played.

NOTE PROCEDURES FOR TERRAPIN LOGO

```
TO C4 :DUR
    PLAY [8] [(:DUR * 10) - 1]
    SILENCE
    END
```

For other notes, substitute the number from the frequency table in the first list after PLAY.

```
TO SILENCE
    PLAY [R] [1]
    END

TO R :DUR
    PLAY [R] [:DUR]
    END
```

## APPENDIX 9B. Bouree by Handel

The program is written for the BBC computer, using note procedures developed in this chapter with inputs for duration and channel. However, provided note procedures have been developed in LOGOs with a multi-channel sound facility requiring the same inputs, this program is translatable, only the appropriate garbage collection command needing to be substituted. The program might be improved by developing note procedures with a volume input, or sound envelopes approximating hapsichords, oboes, etc..

Loading and playing this piece strains the BBC's memory space to its limits. To stop the program running out of memory and crashing RECYCLEs are included at suitable points. The program will only run in Mode 7 on the BBC Micro: use SETMODE 7 before loading it from disk, and run using the command BOUREE

```
TO BOUREE
    REPEAT 2 [PART.1]
    REPEAT 2 [PART.2]
    RECYCLE
    END

TO PART.1
    RECYCLE
    BAR1 BAR2 BAR3 BAR4 BAR5
    BAR6 BAR7 BAR8 BAR9
    END

TO PART.2
    RECYCLE
    BAR10 BAR11 BAR12 BAR13 BAR14
    BAR15 BAR16 BAR17 BAR18 BAR19
    BAR20 BAR21 BAR22 BAR23 BAR24
    END

TO BAR1
    B3 1 2  D4 1 1
    END

TO BAR2
    F#3 1 2  D4 1 1
    G3 1 2  B3 1 1
    EE3 1 2  C4 0.5 1  B3 0.5 1
    F#3 0.5 2  A3 0.5 1
    G3 0.5 2  G3 0.5 1
    END
```

```
TO BAR3
     C4 1 2  EE4 1 1
     D4 1 2  G4 2 1
     A3 1 2  F#4 0.5 1  EE4 0.5 1
     END

TO BAR4
     F#3 1 2  D4 1 1
     G3 1 2  C4 0.5 1  B3 0.5 1
     A3 1 2  A3 0.5 1  B3 0.5 1
     F#3 1 2  C4 0.5 1  A3 0.5 1
     END

TO BAR5
     G3 1 2  B3 1 1
     G3 2 2  G3 2 1
     RECYCLE
     F#3 1 2  A3 1 1
     END

TO BAR6
     G3 1 2  B3 0.5 1  C#4 0.5 1
     F#3 1 2  D4 0.5 1  B3 0.5 1
     EE3 1 2  C#4 0.5 1  D4 0.5 1
     A3 1 2  EE4 0.5 1  C#4 0.5 1
     END

TO BAR7
     F#3 1 2  D4 0.5 1  EE4 0.5 1
     D4 1 2  F#4 0.5 1  D4 0.5 1
     C#4 1 2  EE4 0.5 1  F#4 0.5 1
     A3 1 2  G4 0.5 1  EE4 0.5 1
     END

TO BAR8
     D4 1 2  F#4 0.5 1  G4 0.5 1
     F#3 1 2  A4 1 1
     A3 1 2  A3 1 1
     A3 1 2  C#4 1 1
     END

TO BAR9
     D4 3 1  F#3 3 2
     END

TO BAR10
     A4 1 2  F#4 1 1
     END
```

```
TO BAR11
    A4 1 2  F#4 1 1
    F#4 1 2  D4 2 1
    G4 0.5 2  F#4 0.5 2
    A3 1 1  EE4 0.5 2  D4 0.5 2
    END

TO BAR12
    G4 1 2  B3 1 1
    B4 2 2  G4 1 1  D4 1 1
    EE4 1 2  C4 1 1
    END

TO BAR13
    D#4 1 2  B3 1 1
    EE4 1 2  G3 1 1
    F#4 1 2  A3 1 1
    G4 0.5 2  B3 0.5 1
    A4 0.5 2  D#4 0.5 1
    END

TO BAR14
    G4 1 2  EE4 1 1
    EE4 2 2  G3 2 1
    RECYCLE
    D4 1 2  A3 1 1
    END

TO BAR15
    D4 1 2  G#3 1 1
    C4 0.5 2  G#3 1 1  B3 0.5 2
    C4 1 2  A3 1 1
    C4 1 2  G3 1 1
    END

TO BAR16
    C4 1 2  F#3 1 1
    B3 0.5 2  D4 1 1  A3 0.5 2
    B3 1 2  G3 1 1
    D4 1 2  B3 1 1
    END

TO BAR17
    C4 1 1  EE4 0.5 2  F#4 0.5 2
    A3 1 1  G4 0.5 2  EE4 0.5 2
    D4 1 1  F#4 0.5 2  G4 0.5 2
    C4 1 1  A4 0.5 2  F#4 0.5 2
    END
```

```
TO BAR18
    B3 1 1  G4 0.5 2  A4 0.5 2
    G3 1 1  B4 0.5 2  G4 0.5 2
    F#3 1 1  A4 0.5 2  B4 0.5 2
    D4 1 1  C5 0.5 2  A4 0.5 2
    END

TO BAR19
    G4 1 1  B4 1 2
    B3 1 1  A4 0.5 2  G4 0.5 2
    D4 1 1  F#4 0.5 2  G4 0.5 2
    D4 1 1  A4 0.5 2  F#4 0.5 2
    END

TO BAR20
    EE4 1 1  G4 0.5 2  A4 0.5 2
    G4 0.5 1  B4 0.5 2
    EE4 0.5 1  G4 0.5 2
    F#4 1 1  A4 1 2
    A4 1 1  C5 1 2
    END

TO BAR21
    G4 1 1  B4 1 2
    B3 1 1  A4 0.5 2  G4 0.5 2
    D4 1 1  F#4 0.5 2  G4 0.5 2
    C4 1 1  A4 0.5 2  F#4 0.5 2
    END

TO BAR22
    B3 1 1  G4 0.5 2  A4 0.5 2
    G4 0.5 1  B4 0.5 2
    EE4 0.5 1  G4 0.5 2
    F#4 1 1  A4 0.5 2  B4 0.5 2
    D4 1 1  C5 0.5 2  A4 0.5 2
    END

TO BAR23
    G4 0.5 1  B4 0.5 2
    A4 0.5 1  C5 0.5 2
    B4 1 1  D5 1 2
    D4 1 1  B4 1 2
    D4 1 1  A4 0.5 2  G4 0.5 2
    END

TO BAR24
    B3 3 1  G4 3 2
    END
```

Chapter 10

# CASE STUDY 5: LOGO MUSIC IN THE CLASSROOM

Janice Staines

---

Janice Staines is a class teacher at Delves Primary School, Walsall. She is one of the teachers involved in the work of the Walsall LOGO Project. She gives here an account of her classroom work arising out of the use of LOGO music facilities, first with the Atari 800 and then with the BBC microcomputer.

---

## LOGO Music in the Classroom

My intention in this chapter is to give an insight into how the list-handling potential of LOGO can be used to create computer-generated music, and how this facility has been used in my classroom.

The first thing I must stress is that I am by no means a music specialist. Indeed, when musical talent was being handed out, I must have been hiding under the piano stool! I was thrown out of the choir in my Junior School, being considered a "growler"; and even now, although I enjoy singing, I can only manage to hit the right note perhaps seven times out of ten. My only attempt at learning to play an instrument at school came during compulsory recorder classes. In one whole year I managed to learn to play G, A and B. The rest of the time was spent with me miming as the class made beautiful sounds around me. I was finally shamed into teaching myself to play the recorder about six years ago when some girls in my class wanted to learn to play, but there was nobody available to teach them. I can now play most tunes provided that they are familiar to me and I have two weeks warning in order to practise my fingering. I can also read music after a fashion - at what could be referred to as the "Janet and John" stage! So, from my point of view, anything that can help a musical incompetent like myself to produce music has to be an enormous benefit.

### SEEKING THE FORMULA

I first encountered computer-generated sound when, as part of my activities with the Walsall LOGO Project, I was presented with a specially-written turtle graphics package for the school's BBC microcomputer. It had a TOOT command which would accept inputs for volume, frequency, and duration. The children in my class (3rd year Juniors, 9-10 years old) took great delight in experimenting with this command, including it at various stages in their programs to signal that the turtle had completed its task. They took even more delight in making the TOOT as loud and as long as possible, just to annoy me and the rest of the class. Since the interest was already present, I set about trying to channel it in a direction which would be more productive and less wearing on the nerves.

We discovered that we could create a

procedure to make a simple tune by typing several TOOT commands one after the other, and that we could extend this even further if we used the REPEAT command. Like this:

```
TO SOUND
     TOOT  15  180  50
     TOOT  15  220  30
     TOOT  15  160  40
     END

TO SIMPLETUNE
     REPEAT 5 [SOUND]
     END
```

This is however a very laborious method, and since at this stage we had no idea of the frequencies of the notes, and were therefore guessing the numbers to use as inputs, the results were not always pleasing to the ear.

Shortly afterwards we received an Atari 800 computer to use in the school. This provided the children not only with the turtle graphics they had been used to, but because Atari LOGO has sprites, the facility to produce animations too. Reading through the Atari manual, we discovered that there was a TOOT command similar to the one we had used on the BBC. However, the Atari TOOT needed four inputs: voice number, frequency, volume and duration. Atari LOGO has in fact two voices, and by experimenting we discovered that we could use both these voices at once to create a composite sound. Like this:

```
TO SOUND
     TOOT  0  440  15  40
     TOOT  1  495  15  40
     END
```

By chance, one of the boys in my class had a birthday around this time and he received two Atari games as a present, which he brought into school to show us. Both the games had superb graphics and more interestingly, from our point of view, excellent music running alongside the pictures. This set the children thinking that it should be possible for them to write tunes to play with their own graphics programs. And so started one of the biggest detective hunts since Sherlock Holmes set out to track down the Hound of the Baskervilles!

Whilst describing the TOOT command, the Atari manual told us that the note A had a frequency of 440. We thought we were on our way; we only had to look up the frequencies of the other notes and we could set about writing our tunes. We looked through the Index for the Table of Frequencies, but there was no Table of Frequencies! Having given us the first clue, the rest was obviously going to be up to us.

Fortunately, there was a music specialist on the staff, so we set off to question her.

"There's a formula for working them out." she said, "We learnt it at college, but I've forgotten what it is now."

Undaunted, we waited eagerly for the peripatetic violin teacher to come into school the following week.

"I knew them years ago." she said, "But I've forgotten them now. I think A might be 440."

"Thanks very much." we replied.

So the musicians couldn't help us. Maybe the computer experts could. Again we waited in anticipation, this time for Thursday to arrive, the day on which our Project Co-ordinator was in school.

"We know 440 is A." we told him, "But what are the frequencies of the other notes?"

"I haven't a clue!" he said, "Have you looked in the manual?"

Our hopes and hearts sank as frustrating phone calls followed to the Central Library and Teachers' Centre, with no-one seemingly able to help us. Finally a technician suggested that we should ask someone who used a synthesizer, as they would need to know the frequencies of the notes in order to set it up. Unfortunately, I didn't know anyone who played a synthesizer, so we'd met yet another dead end.

This is where fate stepped in and took a hand. I happened to be shopping in Birmingham two and a half weeks later, and I found myself on the fifth floor of a large department store, where they dealt with Customer Accounts, Bedding, and Electric Organs. And there, on a shelf in front of me, was A Beginner's Guide to Sythesizers - price: £4.50. I opened it, and there, to my delight and excitement, was a table of frequencies. I didn't really need a book all about synthesizers, so I took the lift down to the basement, paid 18 pence for a ballpoint pen, then went back to the fifth floor and copied down the table of frequencies onto the paper bag which the pen had come in. Now that we had the frequencies, we could make the computer play real notes and not just noises.

## PLAYING TUNES

Having experimented previously, we knew that we could write commands one after another to play a series of notes. But this was neither economical on memory space, nor practical if we were going to play a tune of any great length. What we needed was a method of writing a procedure which would look at a list of notes, play the first one, and then automatically move on and play the next one, until it reached the end of the tune. The LOGO primitives FIRST and BUTFIRST, used in list-handling, were just the thing. This is the procedure we developed to use on the Atari:

```
TO TUNE :FREQUENCY :DURATION
     IF :FREQUENCY = [] [STOP]
     TOOT 0 FIRST :FREQUENCY 15 FIRST :DURATION
     TUNE BUTFIRST :FREQUENCY BUTFIRST :DURATION
     END
```

We were actually using two inputs for this procedure, one for the frequency, or pitch, of the note, the other for the duration, or length of time we wanted the note to sound.

IF FREQUENCY = [] [STOP]

tells the computer that if the list of frequencies has no elements left in it (in other words, the end of the tune has been reached), it should stop running the procedure. If this line were not present, when the procedure came to an empty list as input, it would "crash" and an error message would appear on the screen.

TOOT 0 FIRST :FREQUENCY 15 FIRST :DURATION

is telling the computer to use voice 0 to TOOT the first note in the FREQUENCY list, at a volume of 15, for the length of time which appears first in the DURATION list.

TUNE BUTFIRST :FREQUENCY BUTFIRST :DURATION

is telling the computer to repeat the procedure TUNE over again, with FREQUENCY and DURATION lists made up of the previous lists with the first item removed from each, that is, play the note represented by the next frequency and duration on the lists. Because the last line of the procedure

264 297 330 352 396 440 495 528 594 660

Figure 10.1 Note Frequencies for the Atari

TUNE calls itself in this way (this recursion is a powerful feature of LOGO) the process of moving on to the next item on each list will continue until the frequency list is empty. This will be detected by the first line in the procedure, and the process will stop immediately.

I carefully explained the procedure to the children, and showed them how they could load it into their own programs. Using the LOGO screen editor, I then showed them how to put in their own lists of frequencies and durations. Here is one of the tunes made in this way:

```
MAKE "FREQUENCY [495 495 495 440 396 396 440 440
440 528 495 440 396 594 594 594 528 495 495 396
440 440 495 440 396]
MAKE "DURATION [10 10 10 10 20 20 10 10 10 10 10
10 20 10 10 10 10 20 10 10 10 10 10 10 40]
TUNE :FREQUENCY :DURATION
```

The children very quickly understood what was involved in entering frequencies and durations, and I gave them a duplicated sheet so that they could look up their notes and read off the correct frequencies. Figure 10.1 shows the notes which were on this sheet. To calculate the frequencies of notes with sharps and flats we just looked for the half-way number between the notes above and below what was wanted. Thus F# (or Gb) is 374, and Bb (or A#) is 467.5. The children very quickly learnt these numbers off by heart; it was only me who had trouble remembering them!

We experimented with the durations until the tunes sounded about right, and these were then duplicated to go with the list of frequencies. Figure 10.2 shows the durations we used.

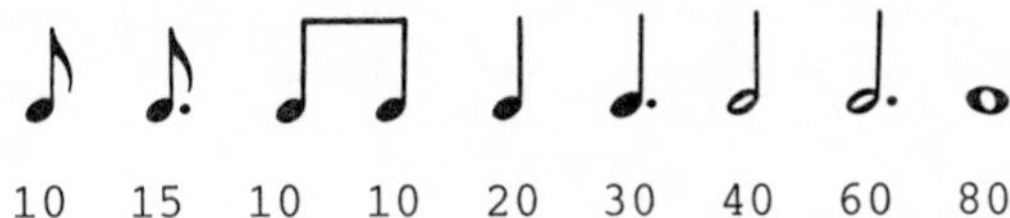


Figure 10.2 Note Durations for the Atari

In order to make the tune work, after they had typed in their lists of frequencies and durations, the children had to type
TUNE :FREQUENCY :DURATION
and then press the RETURN key. We decided after a while that this was a rather tedious way of working, so we created this simple procedure:

```
TO T
    TUNE  :FREQUENCY  :DURATION
    END
```

Using this procedure meant that we only had to type T and press the RETURN key to make the tune play.

One of the problems we encountered when the children were working on long tunes was that they tended to end up with more elements inside the FREQUENCY list than in the DURATION list, or vice-versa; this led to the computer giving us an error message (not a very encouraging occurrence). To avoid this, I simply reminded the children to count carefully the number of items in each list before leaving the LOGO editor, to make sure that the total was the same for each of the two lists.

Another difficulty we found, which kept recurring, was that the children forgot to check for sharps and flats before typing in their tunes. This meant that a lot of editing was required in order to make the tune sound right. A quick reminder before they started work on their tunes usually got over this problem too.

The children very quickly incorporated tunes into their programs, so that we had animals marching into Noah's Ark to "The Animals went in Two by Two", footballers running about the pitch to the tune of "Match of the Day", a lady dressed in pink spiralling around a mountain to the tune of "She'll be Comin' Round the Mountain", and a pirate setting out to bury his treasure to the tune of "Row, Row, Row your Boat". More recently we have been designing computer Christmas cards, where the children have used the tune of a Christmas carol to inspire a picture or animated program.

## NAMING THE NOTES

The wonderful thing abou using LOGO for music from my point of view is the amount of interest and experimentation that it has inspired away from the computer. The children did not really understand what the numbers in the table of frequencies represented, and so, using various stringed instruments, we plucked the different strings to watch the variation in vibrations. This led us on to look at how the length of the string affected the vibration and sound, and how shorter strings vibrated at a much faster rate than longer ones. we then extended this to look at other matrials. We vibrated rulers on the edge of our tables, plucked string of different lengths and thicknesses, and wool and elastic bands. We went on to look at wind instruments, and how the notes are made higher or lower by altering the length of the passage which the air passed through. We even made a row of pop bottles and put various amounts of water in them until we were able to produce a reasonable scale. In order to try and understand what duration meant we used stop-watches to time various activities like how long it took a plucked string to stop vibrating or for how long a note played on the piano could be heard. All of these activities made a very interesting and informative science project.

Whilst attending the British LOGO Users Group conference (BLUG 84) in August 1984, I had an opportunity to demonstrate some of the musical programs the children had produced. I was chatting to one or two people afterwards, and an HMI suggested that it might be possible to simplify the inputs for the children so that instead of typing in a number for the frequency, they would simply have to type in the name of the note.

I must admit that up to that point I had not considered that using frequencies instead of notes

| C | 53 | F# Gb | 77 | TC | 101 |
|---|---|---|---|---|---|
| C# Db | 57 | G | 81 | TD | 109 |
| D | 61 | G# Ab | 85 | TE | 117 |
| D# Eb | 65 | A | 89 | TF | 121 |
| E | 69 | A# Bb | 93 | TG | 129 |
| F | 73 | B | 97 | | |

Figure 10.3 Note Frequencies for the BBC Micro

The frequencies of a wider range of notes are given in Appendix 9A to the previous chapter, or on page 181 of the BBC Microcomputer User Guide.

was a problem; indeed, the children had coped extremely well with the procedure as it stood. When I thought about it more carefully though, I realised that I was working counter-productively, asking them to look at a note, work out where that note was positioned on a stave, and then find out the frequency of that note in order to feed it into the computer and so re-produce that note as a musical sound. It was a bit like me asking them to read a passage from their books to me by translating it first into French and then explaining it to me in English.

At the start of the school year we received a full implementation of LOGO for our BBC computer, and so, rather than using the same method of creating tunes as I had used for the Atari, I decided that it was an opportune moment to change the procedure. It was a relatively simple matter to do this: I merely had to produce a small procedure for each note that would output the frequency of that note to the list that the computer was handling. Here are some examples of these note procedures:

```
TO C          TO F#         TO Bb         TO TG
   OP 53         OP 77         OP 93         OP 129
   END           END           END           END
```

OP is short for OUTPUT: each of these little procedures just issues the right frequency number. TG stands for Top G. Other notes we used and their frequencies are shown in Figure 10.3. The procedures we used were:

```
TO  T
      RECYCLE
      TUNE :VOLUME :NOTES :DURATION
      END

TO TUNE  :VOLUME  :NOTES  :DURATION
     IF  EMPTY?  :NOTES  [STOP]
     TOOT  FIRST :VOLUME  RUN  SE  FIRST
                  :NOTES  []  FIRST :DURATION
     TUNE  BF :VOLUME  BF :NOTES  BF :DURATION
     END

TO TOOT  :VOLUME  :NOTES  :DURATION
     SOUND  1  (-1 * :VOLUME)  :NOTES  :DURATION
     SOUND  2  (-1 * :VOLUME)  :NOTES  :DURATION
     SOUND  3  (-1 * :VOLUME)  :NOTES  :DURATION
     END
```

(These listings are for Logotron (LCSI) LOGO; with Acornsoft LOGO, replace RECYCLE with TIDY, and EMPTY? with EMPTYQ)

The procedure T first performs a garbage collection (TIDY or RECYCLE), and then calls up the main TUNE procedure, to save you having to type

TUNE :VOLUME :NOTES :DURATION

every time you want the tune to play. The TUNE procedure requires three inputs, for volumes, notes, and durations. The first line stops the procedure if the list of notes is empty, i.e. the end of the tune has been reached. The next line calls the TOOT procedure using the first item in the list of volumes, notes and durations. And in the third line the procedure calls itself again, leaving the first item off each list. The TOOT procedure also expects three inputs, for volume, note, and duration; the three SOUND commands then use the three voices available on the BBC micro to play the note at the duration specified and -1 times the volume supplied (this is to avoid having to type in lng lists of negative numbers in the original volume list). So now, when the children use the tune procedures, they simply type

MAKE "NOTES [C C B F G ...

and so on, along with their lists of volumes and

durations. They did find this more convenient than using the frequencies.

One problem we had encountered whilst trying to put tunes into our programs was the rests which occasionally appeared in the music. We overcame this problem on the Atari by putting in a dummy note with a very high frequency so that it could not be heard. in order to overcome this problem on the BBC version of the procedures, we included a volume input so that a dummy note could be put in (any note will do) with the volume set to zero so that it isn't heard.

## VARYING SOUNDS

Probably the biggest advantage in using the BBC computer for music rather than the Atari is that through BBC LOGOs you have access to the full BBC sound facility. This means that you have a choice of four sound channels (one of which generates noise rather than notes), and you can use envelopes to create different sound effects. The BBC User Guide explains in great detail how to set these envelopes and what the various inputs (you need fourteen of them) do, but I found it almost impossible to understand.

What we are doing at the moment, therefore, is experimenting with the numbers in these inputs to see what effects they have on our tunes. We hope eventually to work out a method of plotting these inputs so that they can be visually represented on the screen; maybe then they will become easier to understand. Here are some of the sound envelopes which we have found interesting:

```
TO VOICE1
   ENVELOPE 1 1 0 0 0 0 0 0 126 -4 0 -63 126 100
   END

TO VOICE2
   ENVELOPE 1 1 0 0 0 0 0 0 63 10 0 -63 63 110
   END

TO VOICE3
   ENVELOPE 1 1 0 0 0 0 0 0 63 -4 0 0 63 50
   END

TO VOICE4
   ENVELOPE 1 1 2 3 0 4 0 0 126 -4 3 -63 126 100
   END
```

```
TO VOICE5
   ENVELOPE 1 12 5 10 20 40 80 -3 63 -4 0 0 63 50
   END
```

The main tune procedure for the BBC micro can be modified slightly so that these envelopes can be incorporated into the program, like this:

```
TO TT
  PLAY  :NOTES  :DURATION
  END

TO PLAY :NOTES :DURATION
  IF EMPTY? :NOTES [STOP]
  SOUND 1 1 RUN SE FIRST :NOTES [] FIRST :DURATION
  SOUND 1 1 RUN SE FIRST :NOTES [] FIRST :DURATION
  SOUND 1 1 RUN SE FIRST :NOTES [] FIRST :DURATION
  PLAY  BF :NOTES  BF :DURATION
  END
```

Once the program has been altered and some sound envelopes put in, it is necessary to type the number of the voice the tune is to use before typing TT, for instance

```
VOICE4  TT
```

Using the noise channel, we have found we can generate sounds which are more electronic or "computer" sounding. Experimenting with these has been a lot of fun, and many interesting (and curious) sounds have been added to the children's programs to give them greater effect.

## ROUNDS

Having three sound channels available for music on the BBC micro has greatly increased the scope of the tunes we have been able to create. we can sound all three channels together to produce chords, or we can create tunes with three-part harmonies. We have also found that by using the extra input of volume, and by putting in dummy notes (for rests), we can play rounds.

"London's Burning" is probably the best-known round, so here is the procedure we worked out for playing it. You have first to type in or load the note procedures, as for the TUNE program, and then add these procedures to make the round:

```
TO TUNE :VOLUME :NOTES :DURATION :VOLUME1
                       :NOTES1 :DURATION1
     IF  EMPTY?  :NOTES  [STOP]
     TOOT  FIRST :VOLUME  RUN  SE  FIRST
                 :NOTES []  FIRST :DURATION
     TOOT1  FIRST :VOLUME1  RUN  SE  FIRST
               :NOTES1 []  FIRST :DURATION1
     TUNE  BF :VOLUME  BF :NOTES  BF :DURATION
        BF :VOLUME1  BF :NOTES1  BF :DURATION1
     END

TO TOOT1 :VOLUME1 :NOTES1 :DURATION1
     SOUND 1 (-1 * :VOLUME1) :NOTES1 :DURATION1
     END

TO TOOT :VOLUME :NOTES :DURATION
     SOUND 2 (-1 * :VOLUME) :NOTES :DURATION
     SOUND 3 (-1 * :VOLUME) :NOTES :DURATION
     END

MAKE  "VOLUME1  [0  0 0 0 0 0 0 0 12 12 12 12 12 12
12  12 14 14 14 14 14 14 14 14 15 15 15 15 15 15 15
15 15 15 15 15]

MAKE  "NOTES1  [C C C C C C C C D D G G D D G G A A
B B A A B B TD TD TD TD TD TC B B TD TC B B]

MAKE  "DURATION1 [5 5 10 10 5 5 10 10 5 5 10 10 5 5
10  10  5 5 10 10 5 5 10 10 15 15 15 15 5 5 10 10 5
5 10 10]

MAKE  "VOLUME  [12 12 12 12 12 12 12 12 14 14 14 14
14  14  14 14 15 15 15 15 12 12 12 12 12 12 12 12 0
0 0 0 0 0 0 0]

MAKE  "NOTES [D D G G D D G G A A B B A A B B TD TD
TD TD TD TC B B TD TC B B C C C C C C C C]

MAKE  "DURATION  [5 5 10 10 5 5 10 10 5 5 10 10 5 5
10  10  15 15 15 15 5 5 10 10 5 5 10 10 5 5 10 10 5
5 10 10]
```

The first list, NOTES1, has eight silent notes at the beginning of the list, followed by the notes for the tune. The list NOTES has the notes for the tune, followed by the eight silent notes at the end.

During this period when we at the school were looking at rounds, sound envelopes, and harmonies, our Project Co-ordinator came across an article on Bach, written in an old encyclopaedia of music that his daughter had brought home from a jumble sale at her school. It said that one thing Bach was fond of using was something called a "Crab Canon". What he did was to split the orchestra into two parts; then he would start one half of the orchestra playing a piece of music from the beginning to the end, while the other half of the orchestra started at the end and played through to the beginning.

We were fascinated by this, and determined to see if we could accomplish a crab canon with LOGO. After all, it would be a change from turtles! Using LAST and BUTLAST, we managed to succeed in creating a procedure to add to our basic TUNE. We were now using Logotron (LCSI) LOGO for the BBC computer. Here is the program we used to create a crab canon for "London's Burning". The note and voice procedures should be typed in or loaded, as with earlier programs. Here are the rest of the procedures required:

```
TO T
     TUNE :VOLUME :NOTES :DURATION
     END

TO TT
     PLAY :NOTES :DURATION :NOTES1 :DURATION1
     END

TO PLAY :NOTES :DURATION :NOTES1 :DURATION1
     IF  EMPTY? :NOTES  [STOP]
     SOUND  1  1  RUN  SE  FIRST :NOTES  []
                              FIRST :DURATION
     SOUND  2  1  RUN  SE  LAST :NOTES1  []
                              LAST :DURATION1
     PLAY  BF :NOTES  BF :DURATION  BL :NOTES1
                              BL :DURATION1
     END

TO TOOT :VOLUME :NOTES :DURATION
     SOUND  1  1 :NOTES :DURATION
     SOUND  2  1 :NOTES :DURATION
     SOUND  3  1 :NOTES :DURATION
     END

TO TUNE :VOLUME :NOTES :DURATION
     IF  EMPTY? :NOTES  [STOP]
     TOOT (FIRST :VOLUME) RUN SE FIRST :NOTES []
                               (FIRST :DURATION)
     TOOT  BF :VOLUME  BF :NOTES  BF :DURATION
     END
```

```
TO CANON
     T
     TT
     END

MAKE  "VOLUME  [10 10 10 10 10 10 10 10 12 12 12 12
12 12 12 12 15 15 15 15 12 12 12 12 12 12 12 12]

MAKE  "NOTES [D D G G D D G G A A B B A A B B TD TD
TD TD TD TC B B TD TC B B C C C C C C C]

MAKE  "DURATION  [5 5 10 10 5 5 10 10 5 5 10 10 5 5
10 10 15 15 15 15 5 5 10 10 5 5 10 10]

MAKE  "VOLUME1 [10 10 10 10 10 10 10 10 12 12 12 12
12 12 12 12 15 15 15 15 12 12 12 12 12 12 12 12]

MAKE  "NOTES1  [D  D G G D D G G A A B B A A B B TD
TD TD TD TD TC B B TD TC B B]

MAKE  "DURATION1 [5 5 10 10 5 5 10 10 5 5 10 10 5 5
10 10 15 15 15 15 5 5 10 10 5 5 10 10]
```

The children have indeed found using the names of the notes instead of their frequencies much easier to cope with. Those who were already able to read music could just look at the notes on the stave and type them straight into their lists. Children who were not so proficient at reading music slowly began to recognise the notes and their position on the stave, and so they too may eventually become musically literate. Certainly the advantages of using the TUNE inputs this way have made me adapt our TUNE procedure for the Atari so that it too accepts notes and not frequencies as inputs. Here is the program we now use to create tunes for the Atari; the note procedures are similar to those shown for the BBC computer, but with the appropriate frequency number used, e.g.

```
TO  C
     OP 264
     END
```

... and so on.

```
TO  T
     TUNE :NOTES :VOLUME :DURATION
     END
```

```
TO TUNE :NOTES :VOLUME :DURATION
     IF  EMPTYP :NOTES  [STOP]
     TOOT  1  RUN  SE  FIRST :NOTES []  FIRST
                       :VOLUME FIRST :DURATION
     TUNE  BF :NOTES  BF :VOLUME  BF :DURATION
     END
```

SYNTHESIZING

One thing which has slightly bothered me whilst creating and using procedures with my class is that whilst they are quite happy to use tunes which have been already written, and to incorporate them within their own programs, they have been reluctant to experiment with creating music of their own. Our next step is to encourage the children to develop their own music. The method we have been using, which relies on the computer's own sound chip, offers a very low level of control, since it only has access to three musical sound channels, and is limited by the speed at which LOGO runs the list-handling procedures. Despite this, we would like to extend the programs we have been using to include chords. This would give the children the choice of using either melody or chord accompaniments.

One of the class has already extended the basic TUNE procedure for the Atari to allow us to use the computer as a musical keyboard, like this:

```
TO SYNTH
     MAKE "KEY  RC
     IF :KEY = "A  [TOOT  1  264  15  5]
     IF :KEY = "S  [TOOT  1  297  15  5]
     IF :KEY = "D  [TOOT  1  330  15  5]
     IF :KEY = "F  [TOOT  1  352  15  5]
     IF :KEY = "G  [TOOT  1  396  15  5]
     IF :KEY = "H  [TOOT  1  440  15  5]
     IF :KEY = "J  [TOOT  1  495  15  5]
     IF :KEY = "K  [TOOT  1  528  15  5]
     IF :KEY = "L  [TOOT  1  594  15  5]
     IF :KEY = ";  [TOOT  1  660  15  5]
     IF :KEY = "+  [TOOT  1  352 * 2  15  5]
     IF :KEY = "*  [TOOT  1  396 * 2  15  5]
     IF :KEY = "1  [TEMPO1]
     IF :KEY = "2  [TEMPO2]
     IF :KEY = "3  [TEMPO3]
     IF :KEY = "<  [WHEN  7  []]
     SYNTH
     END
```

```
TO TEMPO1
     CS
     WHEN 7 [TOOT  0  600  15  5
             TOOT  0  400  15  5
             TOOT  0  600  15  5
             TOOT  0  500  15  5
             TOOT  0  400  15  5
             TOOT  0  300  15  5]
     END

TO TEMPO2
     CS
     WHEN 7 [TOOT  0  200  15  5
             TOOT  0  300  15  5
             TOOT  0  200  15  5
             TOOT  0  100  15  5
             TOOT  0  400  15  5
             TOOT  0  300  15  5
             TOOT  0  200  15  5
             TOOT  0  500  15  5
             TOOT  0  400  15  5
             TOOT  0  300  15  5
             TOOT  0  200  15  5
             TOOT  0  300  15  5
             TOOT  0  200  15  5]
     END

TO TEMPO3
     CS
     WHEN 7 [TOOT  0  200  15  5
             TOOT  0  100  15  5
             TOOT  0  50   15  5
             TOOT  0  350  15  5
             TOOT  0  400  15  5
             TOOT  0  300  15  5
             TOOT  0  200  15  5
             TOOT  0  100  15  5
             TOOT  0  500  15  5
             TOOT  0  400  15  5
             TOOT  0  300  15  5
             TOOT  0  200  15  5
             TOOT  0  100  15  5]
     END
```

The TEMPO procedures are shown here as columns of TOOTs, for ease of reading, but can be typed in with single lines of TOOTs:

```
TOOT 0 600 15 5  TOOT 0 400 15 5  TOOT 0 600 15 5
```

and so on.

Moving away in a slightly different direction, we would like to explore music using independent, semi-intelligent sound synthesizers, on which te children can compose and play their own tunes. then, by way of the MIDI interface for the computer, we should be able to write simple procedures to control drum machines, synthesizers, etc. Our project co-ordinator is at present developing extra LOGO primitives that will allow us to "talk" to the MIDI interface, in order to obtain a greater level of musical control and, hopefully, when this is available, we shall be able to explore music for music's sake, and not simply as a method of incorporating tunes into our turtle graphics programs.

Chapter 11

# LOGO IN CONTROL

## CONTROL TECHNOLOGY

It is easy to think of the screen and the keyboard as being the only channels of communication between the computer and the outside world, with the user's eyes and fingers the media for such communication. Yet this is far from being the case. Computers can be linked to a wide variety of "peripheral" devices, from which they can receive information, and to which they can give instructions and information. "Control Technology" is the term used to refer to this ability of a controlling device to interact with its environment.

Although not the only vehicle of control technology, computers are particularly suited for it. Because a computer can be programmed, it possesses a flexibility which other controlling devices do not have. This makes the range of tasks which the computer can be set to perform almost limitless. The limits that are set depend upon the computer's ability to communicate with the outside world, and the size of program and range of instructions it can handle.

Most microcomputers now on the market are equipped with several external communication facilities, in the form of slots or sockets either inside the computer or at the rear, on the sides or underneath the computer's main unit. With the Apple II computers, circuit boards with the extra chips needed to enable the computer to understand the messages coming in from and to send out understandable ones to external devices are plugged directly into slots on the computer's main circuit board. Cables lead from the plug-in boards out through slits at the back of the computer to the external devices. Plug-in boards are required to control disk drives, printers, and colour monitors; however microcomputers now appearing on the market have the chips built in to control these three commonest of peripherals, and offer sockets where cables can be plugged in. Further sockets allow communication with other types of device. The most common "interface" used to link computers with outside devices is the RS232, which carries information in a serial fashion, one bit after another. The Centronics interface, used frequently to link computers to printers, carries data in a parallel fashion, with each byte moving along the cable as a set of eight bits in separate wires. Some computers offer extra interface sockets; the BBC micro, for instance, offers, in addition to RS232 and Centronics interfaces, an "Analogue in" socket, which can receive varying voltages from games paddles, joysticks, and measuring devices, an "8-bit User Port" which supports digital links with many devices, such as robot arms, digital tracers and video-disk units, as well as interfacing boxes which can themselves be linked to further devices, a "1 MHz bus" which allows connection to such items as Prestel and Teletext units, and the "Tube" which permits a second processor to be linked into the BBC Micro system.

As well as the hardware connection (the right slots or sockets) a computer needs a software capability to handle connection to the outside world. With some microcomputers connection to external devices was only possible through machine code programs or through long and complex sequences of POKEs, commands sending particular values to specific memory locations. Others are more helpful, enabling programs to be written in BASIC or using commands built into the computer's operating system. Software difficulties for the user are often overcome however by the producers of peripheral devices, who supply software enabling the user to either use the device directly, or write programs using a simple command language or BASIC.

This is where LOGO comes in, for LOGO can provide a command language which is eminently suited to dealing with control technology. The ease with which new commands can be defined in procedures means that commands can be constructed which are directly meaningful to the naive user (i.e. most of us). When dealing with a single light bulb, commands like LIGHT.ON and LIGHT.OFF are much more meaningful than a series of POKEs or assembly code instructions. Because procedures can be built up to make higher level procedures, more complex sequences of operations can be put together without losing understandability. For instance, a program to make a bulb flicker could look like:

```
TO FLICKER
     LIGHT.ON
     WAIT 5
     LIGHT.OFF
     WAIT 5
     END
```

Repeated flickers can then be achieved by commands such as

```
REPEAT 200 [FLICKER]
```

or by building procedures to control the length or frequency of flicker. LOGO's procedural character has a further advantage: a pool of procedures can be maintained in the computer's memory or on disk, to be drawn on whenever necessary; there is less need for the rigid sequential program structure which a language like BASIC demands, and therefore more flexibility in the way procedures can be employed in any session. Users (children or adult) can easily develop the procedures available in directions which they prefer.

Given the advantages that LOGO offers to control technology, it is not surprising that development of materials and software is taking place. Some examples of work at present under way will give some idea of the possibilities.

## THE STIRLING CONTROL UNIT

The Stirling Control Unit has been developed by Bob Sparkes at the Department of Education, Stirling University. The initial version of the unit consists of a box which is linked to the User Port on the BBC Micro. On the box are four input sources, 2 push buttons, a light sensor and heat sensor, and four output elements, a buzzer and three LEDs coloured red yellow and green. Figure 11.1 shows the arrangement of these.

The basic commands available are extremely simple. For instance RED ON turns the red LED on,

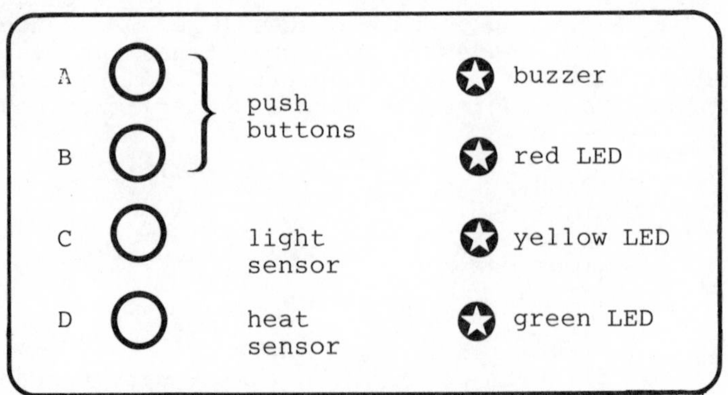


Figure 11.1 Stirling Control Unit

and RED OFF turns it off; SOUND ON turns on the buzzer, SOUND OFF turns it off; IF A detects that button A has been pressed; IF DARK detects that the light sensor is covered; WAIT takes an input in seconds and gives an appropriate delay. The DEFINE command enables procedures to be built. Thus a traffic light sequence can be constructed as:

```
DEFINE TRAFFIC
         RED ON
         WAIT 4
         YELLOW ON
         WAIT 1
         RED OFF
         YELLOW OFF
         GREEN ON
         WAIT 4
         GREEN OFF
         YELLOW ON
         WAIT 1
         YELLOW OFF
         END
```

REPEAT 10 (TRAFFIC) will run the traffic light sequence ten times. Children who are asked to construct this sequence are able to concentrate on the logical sequence of events without needing to be aware of the technical details needed to achieve it.

Direct interaction with the output devices can be simply achieved. A doorbell can be constructed with the line

IF A THEN SOUND ON

or, if the bell is to be activated by either of the buttons,

IF A OR B THEN SOUND ON

or, for activation by both buttons together

IF A AND B THEN SOUND ON

There are clearly good opportunities for work with logical operators, with the results of operations being directly visible or audible.

Simple procedures may be put together to construct more complex ones. A flashing burglar alarm may need several levels of procedure:

```
DEFINE FLASH
        RED ON
        WAIT 0.2
        RED OFF
        WAIT 0.2
        END

DEFINE ALARM
        SOUND ON
        REPEAT 5 (FLASH)
        SOUND OFF
        END

DEFINE BURGLAR
        DARK            i.e. the light sensor
        END                  is covered

DEFINE BURGLAR.ALARM
        REPEAT FOREVER (IF BURGLAR THEN ALARM)
        END
```

A fire alarm can be devised using the same structure, but defining FIRE as WARM (i.e. detection of warmth at the heat sensor) and FIRE.ALARM:

```
DEFINE FIRE.ALARM
        REPEAT FOREVER (IF FIRE THEN ALARM)
        END
```

The Stirling Control Unit is still in the course of development. It was originally developed in BASIC and is now being implemented in LOGO. The unit can be connected to further external devices to make possible a wide range of activities. It will be available by late 1985.(1)

A similar development in England is the CLARE Project, based at the Advisory Unit for Computer Based Education in Hatfield. CLARE stands for "Control LOGO and the Real Environment"; and the objective of the project is to produce a board bearing input and output devices (LEDs, sensors, etc.) and connectable to further devices, and software which will enable the board to be used from existing full LOGO implementations for the Sinclair Spectrum, BBC, and RML 380Z/480Z computers. The software will add a number of new primitives to LOGO enabling easy control of external devices. Control can be directed to numbered switches. Thus

```
TURNON 0
```

switches on relay number 0. Thus, if a light is controlled by switch 0, and if 0 is assigned to the variable LIGHT, using the command

```
MAKE "LIGHT 0
```

then the light can be switched on using the command

```
TURNON :LIGHT
```

and turned off using the command

```
TURNOFF :LIGHT
```

The additional primitives enable sophisticated programming of relations between the computer and objects in the outside world (2).

## CONCURRENT-LOGO

At Edinburgh University's Department of Artificial Intelligence, Paul Chung is currently developing and evaluating an extension to LOGO designed for teaching control applications. This extension, called "Concurrent-Logo", provides new primitives for monitoring and controlling external devices; but it also, as the name suggests, provides a facility for LOGO to undertake more than one task simultaneously. This concurrency has been provided because tasks such as monitoring a receiver or sensor are activities which in real applications would go on whilst other things were happening. Moreover, in real situations monitoring or control of several devices may have to take place at the same time.

Concurrent-Logo can be used to address three different types of object, SWITCH, MOTOR, and RECEIVER. The SWITCHes, MOTORs and RECEIVERs to be addressed are numbered, and an exclamation mark is used to separate object-names from commands addressed to them. Thus

```
SWITCH 2 ! ON
```

will turn on switch number 2, while

```
SWITCH 2 ! OFF
```

will turn it off. Conditions can be attached to switch commands. Thus, if switch 2 is linked to a heating device, the command

```
SWITCH 2 ! ONUNTIL GRE? TEMP 25
```

will turn the heater on until the room temperature is more than 25 degrees Celsius. The object referred to as MOTOR is a stepper-motor, a type of motor which turns by precisely controlled steps, and can therefore be used to power devices needing precise and accurate movement such as turtles, robot arms and cranes. MOTORs can be ordered to turn clockwise or anticlockwise by precise numbers of steps. Thus

```
MOTOR 5 ! TURNC 10
```

will turn motor 5 clockwise by 10 steps. RECEIVERs can be asked to give their current state (ON or OFF) or to count the number of times their state has changed.

New control commands FOREVER and WHENEVER have been added to LOGO. These enable programs to continuously monitor the state of receivers, motors or switches and take action whenever specific circumstances arise. Thus, with a heating device linked to switch 1, a simple thermostat is effected by

```
WHENEVER LESS? TEMP 20
                  (SWITCH 1 ! ONUNTIL GRE? TEMP 25)
```

Concurrent activities are designated by parallel lines between commands. Thus

```
REPEAT 10 (PRINT 'BURGLAR)//REPEAT 10 (ALARM)
```

will sound an alarm whilst printing the word BURGLAR on the computer screen. Up to eight simultaneous activities can be supported.

Three specimen applications have been developed during trials of Concurrent-Logo in a secondary school. These are a turtle, a doll's house, and a miniature lift-shaft and lift, each constructed from Meccano. The turtle is driven by two stepper-motors placed back to back. This means that to make the turtle move forwards the motors should turn in opposite directions. This is achieved by a procedure FORWARD:

```
FORWARD 'X;
  MOTOR 1 ! TURNC :X // MOTOR 2 ! TURNA :X
```

RIGHT, LEFT and BACK are achieved in similar ways. The turtle is fitted with sensors enabling it to follow a black line if suitably programmed. The doll's house demonstrates a security system, with switches attached to the door, windows and doorbell to detect their state, and a motor controlling the sliding front door. Programs have been written to detect intruders and set off various alarms, and to check entry by requesting a password before the door is opened. At top level, the two security systems are combined in the simple procedure HOUSE:

```
HOUSE;
  DOOR // WINDOW
```

The lift-shaft and lift is a more complex system designed to demonstrate the value of concurrent programming; a detector constantly monitors the lift position, whilst a controller sends it to required floors. Development work and evaluation of Concurrent-Logo is still under way, but its value can be seen from these examples. (3)

## CONTROL LOGO IN SCHOOLS

The developments described above show some of the work which is being done in enabling LOGO to become a vehicle for the exploration of computer-based control technology. But these only represent a small part of a rapidly growing area of interest. An important application not touched upon in this chapter has already been raised in chapter 4, namely the control of turtles and buggies. Another is that of robots. However, hopefully enough has been mentioned to give an idea of the potential of LOGO for control applications in schools.

There is much support for the introduction of control technology into the primary as well as the secondary schools, since it is felt that this would give children a greater appreciation of the nature of technology and the links between the theory and practice of its application. The problem has been to discover the appropriate vehicle through which control technology can be introduced into schools to a general audience (i.e. other than senior science pupils) whilst remaining meaningful. LOGO, with its flexibility, and its simple yet powerful structures, could offer this vehicle.

## NOTES

1. For up-to-date details, contact: R. A. Sparkes, Department of Education, University of Stirling, Stirling FK9 4LA, Scotland.
2. For up-to-date details, contact: CLARE Project, AUCBE, Endymion Road, Hatfield, Herts AL10 8AU, England.
3. For up-to-date details, contact: Paul Chung, Artificial Intelligence Applications Institute, University of Edinburgh, Hope Park Square, Meadow Lane, Edinburgh EH8 9NW, Scotland.

Two publications are:
P. Chung, _Terak Concurrent-Logo Manual_ DAI Occasional Paper No. 49. Department of Artificial Intelligence, University of Edinburgh. 1984
P. Chung, "Concurrent-Logo: A Language for Teaching Control Applications." _LOGO Almanack_ Vol. 2 (1984).

# Chapter 12

# LANGUAGE WITH LOGO

Computers are often seen as mainly suitable for scientific or technical applications. In secondary schools the maths or physics specialist is often given charge of computing because he is thought to have "the right sort of experience". The scientific image has been supported by the obscure and often mystifying commands which are sometimes required just to run a piece of software, and the arcane conventions of some programming languages. Computers are however becoming more "user-friendly"; and this helps applications outside the realm of numbers to be appreciated more fully. LOGO is part of the trend for computers to become more accessible and understandable. As a descendant of LISP, it allows simple handling of lists. Since lists may contain any collections of characters, including other lists, there are implications for LOGO's ability to deal with words and sentences. And an aptitude for handling language raises possibilities for applications in the humanities. This chapter will consider some of the ways in which LOGO can be used in this area; some others will be mentioned in chapters 14 and 15.

## LIST-PROCESSING IN LOGO

LOGO has a powerful armoury of primitives for dealing with lists. An example will give an idea of how these can be used. The command

```
MAKE "PERSON  [[HEAD [EYES NOSE MOUTH
          EARS]] [BODY [ARMS LEGS TORSO]]]
```

assigns a list containing parts of a drawing of a person to a name PERSON. The command
PRINT :PERSON

will result in the whole list being printed out on the screen, just as it was typed in, except that the outermost layer of brackets will be removed:

```
[HEAD [EYES NOSE MOUTH EARS]] [BODY [ARMS
LEGS TORSO]]
```

At this level, the list only contains two elements. So if we type
PRINT FIRST :PERSON
the first element of the list will be printed:

```
HEAD [EYES NOSE MOUTH EARS]
```

and if on the other hand type
PRINT LAST :PERSON
the last element of the list will be printed:

```
BODY [ARMS LEGS TORSO]
```

Each of the two elements of the list itself contains two elements, the first a word (e.g. HEAD) and the second a list (EYES NOSE MOUTH EARS). Thus typing
PRINT FIRST FIRST :PERSON
will produce on the screen

```
HEAD
```

i.e. the first (and only) item of the first element of the list, while
PRINT LAST FIRST :PERSON
will produce

```
EYES NOSE MOUTH EARS
```

BF is short for BUTFIRST, and returns all the elements of a list except the first. So if we type
PRINT BF LAST FIRST :PERSON
we will see on the screen

```
NOSE MOUTH EARS
```

Some LOGOs have an ITEM primitive which allows a numbered element of a list to be delivered. So if we type
PRINT ITEM 3 LAST FIRST :PERSON
we will see on the screen

```
MOUTH
```

These are powerful tools to deal with collections of words, and they are only a few of the list-handling primitives LOGO offers. Here is a program HEADLINES which shows some of these primitives in action:

```
TO HEADLINES
     SETLISTS
     STORIES
     END

TO SETLISTS
     MAKE "PEOPLE1 [POSTMAN FIREMAN GARDENER
       POLICEMAN TEACHER BURGLAR]
     MAKE "PEOPLE2 [COOK BUTCHER LUMBERJACK
       POACHER [RUGBY TEAM] [CROWD OF S.A.S.
       PERSONNEL] [CABINET MINISTER]]
     MAKE "BARRIERS [WALL FENCE HEDGE
       TREETOPS PARAPET [WINDOW LEDGE]]
     MAKE "ACTIVITY [[DANCING WITH] [WRESTLING
       WITH] [STARING AT] CHASING EATING
       [CUTTING UP] [TALKING TO]]
     MAKE "OBJECTS [PORCUPINE. CUCUMBER. SOFA.
       CROCODILE. CHEESECAKE. [TEDDY BEAR.] [LAMP
       POST.]]
     END

TO STORIES
     CHOOSEWORDS
     PRINT (SENTENCE [THE] :PERSON1 [LOOKED
       OVER THE] :BARRIER [AND SAW A] :PERSON2
       :DOING [A] :OBJECT)
     STORIES
     END

TO CHOOSEWORDS
     MAKE "PERSON1 PICKRAND :PEOPLE1
     MAKE "PERSON2 PICKRAND :PEOPLE2
     MAKE "BARRIER PICKRAND :BARRIERS
     MAKE "DOING PICKRAND :ACTIVITY
     MAKE "OBJECT PICKRAND :OBJECTS
     END

TO PICKRAND :LIST
     OP ITEM (1 + RANDOM (COUNT :LIST)) :LIST
     END
```

These procedures create sentences by picking words at random from lists. The structure of the program is shown in Figure 12.1. The procedure SETLISTS assigns to a number of variables lists of

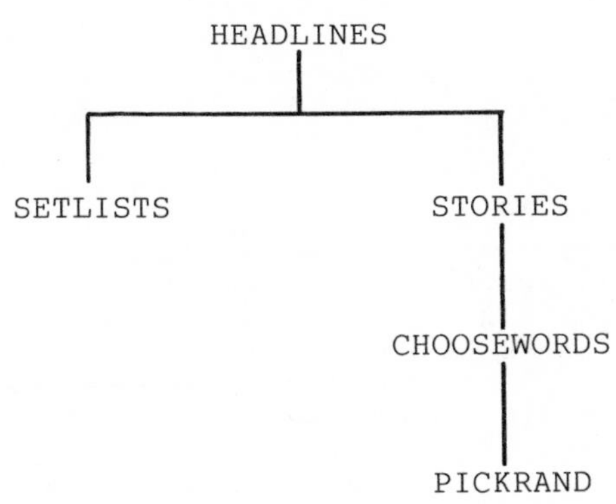


Figure 12.1 Procedure calls for HEADLINES

items selected by the user. Notice that these items can be either words or lists. CHOOSEWORDS picks one item at random from each list (PICKRAND being a procedure to pick at random an item from a list). STORIES, after calling CHOOSEWORDS, places the words chosen into a template to create the finished sentence. Notice that the primitive SENTENCE (often used in its shortened form SE) is employed to join together lists, including those referred to by variable names. Here are some examples of sentences produced by this program:

THE FIREMAN LOOKED OVER THE FENCE AND SAW
A POACHER CUTTING UP A CHEESECAKE.

THE GARDENER LOOKED OVER THE TREETOPS AND SAW
A RUGBY TEAM DANCING WITH A SOFA.

THE FIREMAN LOOKED OVER THE PARAPET AND SAW
A CROWD OF S.A.S. PERSONNEL CHASING A TEDDY BEAR.

THE BURGLAR LOOKED OVER THE WINDOW LEDGE AND SAW
A CABINET MINISTER WRESTLING WITH A CUCUMBER.

Because items can be either words or lists of varying length, considerable variation in the sentences produced is possible. The possibility of generating, for example, creative writing suggestions or poetry, by developing programs of this type suggests that LOGO has something to offer language work in the classroom. Most work with LOGO in schools has so far been graphics-oriented, but some experimenters with LOGO are now asking how LOGO's powerful list-processing ability can be put to good use.

## POETRY AND GRAMMAR

One of the earliest experiments with LOGO list-processing in the classroom was carried out by Mike Sharples at Edinburgh University. In his "Poetry from LOGO" project, Sharples worked with three 14-year-old boys in an Edinburgh school. Two of the boys had some familiarity with LOGO. Having discussed with the boys the way in which LOGO might be used to generate poetry, Sharples then wrote three successive LOGO programs, to create poems at different levels of sophistication. Each program was experimented with by the boys, and its effects discussed, and improvements suggested. As Sharples intended, however, the boys were using LOGO to talk about the nature of language and poetry, for in criticising the poems produced by the LOGO programs, they had to compare what they saw with their own understanding of how language worked, and had to articulate and reflect upon that understanding.

The first program, POEM1, would accept a list of words and produce items from the list in random order. Discussion centred upon which combinations succeeded, and particularly, why failed combinations did not make sense. Out of this discussion came suggestions for improving the procedures, so that they would avoid some of the failures. POEM2 generated poems using a template specifying the number of words in each line and the part of speech required at each position in a line. Discussion moved on from mechanical aspects to those of meaning, since correct word order and plausible vocabulary was not seen as sufficient to make acceptable poetry. The final program, POEM3, used a template; however each word in the available vocabulary carried with it a list of "meaning words", descriptors indicating some associations of the word, and selection of words from the vocabulary, although still random, was now constrained by the need for words used to share "meaning words". Material generated was still a mixture of the bizarre and the profound:

DRY PATH

LONELY MOON FADES SUBTLY
IN COLD PLAINS
BLACK CLOUDS
FROST FADES BY WISH

WE FEED SLOWLY

BLACK PATH FADES TO RED ROCKS
I FEED.

Alongside the work with the computer, the same procedures were simulated using slips of paper in boxes. This was very helpful in conveying an understanding of how the procedures worked; but as the level of complexity rose, the paper simulation became more tedious and inconvenient.

Sharples concluded that this type of exercise could be a useful part of a "creative linguistics" in schools, where English language and literary awareness can be learned through creation and reflexion rather than through the application of mechanical rules without reference to meaning and context.

Following the Poetry Project, Sharples developed a "language workshop" employing a suite of four programs of increasing sophistication (as in the Poetry Project) to create text. The simplest, GRAM1, is a text generator which places words supplied to it into a random order. This program can be used to show children the elementary fact that language is more than just a random sequence of words. The second program, GRAM2, is a grammatical sentence generator, in which words are classed by part of speech and sentences are produced, in accordance with part of speech templates. Using this program, basic, or more complex, "context-free grammars" can be constructed from simple rules. The notion of a context-free grammar has wide implications: it can be used to generate expressions in any language, including that of mathematics. TRAN is a sentence transformer program which enables sentences to be changed according to the rules supplied. GRAM3 allows meaning descriptors to be associated with groups of related words in the vocabulary. Thus the descriptors "animal" and "small" can be associated with the noun group "lion/tiger". This poem was produced (and titled) using GRAM3:

<u>You</u>

Why does my waiting child like to talk ?
Why does my girl wish to dream of my song ?
You are like a song.
By herself my waiting girl dreams.

The language workshop was tested with primary schoolchildren. It was programmed using the computer language POP 2 on a computer at Edinburgh University. POP 2 is not available to most schools; but the same suite could (as the Poetry Project showed) be written in LOGO. The technical problem which might then emerge is the limited memory available to LOGO on most microcomputers used in schools.

Mike Sharples describes the language workshop as "a set of building blocks for the language architect"; it permits exploration of fundamental elements of communication and understanding in a way which is creative and enjoyable.(2) Sharples has speculated on additional elements which may be built onto the language workshop, such as a story planner and spelling checker.(3) In his view the language workshop would be situated in a school resource area, to be used by pupils as required, alongside the other forms of language resource available to them. It should be noted that in testing the language workshop Sharples was careful to mingle computer-based and non-computer-based learning tasks, with activities on and off the computer interacting and complementing each other.

## TRANSLATION MACHINES

As an example of a simple language toolkit, here is the program for a French "translating machine" in LOGO. It will translate only extremely simple English sentences into French, but shows how this can be achieved using LOGO.

```
TO FRENCH1
    SETUP
    TITLE
    DISPLAY
    END
```

```
TO SETUP
     MAKE "PRONS [I  HE  SHE  WE  YOU  THEY]
     MAKE "FPRONS [JE  IL  ELLE  NOUS  VOUS  ILS]
     MAKE "VERBS [FIND  GIVE  SEEK  SING  TALK]
     MAKE "STEMS [TROUV  DONN  CHERCH  CHANT PARL]
     MAKE "ENDS [E  E  E  ONS  EZ  ENT]
     CT
     END

TO TITLE
     PRINT [AUTOMATIC FRENCH MACHINE]
     PRINT []
     PRINT [Translates English into French]
     PRINT []
     PRINT [Use form: PRONOUN VERB (eg he gives)]
     PRINT [Note: limited vocabulary available]
     PRINT []
     PRINT [Enter text, press RETURN key]
     PRINT [Press Z then RETURN to finish]
     END

TO DISPLAY
     PRINT []
     PRINT [Text please ...]
     PRINT []
     PRINT  SEARCH  RL
     DISPLAY
     END

TO SEARCH :LIST
     IF (FIRST :LIST) = "Z [TOPLEVEL]
     MAKE "EL1  DEL :PRONS  FIRST :LIST :FPRONS
     IF (LAST  LAST :LIST) = "S [MAKE "LASTWORD
       BL LAST :LIST] [MAKE "LASTWORD  LAST :LIST]
     MAKE "EL2  DEL :VERBS :LASTWORD :STEMS
     MAKE "EL3  DEL :PRONS  FIRST :LIST :ENDS
     OP  SE :EL1 (WORD :EL2 :EL3)
     END

TO DEL :LIST1 :ITEM1 :LIST2
     IF (FIRST :LIST1) = :ITEM1 [OP  FIRST :LIST2]
     OP  DEL  BF :LIST1 :ITEM1  BF :LIST2
     END
```

The structure of this program is shown in Figure 12.2. The master procedure FRENCH1 calls three sub-procedures, SETUP, TITLE, and DISPLAY. SETUP assigns lists of pronouns, verbs and endings to appropriately named variables, TITLE presents the instructions for using the program on the screen, and DISPLAY accepts English text and delivers its

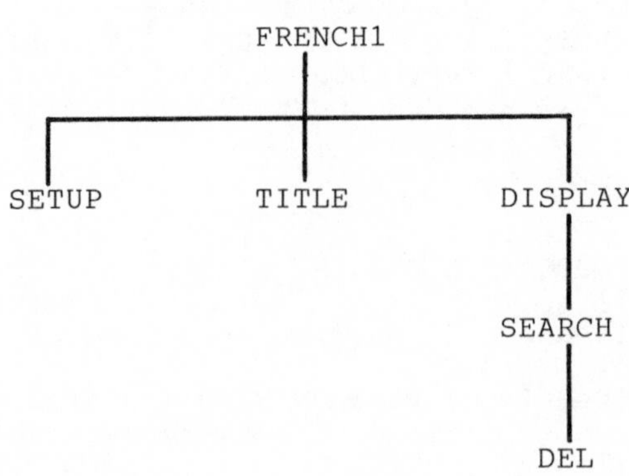


Figure 12.2 Procedure calls for FRENCH1

French equivalent. Two further procedures are necessary to achieve this. SEARCH looks for the entry of a Z as the signal to end the program run; the letter S is stripped off the English verb if present, to give the stem; then the procedure DEL is used to select the correct pronoun, verb-stem and ending; and finally the three elements are joined together and sent back to DISPLAY to be printed out. DEL (short for DELIVER) is a useful utility which accepts an item and two lists as input: the first list is searched until the item is found in it; then the element at the same position in the second list is returned. It should be noted that the program as shown does not include error-trapping devices and will work as long as input obeys the rules.

What value might this program be in the classroom? At one level, it functions as a black box translator, although it operates within very strict limits. The program shown only works with expressions of the form (pronoun - verb), and with an extremely limited number of regular verbs. However, editing the procedure SETUP can enable extra or different verbs to be included, and a procedure could be added to enable a modified SETUP to select one of a number of collections of verbs held on disk. It may then have a useful function as a revison-aid or vocabulary store. Modification of the whole program can enable the same principle to apply to different expressions. For instance, substitute these procedures for those with the same names in FRENCH1 to translate expressions of the form (subject - verb - object):

```
TO SETUP
     MAKE "FVERBS [MANGE CHERCH REGARDE]
     MAKE "VERBS [EATS SEEKS WATCHES]
     MAKE "FNOUNS [[LE CHAT][LE CHIEN][LA FILLE]
             [L'HOMME][L'ARBRE]]
     MAKE "NOUNS [CAT DOG GIRL MAN TREE]
     CT
     END

TO TITLE
     PRINT [AUTOMATIC FRENCH MACHINE]
     PRINT []
     PRINT [Translates English into French]
     PRINT []
     PRINT [Use form: SUBJECT VERB OBJECT]
     PRINT [(e.g. the man watches the dog)]
     PRINT [Note: limited vocabulary available]
     PRINT []
     PRINT [Enter text, press RETURN key]
     PRINT [Press Z then RETURN to finish]
     END

TO SEARCH :LIST
     IF (FIRST :LIST) = "Z [TOPLEVEL]
     MAKE "EL1 DEL :NOUNS (FIRST BF :LIST) :FNOUNS
     MAKE "EL2  DEL :VERBS (ITEM 3 :LIST) :FVERBS
     MAKE "EL3  DEL :NOUNS (LAST :LIST) :FNOUNS
     OP (SE :EL1 :EL2 :EL3)
     END
```

Clearly, modifying the procedures requires understanding of both the French and English languages, as well as some LOGO. As with much learning development work with or without computers, a team approach can be the most productive, and can encourage co-operation between different areas of specialism. But, as with Sharples' poetry programs, the process of consructing variations which deliver sensible and correct responses will develop skills in all three areas. Examining the mechanics of translation, and the limitations of mechanical translators, will indicate the complex nature of the process, and point to the importance of contexts in giving meaning to words.

## POSSIBILITIES AND A PROBLEM

One area in which LOGO's list-processing facilities could be made use of in the classroom has been explored. Other areas have not been touched upon here. LOGO is well-suited for writing adventure games, for setting up and interrogating databases, for supporting interactive quizzes and conversation programs; space does not permit the exploration of all of these, although some related possibilities are considered in Chapters 14 and 15.(4) As teachers and researchers look beyond turtle graphics at the capabilities of full LOGO implementations, many of these directions are being explored and developed.

A major problem however is the limited capacity of currently available school computers. LOGO is a powerful language, originally developed on large computers. The LOGO implementation occupies a sizeable part of the memory of a school microcomputer, leaving comparatively little for holding users' procedures. For instance, on the Apple II (with added language card bringing total memory up to 64K) there is slightly over 11K available for users' programs; and on the BBC microcomputer just over 20K is available, but only in the non-graphics Mode 7. With turtle graphics, this does not usually pose a problem, since programs are usually very terse, and plenty can be accommodated in a small amount of memory. But text-oriented programs fill space very quickly, especially if lists have to be stored; and when programs are run, especially if recursive processing procedures are being used, remaining memory can be very quickly used up.

Various strategies can be adopted to make the most of memory, but all operate at the cost of the simplicity and elegance of programs. Numbers of short procedures can be combined with others, saving space but leaving programs which are untidy and dificult to read. Recursive loops can be replaced by non-recursive loops, saving memory when the program runs but losing what is often the best way to carry out a processing operation. Chunks of the program can be read in from disk, run, then immediately deleted, leading to long delays while the disk drive whirrs busily but nothing else happens, and tremendous inconvenience in writing and testing the program. Or all the decorative frills that make a program look attractive on the screen can be abandoned, leading to a program that works but looks fairly basic on the screen. Several of these strategies may have to be adopted at once, resulting in the program developer spending more of his time trying to fit the program into the computer's memory than he spent designing it to do what he wanted!

This situation will persist so long as the current generation of computers inhabit the schools. This means that, although interesting and useful language applications in LOGO will be developed, large systems (such as that described in Chapter 15) will be difficult to construct so that they will run. LOGOs already running on bigger microcomputers with more memory (such as the IBM PC or Apple Mackintosh) show that this is a problem limited to small systems. And the fact that computer memory continues to become cheaper month by month shows that the current situation is a temporary one. In 5 years time the present generation of school computers may have been replaced, or at any rate supplemented, by computers which will give LOGO's list-processing facilities the chance to support extensive and powerful language-handling programs.

## NOTES

1. The LOGO Poetry Project is reported in: M. Sharples, Poetry from LOGO DAI Working Paper No. 30. Department of Artificial Intelligence, University of Edinburgh. 1978
and: M. Sharples, A Computer Based Language Workshop DAI Research Paper No. 135. Department of Artificial Intelligence, University of Edinburgh. 1980

2. The language workshop is reported in: M. Sharples, A Computer Written Language Lab DAI Research Paper No. 134. Department of Artificial Intelligence, University of Edinburgh. 1980

3. M. Sharples, "Microcomputers and Creative Writing" pp. 138-157 in J. Howe & P. Ross, (eds) Microcomputers in Secondary Education: Issues and Techniques London Kogan Page 1981

4. Many language-related areas of LOGO-use are considered in a forthcoming book: Wallace Feurzeig & Paul Goldenberg, Exploring Language with LOGO New York Harper & Row 1985

Chapter 13

# LEARNING PROGRAMMING THROUGH LOGO

"Computer Studies", as a subject in its own right, is now becoming established as a part of the secondary school curriculum. Examination syllabuses have been or are being developed at all levels, so that Computing can be among the certificated skills of school-leavers. One of the components of such courses is always computer programming, since it is generally felt that an essential element in studying computers is examining the way in which instructions are given to the computer in order to make it carry out the tasks required of it. Including a programming element in a course immediately raises a question: which programming language should be adopted as the medium for the programming element of the course? In this chapter we will suggest that LOGO is a valuable medium for the formal teaching and learning of programming.

## TOP-DOWN AND BOTTOM-UP

It is often claimed that there are two distinct styles of writing computer programs: "top-down" and "bottom-up". Top-down programming is considered the better style by computer academics; this style is taught at colleges and universities, and programming languages such as Algol and Pascal have been specifically developed to foster its use. By contrast, bottom-up programming is seen as the sort of style developed by self-taught computer hobbyists, usually using BASIC.

The top-down style involves starting with the goal or task which the program is intended to achieve. This may be presented to the programmer by his superiors. The goal may require clearer definition and expression in terms, for example, of the types of inputs and outputs needed and the limits which need to be set on input and output. Moving on from there, the major component modules or parts which are necessary to achieve the goal will be set out. These modules are themselves then broken down into progressively smaller units, so that a pyramid-like structure may emerge. These small units are then coded, that is, written into the statements of a particular programming language. The programming task thus ends at the keyboard (although testing and refinement will follow). It is thought that this sort of programming is usual where clearly set goals, often set by non-programmers, have to be achieved, as in business or administrative applications.

The "bottom-up" style, on the other hand, begins at the keyboard, as the user "hacks around" some lines of code to find out what his computer can do. Having joined some commands together to create an interesting effect, he may add this to another effect. So, for example, a spectacular graphic sequence may be attached to some dramatic sound effects. Another feature may then be added; in the example, the programmer may decide to add some user-interaction to his program, so that the user is asked his name, how many colours he wants in his effects and how loud he wants them to be. In this way, more and more refinements and options may be added until a very complex program has been built up. This program will have grown from the features of the hardware, and the inclination of the programmer. This sort of programming is thought to occur when the programmer is not working with pre-set goals, but rather is exploring the possibilities of the hardware or software at his disposal, or indulging his own whims. Such "playing" rather than "working" is thought typical of the computer hobbyist, creating programs written in a "spaghetti" manner which cannot be understood by anyone else.

The choice of programming languages is tied up with assumptions about programming style. "Structured" languages, like Algol and Pascal are held to be especially suitable for top-down or "structured" programming, since they encourage the programmer to think everything out before starting any of the coding, and to break the program up into clearly-defined elements with inputs and outputs specified at the start. They also possess powerful looping structures making the nesting of sections of program inside others straightforward (using commands like REPEAT ... UNTIL or WHILE ... DO). Since these languages are usually "compiled" languages, where the whole program has to be compiled (i.e. converted into a machine code file) by a special piece of software, testing little bits as you go along and making minor alterations until it looks satisfactory, is inconvenient and time-consuming.

On the other hand, the computer language BASIC, which tends to be the most frequently available language on home microcomputers, is held to encourage bottom-up "spaghetti" programming. This is because of its linear layout (as a long list of command lines, each with a line number) which encourages the programmer to start at the beginning and work towards the end, without seeing the whole program in perspective. Line numbers also make it difficult to transfer parts of one program to another. BASIC has looser looping structures, especially GOTO, which enables the programmer to direct the "flow of control" into any part of the program he likes, even right into the middle of a completely different section. Because it is an "interpreted" language, where the language software executes each command as it comes to it, without reference to those that lie further ahead in the program, minor alterations can be constantly made as the program is being developed at the keyboard. "BASIC is bad for the brain" is a cliche that comes easily to the tongue of the Pascal enthusiast.

However, if we consider more carefully the two supposed types of programming, it becomes clear that, far from being opposed (so that doing one makes you bad at the other), they are complementary styles of approach to the programming task, and an awareness of both styles is necessary to successful programming. At all stages in the top-down method, as the program is progressively refined and made more specific, decisions have to be made. For example, what sort of input is required, what messages will appear on the screen, what graphic and sound effects are required, how much information is to be manipulated, whether a printer is to be attached, and so on. To make these decisions, the programmer has to know what the hardware he is using will achieve, not just in general terms of its memory limits or the number of colours offered, but whether particular effects or sequences are possible. He needs to know his

The Stereotype

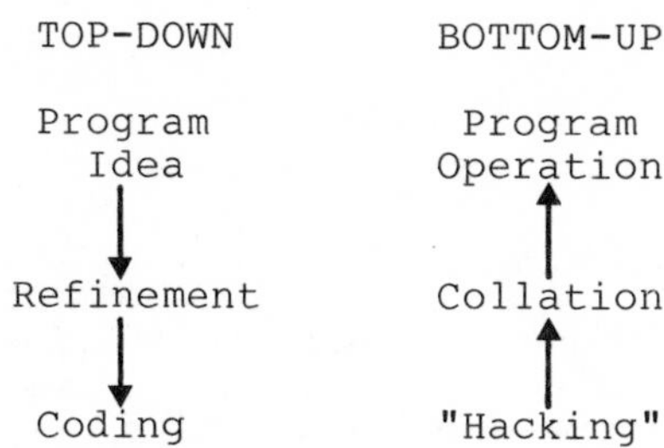


The Reality

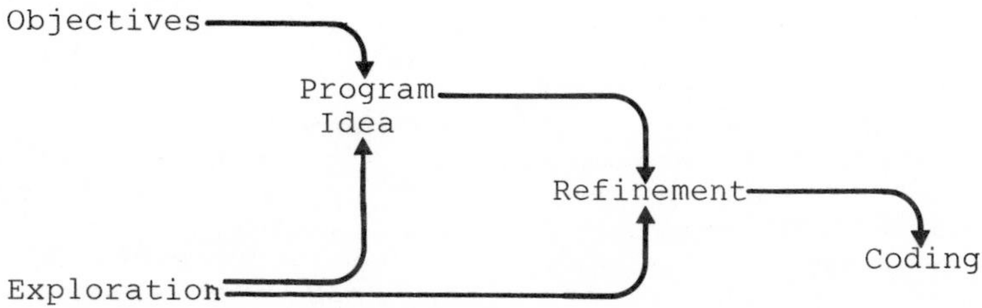


Figure 13.1 Program Design: Image and Reality

equipment, and the best way to get to know it is to explore it from the keyboard. Likewise, the bottom-up programmer building up a program at his keyboard does not follow a process of random exploration; he has interests and lines of development which he wishes to follow, ad his piecemeal program construction, although it may have a less organised look about it, may have a fairly clear end in view. In fact the good programmer needs to be able to use both styles, setting out the structure of his program in order to plan it clearly, and exploring the possibilities which his hardware and software offers in order to select the features most appropriate. He must be able to work from the top down and from the bottom up; both planning and exploration play a part in good programming. Different "styles of programming" reflect the different balances which individuals reach between the activities of planning and exploration. Figure 13.1 contrasts the images and the reality of program design.

## PROBLEM-SOLVING

Books on programming often include the phrase "problem-solving" in the title. This is to indicate that computer programming is usually a means to an end. The end may relate to one of a wide range of computer-based activities: the intended product may be a game, a statistical program, a diagnostic test, a graphics utility, or a set of commands to operate a robot-arm. It may be more or less clearly definable. But in all cases, reflecting about how the end can be attained, before sitting down at the computer, can be a very productive exercise. It is this process of reflection to which the term "problem-solving" refers.

The treatment of "Good King Wenceslas" in Chapter 9 gives us an example of how thinking about a task helps to achieve it. It would be possible to sit down at the computer, start with the first note, and go through, note by note, until the end of the tune had been reached. However, this process has two disadvantages. First, it takes a very long time, and since every note is entered, whether it is part of a repeated phrase or not, it can also take up a lot more of the computer's available memory than a more carefully planned program. It may occupy so much memory that the computer is unable to run it. Second, programming the tune this way gives us no understanding of the music, since we do not see the patterns into which it falls. Thinking about the nature of the tune helps to make sense of the music, and to program it. Thus the tune was first divided up into phrases, each phrase occupying a line of the verse:

```
GOOD KING WENCESLAS
   PHRASE A
   PHRASE A
   PHRASE B
   PHRASE C
   END
```

The statements written down at this stage do not need to be in any particular programming language.

They must only indicate clearly the elements making up the task which the program is to achieve. This initial list of elements makes up what some programmers call the "main program". For instance, the main program for a diagnostic testing program might be written as follows:

```
DIAGNOSTIC.TEST
   SET LIMITS
   INSTRUCTIONS
   TEST
   STORE RESULTS
   FAREWELL
   END
```

This formulation does not use the syntax of any particular programming language, but is intended to be concise and well-organised enough to be translatable into a suitable language when the time for this comes.

Having specified the program elements at "top level", the program designer can now examine each element, considering it as a separate procedure, i.e. almost a program in its own right. Thus, in the "Good King Wenceslas" program, the first phrase, which is repeated, could be shown as:

```
PHRASE A
   BAR 1
   BAR 2
   BAR 3
   BAR 4
   END
```

Remark statements may be added to make the operation of each element clear. Thus, in the diagnostic test program, the first element might be:

```
SET LIMITS
   SHOW LIMITS  (list parameters to be set)
   ASK SETTINGS  (teacher inputs settings)
   SET VARIABLES  (sets relevant variables)
   END
```

The constituent elements or procedures making up each second level procedure are then broken down in the same way, and the process continues in the same vein until every operation required is clear. In the "Good King Wenceslas" program, each bar was seen as made up of individual notes. In the

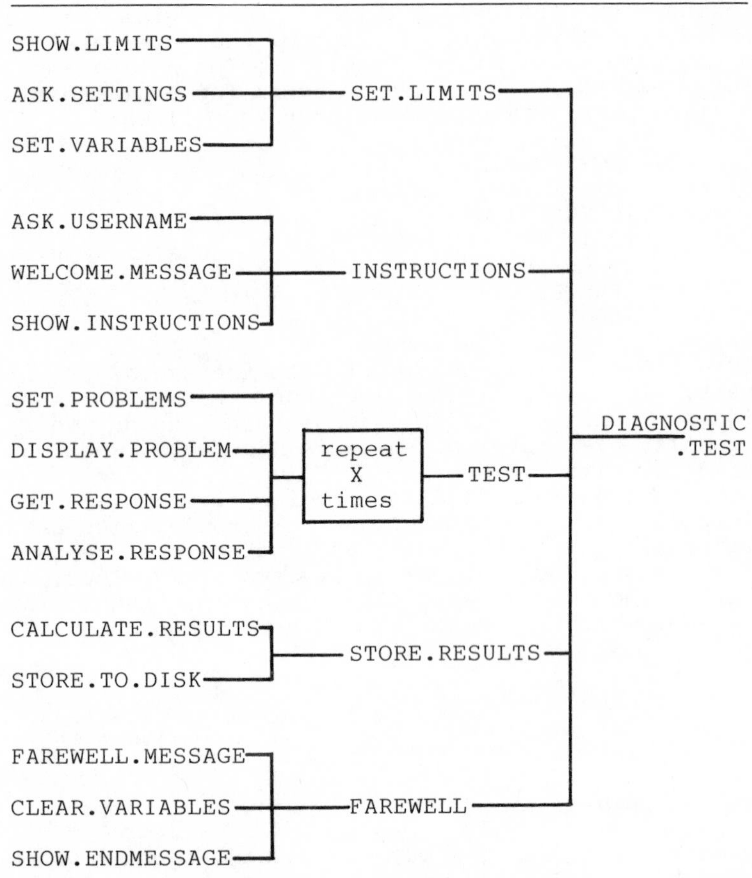


Figure 13.2 Structure Diagram for Notional Diagnostic Test Program

diagnostic test program, the next stage of planning the element SHOW LIMITS might be to draw a plan of what the screen display should look like. The types of information which need to be passed from one procedure to another, the inputs to and outputs from the computer and its peripherals, and the variables required to store information during the running of the program can now all be worked out. All of this can take place before any coding (i.e. writing the program lines in a specific computer language) need be done.

Indeed, the designer may not decide which programming language is most appropriate to his needs until the process of design is well under way. The structure of the program can be demonstrated through modular or hierarchical diagrams of the type which are seen in a number of chapters in this book. Figure 13.2 shows a possible structure chart for the diagnostic test program considered above.

In the case of many tasks, the process of breaking down into parts may not be as simple as in the examples quoted above. The structure chart becomes more confused if the same module is used in different parts of the program, which may often happen, particularly if a program offers a number of not dissimilar options. The act of spelling out just what is involved in achieving the goal of the program may indicate that the goal itself has not been adequately formulated. Or it may not be practicable with the hardware available; the computer available may not have enough memory, or may not offer the graphics capability to handle the sort of display required.

Thinking about the objective of the program, and putting thoughts onto paper in the form of plans, diagrams, or lists of modules, is an essential aspect of good programming. It enables the programmer to see where each bit of his coding fits into the overall scheme, and to see at any time just how far he has proceeded towards completing his task.

## COMPUTER LANGUAGES FOR STRUCTURED PROGRAMMING

Good programming, which involves the effective combination of planning and exploration, is possible in most computer languages. Having thought out the overall intention and shape of the program, and expressed it in a clear plan, the modules making up the program can be implemented in whatever language is available to the programmer. However, some languages make the task of planning and executing a program easier than others. We will look at three of the most popular languages in use in educational systems, BASIC, COMAL, and Pascal, to see how easily they permit good programming practice, before considering what LOGO can offer.

To show some of the differences in syntax at a simple level, a specimen program has been coded in each of these languages. This program, Anytable, generates "times tables" for whole numbers. It asks the user to give a whole number, then displays on the screen the "times table" for that number. The elements of the program are as follows:

```
ANYTABLE
   TITLE    (prints a heading on the screen)
   ENTRY    (asks for number to be entered)
   DISPLAY  (calculates & shows table on screen)
   END
```

TITLE will place the heading "Tables Produced for any Integer" on the screen. ENTRY will ask the user to enter the number for which he requires the table, and will store that number as a variable. DISPLAY will calculate the values for the table by multiplying the number entered by each number from 1 to 12, and display the table on the screen.

BASIC (short for "Beginners All-purpose Symbolic Instruction Code") was developed at Dartmouth College, in America, in the 1960s. It was developed out of an earlier language (still used today), Fortran (short for FORmula TRANslation); the object was to create a language with commands as close to normal English as possible. Being interpreted, it allows program development at the keyboard. BASIC has rapidly become the principal language used in teaching programming in secondary schools, and it has also become the most popular language among home computer enthusiasts. Figures 13.3 and 13.4 show the Anytable program, first in the sort of BASIC common on machines like the Apple and the PET until recently, and then in one of the now common structured BASICs. Probably the most noticeable feature of a BASIC program is that it has line numbers. Use of line numbers (in GOTO or GOSUB statements) is the most common method of directing the flow of program control in an unstructured BASIC. This makes the program difficult to read, as can be seen from Figure 13.3, and encourages the programmer to visualise his program in one-level terms, like a sort of horizontal Snakes and Ladders. Nevertheless, structured programming is possible in unstructured BASIC, although more work is needed to keep the structure visible.

More recent "structured BASICs" permit the user to define separate program elements as procedures, making well-planned programming much

```
10  REM**  Anytable  **
20  REM
30  REM         *** main program
40  GOSUB 100; REM title
50  GOSUB 200; REM entry
60  GOSUB 300; REM display
70  END
80  REM
100 REM title
110 PRINT "TABLES PRODUCED FOR ANY INTEGER"
120 PRINT
130 RETURN
140 REM
200 REM entry
210 PRINT "WHICH TABLE DO YOU WANT ?"
220 PRINT
230 PRINT "ENTER INTEGER NOW ..."
240 PRINT
250 INPUT N
260 RETURN
270 REM
300 REM display
310 PRINT
320 FOR K = 1 TO 12
330 PRINT K;" X ";N;" = ";K*N
340 PRINT
350 NEXT K
360 PRINT "END OF TABLE."
370 RETURN
```

Figure 13.3   Anytable in unstructured BASIC

easier. Procedure calls can now replace line number redirections in controlling the program sequence. The structure of programs can be seen more clearly in the listing. The difference is visible in Figure 13.4. Structured BASICs also have a wider range of looping structures, adding REPEAT...UNTIL and sometimes WHILE...DO to the FOR...NEXT and GOTO of earlier BASICs. Being interpreted, BASIC programs can be tested as they are developed; however, some BASIC compilers are available which can speed up execution of BASIC programs. Structured BASIC facilitates structured programming, but also allows exploratory activity at the keyboard.

COMAL was developed in Denmark in 1973-4, as a response to the criticism that the BASICs then

```
10  REM**  Anytable  **
20
30  REM main program
40  PROCtitle
50  PROCentry
60  PROCdisplay
70  END
80
100 DEF PROCtitle
110   PRINT "Tables Produced for any Integer"
120   PRINT
130 ENDPROC
140
200 DEF PROCentry
210   PRINT "Which table do you want ?"
220   PRINT
230   PRINT "Enter integer now ..."
240   PRINT
250   INPUT num
260 ENDPROC
270
300 DEF PROCdisplay
310   PRINT
320   FOR k = 1 TO 12
330     PRINT k;" x ";num;" = ";k*num
340     PRINT
350   NEXT k
360   PRINT "End of table."
370 ENDPROC
```

Figure 13.4   Anytable in Structured BASIC

in use discouraged good programming style. COMAL (short for COMmon Algorithmic Language) was intended as a language retaining the ease of use of BASIC, but adding to it facilities to enable more structured planning. Thus many of the commands are those of BASIC; and COMAL is interpreted, making program development easy. But procedure-defining, and more sophisticated control structures, such as REPEAT...UNTIL, WHILE...DO, and the CASE statement, which makes situations where a decision must be made within a program between several options easier to achieve, have been adapted from the more structured language Pascal. Some COMALs have done away with line numbers, as an unnecessary and confusing distraction, others have retained them. In the

```
10  //  Anytable
20  //
30  // main program
40  title
50  entry
60  display
70  end
80  //
100 PROC title
110   PRINT "Tables Produced for any Integer"
120   PRINT
130 END PROC title
140 //
200 PROC entry
210   PRINT "Which table do you want ?"
220   PRINT
230   PRINT "Enter integer now ..."
240   PRINT
250   INPUT num
260 END PROC entry
270 //
300 PROC display
310   PRINT
320   FOR k := 1 TO 12 DO
330     PRINT k;" x ";num;" = ";k*num
340     PRINT
350   NEXT k
360   PRINT "End of table."
370 END PROC display
```

Figure 13.5   Anytable in COMAL

late 1970s COMAL gained much support as a language which could supersede BASIC but still be "user-friendly" enough to be used in schools. However, microcomputer manufacturers and software houses seem to have felt that buyers would prefer an improved version of what they knew, rather than something with a new name, and COMAL implementations were very slow to appear. Meanwhile, the development of structured BASICs has removed much of the advantage which COMAL was seen to possess. COMAL now differs little from a good structured BASIC. Figure 13.5 shows the Anytable program in Acornsoft COMAL. COMAL continues to be used in secondary schools in Denmark and Eire, and has been chosen recently as the language in which programming will be taught

```
program anytable (input, output);
var num, k: integer;

procedure title;
begin
  writeln('Tables produced for any Integer');
  writeln
end;

procedure entry;
begin
  writeln('Which table do you want?');
  writeln;
  writeln('Enter integer now ...');
  writeln;
  read(num)
end;

procedure display;
begin
  writeln;
  for k := 1 to 12 do
  begin
    writeln(k,' x ',num,' = ',k * num);
    writeln
  end;
  writeln('End of table.')
end;

begin {main program}
  title;
  entry;
  display
end.
```

Fig 13.6  Anytable in Pascal

in Scottish secondary schools. But it no longer seems the breakthrough which it did in the late 1970s.

Pascal was first implemented in Switzerland in 1970; it is named after the great 17th-century French philosopher, scientist, and inventor of calculating machines. It was designed as a vehicle for teaching well-structured programming, and is now the language most commonly taught in universities. In accordance with the aims of its inventor, it permits highly structured programming, and encourages detailed planning before coding by having very rigid rules about program layout. All variables, constants, and data types must be declared at the beginning of the program, and all functions and procedures must precede the main program. Pascal is a compiled language, and therefore writing the program as you code it, and making frequent adjustments, are somewhat tedious, since each new version of the program must be compiled before being run. It lacks the convenient string- and array-handling of BASIC, but has powerful looping and program control features, and offers user-defined data types. It is more powerful than BASIC or COMAL, but not easy to learn and to use effectively. It encourages top-down program organisation, but makes exploration of hardware facilities difficult and inconvenient. Figure 13.6 shows the Anytable program in Pascal.

We are discussing the suitability of programming languages for well-planned and structured programming, however the point should be made that, although structured languages encourage or help structured programming by offering appropriate features, ill-planned and confused programming is still possible with all of them. The programming language used will make good programming more or less convenient to implement; but it will not create a good programmer. This can only be achieved by good teaching, good learning, practice, and experience.

## GOOD PROGRAMMING IN LOGO

Having looked at some other programming languages, we should now consider LOGO. How useful is LOGO as a vehicle for learning good programming practice? In focusing on learning programming, we should ask how easy it is to design and implement LOGO programs while retaining good style. To be useful in learning programming, a language should be clear, convenient to use, flexible, and easy to experiment with.

The first thing we must consider is LOGO's "procedurality". It was intended as a language which would be powerful, yet easy to learn. By "easy to learn" the inventors of LOGO were not thinking about simple linear program arrangements with easily grasped control direction commands like GOTO. Rather, they were thinking about the way LOGO would resonate with the patterns of thinking we use. Thus, small and understandable pieces of program can be created almost immediately, using the primitives which LOGO provides. But they can then be joined with others to build bigger programs with a clear structure, rather than being attached to the end of a linear program. Each unit making up the program can be given its own name, and called up by using this name. This procedural nature means that in LOGO programs can be built up in blocks after the structure has been worked out, and unit-names used in the design phase can be retained as procedure-names in the coding phase. The program can then be easily compared with its outline plan, and more readily thereby understood. Figure 13.7 shows the Anytable program in LOGO.

LOGO has a flexibility which many other languages lack. The fact that LOGO maintains in its workspace a reservoir of procedures, some of which draw upon others, means that several programs may share some of the same constituent procedures, without the duplication and matching of line numbers which using a collection of subroutines (and even procedures) involves in BASIC. LOGO's flexibility is lacking not only in linear languages like BASIC, with their programs determined by line number, but in some procedural languages like Pascal, with their strict rules about declaring variables, constants and data types, and about the order in which program elements should be placed.

Because LOGO is an interpreted language rather than a compiled one means that experimentation and testing of small elements during program development is conveniently done. Having defined a procedure, you can immediately see if it achieves what was intended; if not, adjustments can be made and the new version immediately tried out again. Exploration of what the language offers, and trial-and-error program refinement are both easily done without having to pass everything through a compiler before running. The use of procedures which can be isolated from the rest of a program enables exploration of particular parts to go on without requiring constant adjustment of the rest of the program.

LOGO possesses convenient and powerful command and data structures. Looping ability is provided by the REPEAT command and by the possibility of recursion. REPEAT enables

```
TO ANYTABLE
     TITLE
     ENTRY
     DISPLAY
     END

TO TITLE
     PR [Tables Produced for any Integer]
     PR []
     END

TO ENTRY
     PR [Which table do you want ?]
     PR []
     PR [Enter integer now ...]
     PR []
     MAKE "NUM  FIRST  RL
     END

TO DISPLAY
     PR []
     MAKE "K  1
     SHOWTABLE
     PR [End of table.]
     END

TO SHOWTABLE
     IF :K > 12 [STOP]
     PR (SE :K [x] :NUM [=] (:K * :NUM))
     PR []
     MAKE "K :K + 1
     SHOWTABLE
     END
```

Figure 13.7 Anytable in LOGO

fixed-number loops to be achieved simply, while recursion allows more open-ended looping. The inclusion of conditional elements into REPEAT and recursive loops can give structures achieved in other languages by WHILE...DO or DO...UNTIL. Data assembly and processing is achieved in LOGO through manipulation of lists. Because they may contain other lists, as well as words or numbers, lists are very versatile data-carriers. For instance, handling of text when items are of variable length presents no problems.

No computer language can be perfect for all

purposes, and LOGO is no exception to this rule. WHILE and UNTIL would be useful additions to the looping primitives (although they can be implemented as procedures); and the ability to set up arrays or define new data types would be welcomed. Since LOGO is interpreted, this helps program development, but it also means that complex programs, especially those with a lot of recursive list-processing, can run apparently very slowly. A LOGO compiler would therefore be a very useful aid in running large programs. It cannot be suggested that LOGO is a good language for business applications programs.

But LOGO does seem particularly suited to learning applications. It is a language for learning good programming habits as well as for learning through programming. "Good programming habits" include the exploration of computer facilities and the testing of improvisations on existing program elements, as well as elegant top-down design. And as computer memories grow and LOGOs themselves evolve, many of the irritations which large-scale programming in LOGO involves may soon disappear.

Chapter 14

# SOFTWARE IN LOGO

## LOGO TOOLKITS

LOGO was envisaged by its creators as a computer language which would enable the user to learn by programming. By exploring the possibilities of the various facilities which LOGO can offer (turtle graphics, music, and so on), the user can make discoveries about the microworlds which they sustain. Learning proceeds through the construction of procedures out of the building bricks available (that is, the primitives offered by the version of LOGO being used), and the testing out of procedures through the examination of their effects. So far, in what we might call the first phase of LOGO-use, this process has been largely concerned with turtle graphics and the microworld of plane geometry, although of course many other microworlds have been demonstrated by pioneers (and are discussed in this book). Turtle graphics has normally been seen as sustaining a microworld which can be explored with only the primitives available to hand: using FORWARD, BACK, RIGHT, LEFT, and so on, simple procedures can be understood, and then built up into more complex ones.

However, in developing learning possibilities with other LOGO facilities, a different strategy for learning has sometimes been used. This involves presenting the user with a collection of "black box" utilities, procedures which the user is not expected to understand at the start, but only to use for exploration and further procedure-building. A notable example is Mike Sharples' work on poetry and language toolkits, described in chapter 12. The music programs described in chapters 9 and 10 could fall into the same category. In these cases, the learner begins his LOGO work with prepared procedures, and only at a later stage in learning, when his conceptual grasp of LOGO-use has reached an appropriate level, does he approach a fuller understanding of how the black box procedures work.

The contrast between these two strategies is to some extent illusory, since in both cases the facilities are used by the beginner as if they were primitives, whether they are or not. So to this extent, the journey to knowledge by exploration proceeds the same way. There still however remains some difference, for the toolkit utilities are not usually as open-ended as the primitives available to the turtle graphics user: they set constraints on the directions in which exploration may take place. So, as the process of exploring with the utilities develops, a concurrent process may emerge of exploration within the utility procedures themselves, a process which yields new tools for wider exploration in the form of their constituent primitives. Discovery and assimilation of the primitives makes possible more open-ended construction than the utilities permitted, but using the constructive techniques which were developed through the use of the utilities. Thus, discovering how some of the poem-generating procedures work will permit development of programs which generate other forms of textual material.

## BLACK BOX PROGRAMS

Most commercial computer programs, whether to be used for education, business or pleasure, can be described as "black boxes". The user is presented with a piece of software which achieves certain objectives. It may be an arcade game requiring fast responses to knock out oncoming aliens, or an adventure game where the player must make his way through caverns, passages and rooms in a castle or labyrinth in search of treasure, a word processor where text can be manipulated on the screen then sent to the printer, a spreadsheet where statistics can be collated, a database where collections of information may be stored and searched, a cloze procedure exercise where missing words have to be inserted into a passage, a simulation of a battle from history, or an arithmetic program which generates subtraction problems and diagnoses the students particular learning difficulties. It may be very "user-friendly", asking the user in everyday language to enter information or press certain keys, or it may be more difficult to use, requiring what seem to the outsider strange formulas and odd passwords to achieve what seem simple outcomes. But all such "applications" software has in common the fact that the user does not see how the program operates. A "black box" program is one which delivers results without letting the user see how it does so. The "works" are not visible.

In many cases this does not present a problem for anyone. The businessman is not interested in <u>how</u> his spreadsheet program works, only <u>whether</u> it works. If it doesn't do what he wants, he will send it back to the supplier and complain. Similarly, the teacher may only be interested in using a cloze procedure program, rather than seeing how it has been programmed. Providing a particular educational experience will be her objective, rather than understanding how computer programs work for their own sake.

Taking further the idea of toolkits of useful procedures, we can consider the possibility of LOGO programs which, at their initial level of usage, are in effect complete black boxes, as far as learning by LOGO programming is concerned. LOGO is a powerful list-handling language, available on most microcomputers, and is easier to use than BASIC or machine code. Spelling games, multiple-choice tests, adventure games, and cloze procedure exercises are all examples of programs which can be straightforwardly produced in LOGO. Being written in LOGO does not mean that they are therefore necessarily educationally valuable: a drill-and-practice program testing retention of rote-learned facts (kings and queens, state capitals, etc.) might well be of no value at all as a vehicle for learning (except for the person who wrote it, who may have got some good LOGO programming practice). However, a simulation exercise giving the user the decision-making role at each stage, or a creative graphics or music facility could be of great worth as an educational experience offering the same style of learning as LOGO programming: exploration and discovery, problem-solving, decision-making, interaction and collaboration.

## TRANSPARENT SOFTWARE

Very often the user of an educational program is keen to know a little about how the program works. Sometimes this is because it does not quite suit the situation the he is presented with. Commercial software must be aimed at large numbers and therefore must try to fit an average situation (if such a thing exists). In this way, many people may get something that is close to what they want, but not _precisely_ what they want. Many teachers are keen to learn just enough about how programs work to be able to make slight adjustments which they feel will make a program more suitable to their class. This may mean altering the speed at which the program runs, or changing the wording of some of the messages on the screen, which may not be at an appropriate reading level, or changing the names in an adventure game to make it seem more local.

Learning enough programming to make even minor changes to software is not an easy task. Most educational software is written in machine code or BASIC. Machine code programs are complex collections of arcane instructions which operate at the level of the microchip itself. Listings of machine code programs are virtually impossible to read, being difficult even for experts. Altering machine code programs is thus a dangerous pursuit for all but the expert, since a minute alteration may have disastrous consequences.

Programs written in BASIC seem more amenable to adjustment, since BASIC listings are a lot easier to read than machine code. However, even though you may be able to read BASIC program listings and recognise some of the commands, understanding what the program actually does is a different matter. BASIC programs are often written in a serial manner, starting at the beginning and going through everything, in order of occurrence, to the end. This sounds reasonable as a way of working, but it means that activities of many different levels of importance are happening in intermingled lines, so that it is not easy to work out what is doing what. The GOTO statement sends the flow of control of the program to another section which may be a hundred or a thousand lines further on or further back. Plenty of GOTOs leads to a "spaghetti program" which is all but impossible to disentangle. Manipulations of variables and arrays are also difficult to follow. Usually, knowing enough to make minor adjustments means searching through the program for DATA or PRINT statements, altering these, and hoping for the best.

Customising of programs is also getting more difficult because of measures taken by the publishers to protect their wares from unauthorised copying. Both machine code and BASIC programs will have security devices built in to prevent the program from being listed or copied. Putting a program onto a ROM cartridge makes it even more difficult to copy. All these measures may be effective against casual copiers; but they do not prevent expert copiers who regard any new security device as a professional challenge. However, they do have the side-effect of "freezing" programs in their published state, making customisation impossible.

By contrast to the "black box" inaccessibility of programs in machine code or BASIC, LOGO programs are more likely to be "transparent". Its inventors intended that in LOGO programs the works should be visible. Programming computers should not, they believed, be a hidden art reserved for a few. Building up programs from user-defined procedures which can be easily called should make the structure of a LOGO program clear. This does not mean of course that it is impossible to write obscure and mystifying programs in LOGO: long strings of RIGHTs, LEFTs, FORWARDs, PENUPs and PENDOWNs which create pictures of monkeys, penguins or aeroplanes. But the philosophy of LOGO should encourage teachers and pupils to view such products as transitional products of an initial level of exploration, rather than end products to be aimed for. LOGO is not just a programming language but a collection of ideas about how it should be used. (This is not to say that there is anything wrong with pictures of monkeys, penguins or aeroplanes; just that there are different ways of getting to those pictures.)

Applications software written in LOGO should be easier to understand and therefore to customise. The author of a large program in LOGO can develop his program in clearly identified modules, with each function which contributes to the whole encapsulated in an appropriately-named procedure. The top level procedure contains the main elements of the program; and the function of each is clear from its name. Within each of these modules the same is true: the name gives a good indication of what each procedure does. Because LOGO programmers are encouraged to keep procedures short, if the name is not quite clear or not specific enough, the shortness of the text should enable it to be read through line by line. Customisation or extension can therefore be possible. This does not necessarily mean easy, for modification of any software requires careful thought and planning before it is undertaken.

## LOGO SOFTWARE PACKAGES

What LOGO can make possible is a level of usage beyond that of the black box, as the routines making up the program can become a focus for exploration, in addition to what can be done with the program itself. Because the program is constructed in LOGO, the lid can be taken off the black box. At a first level of usage, the program is utilised as a black box, offering the simulation, language game, animation facility, or whatever. At a second level of usage, however, the construction of the program is explored: this makes possible the discovery of powerful LOGO procedures and primitives, along with functioning exemplars demonstrating their capabilities. But it also deepens understanding of what the black box program was set up to do, because it reveals the decisions which have been taken in creating the environment it provides. The reasons why the program does what it does can be investigated, and the limits on action which have been built into it can be understood. This twofold knowledge forms the foundation for a third level of usage, at which the black box can be amended, extended, re-designed and re-created.

These two further levels are not necessarily approached in strict order of sequence, with the workings of the program being fully mastered before adjustments can be made. As simple elements of the program are mastered, they can be experimented with to make minor adjustments; as deeper procedures are investigated more fundamental changes can be enacted. Thus understanding and amendment of the program run side by side. The process is complicated by the presence of various levels of users. Thus a teacher may begin to delve into the program and customise it for her class, whilst the class still face the program as a black box. Eventually some members of the class may gain understanding of the program's innards whilst others still have much to benefit from black box usage. Some members of the class may revert to using the program in its black box state to test out modifications which some of their colleagues have made.

A piece of educational software written in LOGO already available is Tillie the Turtle. This is a software package developed for Atari LOGO; it will however be available for the BBC computer for those who have a "sprite board" fitted. It is essentially a story with graphics: the package includes a book, the original story on tape, and a disk. The software provides animated pictures of Tillie the Turtle in her own environment, with scenes from the story being shown, using Atari LOGO's sprite facility. The sprites, moveable shapes which can be easily shifted around the screen without affecting the background, can be controlled easily. The ease of sprite control enables the action on the screen can be altered; different stories can then be developed by adult and child out of the new patterns which emerge. The storybook becomes the springboard for new stories.(1)

## THE MICROWORLD OF THE VIKINGS

These possibilities can also be demonstrated by a rather different package called The Microworld of the Vikings (2). The package, currently in course of evaluation, is designed as a computer-based classroom simulation. Its aim is to allow children of about 9 to 13 to gain something of the perspective of the Vikings, men who traded, raided, fought, farmed and explored their way across the mediaeval Northern Hemisphere, from Byzantium to Newfoundland. Used at what we can call Level I, the program is a black box movement and incident simulator. The class is divided into groups, each of which directs the movements of a Viking ship around the North-West Atlantic Ocean and the North Sea. When the ship is off land, there are opportunities for raiding, trading, or visiting existing Viking settlements. These activities do not however always come off as anticipated, for friends, if drunk, may turn ugly, and empty villages may not always be what they seem. Out at sea, too, unexpected things can happen: bad weather may send a ship off course, or Frankish pirates may show up, spoiling for a fight. A constant flow of decisions is required, decisions which are taken by the group after discussion amongst themselves.

In between their turns at the computer (which stores their situation ready for their next turn), group members return to their table to carry out further study of the Viking epoch. some of this work will be directly related to the progress of their ship: they may chart their route on a map, write up a log book or journal, dramatise incidents on tape or for class performance, or discuss future strategy. Other work will be indirectly related to the group's voyage: reading a novel (such as Henry Treece's Viking's Dawn ) or a Norse saga (like that of Eirik the Red), modelling a trading ship or a warship, asking how the Viking sailors could navigate. Further work may deal with other aspects of Viking life: compiling a dossier on domestic life or religious ideas, modelling a village, writing stories or poetry. In this way what is being supported by the computer is fully integrated into work away from the computer; the computer is seen as a normal classroom resource and not as a freakish novelty or extra. Using a computer in this way does not replace the teacher; nor does it make good preparation unnecessary. As with any topic-based group work, if the teacher is well-prepared, her intervention is low: she is a provider of resources and (where necessary) ideas. Learning is active, stimulating, enjoyable.

At other levels, however, further possibilities are available. The program has been written in LOGO, partly because LOGO is good for list-processing, and partly because, at what we can call Level II, the LOGO code can itself become an environment for exploration. Particular areas of the program can be examined: presentation of messages on the screen, creation of incidents, maintenance of cargo records, and so on. Procedures may be extracted to experiment with on other data: adding items to and deleting them from a shopping list, printing messages and menus on the screen, etc. Learning about how the LOGO works can lead to questions about why the particular outcomes set for the program were chosen: why these incidents, why this frequency of occurrence, why this extent of movement? Understanding of the structure and form of the program prepares the learner for what we can call Level III of program usage: re-creation of the program itself. This may take many forms, from alteration of the names of ships and their captains to those chosen by the groups themselves and addition of new items to the cargo list to modification of incidents and the addition of new zones to the possible sailing area. For instance, the program as supplied only permits travel as far as the Western side of Iceland; but extra zones can be added allowing ships to travel to Greenland and to America. An ultimate modification would be the dismantling of the substantive form of the simulation, and its replacement by another: thus the Viking ships may become wagons crossing the interior of North America, pirates in the Caribbean, or Arab traders in the Indian Ocean.

## SIMULATION-DATABASE PACKAGES

The development of a context-free simulation shell in LOGO, which would enable these possibilities to be realised, is being carried out at the Simulation-Database Project at St. Andrew's College, Glasgow.(3) The type of package being evolved (termed a simulation-database ) consists of three software elements, a movement-simulator based on the "adventure game" model, enabling participants to move around, between "zones", encountering various situations and incidents, within a particular "micro-world", and two databases, one of files relating to the zones of the simulation-structure (which could contain passages, lists, diagrams, etc.), and the other a list of further references and sources, book and non-book. However, it is assumed that these will be accompanied by appropriate ancilliary materials (handbooks, maps, documents, pictures, etc.), as computer-use is not seen as isolated from other classroom activities. A computer-based learning package cannot consist merely of software if it is to be fully integrated into classroom activities.

A simulation-database package could form a continuity element as well as a key resource for topic work in primary or subject-focused activity in secondary classes, running for up to a term, or even longer if desired. The movement-simulator will provide a framework of movement and incident, and the databases will make available a collection of information for investigation, and enable the user to pursue his/her enquiries through further sources. Each of these facilities gives the user (either teacher or pupil) a wide range of choice; and therefore the opportunity to explore widely a particular learning environment.

A class using a package may be divided into up to six groups. Each group takes on the identity of a particular character, and is presented with a scenario requiring their character to make a journey. The journey is planned, then movement is made using the movement-simulator which forms part of the package. During movement, incidents may befall the characters. After the movement phase, investigative work may take place concerning the zone arrived at, making use of all the resources which the school can muster. During this phase the two databases may be consulted. Activities arising out of trials with specimen packages include mapwork, creative writing (diaries, newspaper reports, descriptions), drama (plays, taped interviews with characters), discussion, historical and geographical research and the compilation and presentation of findings, art and craft work (drawings of scenes and situations, friezes, models), field trips and visits by outside speakers. These activities include language, both written and oral, and number work. Group interaction and co-operation plays a major role in project-based activity.

This package would not be used in isolation from other teaching resources; it would be one of a range of learning activities made available in the context of a particular topic area. "Hands-on" time at the computer would be very small, since it is intended that most learning should occur away from the computer, whose only function is as a tool available (among others) should its services be required. For this reason, simulation-database packages require the use of a printer, in order that material generated by the computer (passages of text, references, maps, diagrams, instructions and progress reports, etc.) may be taken to the work-tables to form part of learning activities. It is assumed that one computer per classroom is a likely optimum.

An important feature of a simulation-database is that it should be easily adaptable and extensible by the user. New zones and data should be easily added, and existing zones and data easily replaced. It could thus be adjusted to local conditions or to the particular objectives and interests of a particular school and its teachers and pupils. Using LOGO as the programming environment will facilitate such alteration possibilities, and make the simulation-database open-ended on a multi-level use basis, since adaptation could involve exploration of the LOGO program itself.

The main objective of the project is to develop a "Do-it-yourself Kit" which will enable any individual or group of individuals to construct their own simulation-database package for use in any curricular area. A small simulation-database might be based on "Our School", and permit movement between the different parts of the school. "My house" could be a package developed by a group of children. "Our Town" might be a more ambitious project, fostering local studies work; use of the simulation-database could be combined with field studies. Packages could represent countries or regions. However, the simulation-database can be of value in curricular areas beyond the historical or geographical: "Inside the atom", or "Journey through the human body" could become the self-developed simulation-database packages of the future. Once created, packages may be exchanged, updated, merged or further developed. The range of possibilities is limited only by the imagination and the resources available. The package-making kit is currently being prepared for the Apple and BBC microcomputers, and versions for other computers will follow.

An important element of the project's work is to produce ready-made packages in relevant curricular areas. A package on Scotland a Hundred Years Ago is currently being evaluated in use in primary and secondary schools. This package is described and discussed in Chapter 15.(4) At present work is under way on the construction of two further packages, Palestine in the First Century , for use in the religious education area, and The River , for the environmental studies/ geography area.

## CONTINUITIES OF STYLE

The continuity of style that is possible between LOGO and non-LOGO activities in the examples above is of profound importance. First, it should warn us that LOGO, like any open-ended resource, can be used in many ways, and incorporated into different styles of teaching. If used insensitively, it may become another collection of signs and rituals force-fed to clients who do not have the key, and tested with a drill-and-practice exercise (which could be written in LOGO). Second, it shows us that LOGO, used sensitively, is one way in which a user-centred learning situation may be created, but that there are other ways too; and the LOGO experience will be most successful in the context of a whole curriculum which is consonant with it. Finally, it reminds us that a roomfull of computers is not a precondition for the building of a rich learning environment. For most primary or elementary schools, one computer per classroom is an enviable situation still far off; and teachers must make the most of whatever is available to them at whatever times they have access to it.

Applications programs written in LOGO have a role to play in supporting rich learning environments which include the exploration of LOGO itself. As LOGO becomes more widespread, more of these will be produced. And as more powerful machines than the current generation of school computers find their way into classrooms over the next few years, larger and more comprehensive LOGO applications will become available.

NOTES

1. For details, contact: Interactive Storybooks Ltd., London New Technology Network, 86-100 St Pancras Way, London NW1 9ES.

2. For details on availability, contact: Allan Martin, Project Director, Simulation-Database Project, St. Andrew's College of Education, Bearsden, Glasgow G61 4QA, Scotland.

3. The Simulation-Database Project was established at St. Andrew's College of Education in April 1983; it is funded by the Scottish Education Department.

4. See also: A. Martin, "Journeys into a Microworld" <u>Interactive Learning International</u> Vol.1, (1984-85) No. 2., pp. 7-8. Further information available from the Simulation-Database Project (address in Note 2).

Chapter 15

# CASE STUDY 6: A HUNDRED YEARS AGO

Mary Scott, Maria Shields and Joan Wilson

---

Maria Shields and Joan Wilson, both trained teachers, are research assistants with the Simulation-Database Project, St. Andrew's College of Education, Glasgow. Mary Scott is a class teacher in one of the primary schools where the Project's package *Scotland 100 Years Ago* was piloted. In this chapter, they describe the classroom implementation of a major piece of software written in LOGO.

---

## ENVIRONMENTAL STUDIES IN SCHOOL

The Scottish Primary Memorandum of 1965 drew the attention of primary schools to "Environmental Studies", suggesting a co-ordinated focus of studies in Arithmetic, History, Geography and Science, "since they all in some degree involve activities which are grounded in the child's observation and investigation of his surroundings."(1) In fact, arithmetic was never successfully drawn into what teachers saw as Environmental Studies, and it is now accepted that the term refers to an amalgam of history, geography, and science, with smaller elements of economics, health education and civics.

In its policy statement, published in 1981, the Scottish Committee on Environmental Studies in the Primary School (SCES) reaffirmed the importance of Environmental Studies:

> In every school environmental studies should be given a status at least equivalent to that traditionally given to language, mathematics and expressive arts. Indeed, when one considers, not only the opportunities that environmental studies provides for realistic and relevant work in language, mathematics, and expressive arts, but also the many incidental day-to-day opportunities for the discussion of matters affecting behaviour, relationships, health habits, it is arguable that environmental studies should of necessity comprise the major part of the child's school life. (2)

With regard to the way in which Environmental Studies should be presented, skill and concept development was to be seen as the major objective:

> A series of content topics should be treated in such a way as to ensure that learning involves activity and experiment, and that teaching is interesting, outward looking, and concerned with understanding rather than merely remembering. (3)

With the gradual adoption of co-ordinated Environmental Studies in primary schools, studies of particular localities have assumed more importance. Education through history has long been a part of the primary curriculum; however, as historical environmental studies, the emphasis has been increasingly placed on recent history. In particular, more attention has been given to the last one hundred years than previously.

Taking this into account and the fact that there was a distinct lack of materials covering this period and suitable for primary school pupils (in terms of reading level, amount of detail, relevance of content, and style of presentation) the Simulation-Database Project decided to develop a package on the theme of Scotland 100 Years Ago. The heart of the package would be a computer-supported simulation exercise representing journeys through late 19th-Century Scotland by six characters. This package has been piloted in primary schools since February 1984.(4)

## SCOTLAND 100 YEARS AGO

The Scotland 100 Years Ago package consists of a box of disks, three handbooks and various other printed materials. The software, written in LOGO, consists of a movement-and-incident simulator, which enables the user to move around a notional map of Scotland, divided into locality zones on a grid pattern, and two databases, one containing a large number of passages relating to the zones, and the other consisting of a wide variety of book and non-book references. The handbooks are a general teacher's handbook, describing the materials and suggesting how they might be used, a "Zone Information Handbook" providing further information and sources of information regarding each of the zones, and an annotated printout of the contents of the reference database. The other printed materials have been designed to encourage the children to relate to the character roles they are to take on in the simulation. Included are four sets of six character storysheets; six documents which give a pseudo-authentic backing to the characters and their quests; a coded message; a pack of twenty photographs; a map of Scotland with the simulation zones marked out for reference; and record sheets for teachers and pupils to record their movements. Required to use the software are a computer with disk drive and printer.(5)

The package aims to provide a vehicle which enables a class to study Scotland 100 years ago by taking part in a series of simulated journeys around the country, and studying the places passed through. It may form the core of a programme of investigation continuing for several weeks, and involving a wide range of associated (but not necessarily computer-based) activities. In terms of skills and qualities, it is intended that activities carried out in connection with use of the package may contribute to the development of:

1. <u>Intellectual Qualities</u>

a] Conceptual understanding: particularly of development, change, variety, continuity and similarity.
b] Comprehension skills.
c] Inference making and deduction: drawing conclusions from study of given information.
d] Decision-making and planning.

2. <u>Practical Skills</u>

a] Recording material in an appropriate form and pursuing inquiries independently.
b] Presentation of material, both written and oral, in a clear and precise manner.
c] Correct use of technology.

3. <u>Acquisitional Abilities</u>

a] Factual recall of relevant and significant items of information.
b] Contextual knowledge which aids the approach to more specific items of information.

4. <u>Imaginative Qualities</u>

a] Ability to place oneself in the role of another, accepting the limitations on evidence and background knowledge of the role.

5. <u>Interactional Qualities</u>

a] Co-operation in a group working to achieve a common goal.
b] Ability to exchange information and opinions with others.

The package was designed with the middle-school age range (9-13 years) in view; however, it also has applicability further up the secondary school. The wide range of applicability is made possible by the flexibility of the materials and the teacher-adjustment possibilities incorporated.

The main software element of the package is the movement and incident simulator. This provides a means of notionally moving around Scotland, a short distance at a time, thus permitting frequent stops. Movement is possible only between adjacent zones, so that progress on the journey is clearly visible to the child. At each zone, a map of Scotland may be printed out, pinpointing the current location. Direction and structure is provided through scenarios based upon the situations of six pseudo-authentic characters, three male and three female, chosen to represent the range of social statuses which might have been encountered in the late nineteenth century.

A class using the package may be divided into groups. It is suggested that these be mixed-ability, as this provides opportunities for the sharing of experience and for both independent and co-operative activity. Each group takes on the identity of one of the characters, and is given a storysheet requiring their character to make a long journey across Scotland. The journey is planned, then movement made using the computer-based movement-simulator. The scenarios provide pupils with a foundation for building up and developing their group's adopted character and become the basis for much non-computer work.

Included in the movement-simulator are incidents designed to provide real-life events which could have occurred in Scotland a hundred years ago. They also place pupils in situations where they must make decisions which will affect both themselves and others. There is opportunity for group discussion and decision-making in regard to how to move and react to the incidents which occur. The incidents have been chosen to provide the teacher with the choice of using them as a starting point for further activity lessons. As the children travel through the different zones, they may encounter incidents related to the type of area they are in. General incidents can occur in any area. An example of one of the incidents as it is printed out is given in Figure 15.1.

After the movement phase, investigative work may take place concerning the zone arrived at, making use of all the resources which the school can muster, including the two databases included in the package. The databases provide additional information which will be of value as different zones are reached. Database 1 contains passages relating to the zones, which can be used as stimulus for study activities; there are currently six data disks for Database 1. As the groups move around the country it is recommended that they have planned the stopping places to study along their route. After the group has arrived at their stopping place and typed the name into the computer a list of passage headings applicable to that zone will appear on the screen. The group select a passage, which will

A Hundred Years Ago

---

You meet a poor crofter who is very distressed. He tells you that tomorrow the Factor and his men will come to throw him and his family out of their house if they cannot pay him 1 pound for their rent. Nearly in tears, the crofter explains that his crops are not yet ready to be sold, and that he has no money to give to the factor. To save his family and his home, the crofter begs you for 1 pound to pay his rent for the next Quarter. By then his crops will be ready for sale. Will you help him?

[If response is Yes:]
The crofter gives the pound to the Factor and is given permission to stay on his croft. The family are very happy and thank you with all their hearts.

[If response is No:]
The crofter and his family are thrown out of their home and left to wander in search of food and shelter.

Figure 15.1 Specimen Incident Printout

---

automatically be printed out. Each passage has been examined for readability: all fall within the reading age range 8.5-13 years.

Database 2 is a collection of book and non-book references related to Scotland 100 years ago. This database provides the user with further sources of information, along with details of the references found at the end of each passage in Database 1. The teacher can use Database 2 to prepare work in advance. By keeping a record of each group's movements, she can plan ahead, looking at the passages they will come across in Database 1 and using Database 2 to provide herself with relevant material for follow-up work. The printout of the details of each reference can be taken to a teachers' centre or public library if books are to be ordered. The teacher can also input new references to the database, such as those in school or local libraries. She can in this way provide opportunities to enhance the children's research and library skills. This also allows them to explore their own school and public libraries and collate material from additional sources.

The package does not in itself constitute a total programme of work for a class. A certain amount of preparation is necessary by the teacher in order to make the most of it. Thus, particularly at the beginning of its use, the teacher's knowledge of the history of the school's locality will be important in getting the work off to a good start.

## INTO THE CLASSROOM

The schools involved in piloting the project ranged from traditional closed classrooms with a more didactic teaching mode to more modern open plan schools with an integrated curriculum and co-operative teaching. The class teachers who were to use the package, together with their head teachers and appropriate local authority advisers, were given a demonstration, and the use of the materials in the classroom were discussed. To familiarise themselves with the project materials the teachers studied them in depth before introducing them to the children. Only through personally examining and using the materials did the teachers become to some extent aware of what lay ahead.

Their next task was to prepare the children for the project. With the help of two specimen introductory lessons provided in the teachers' handbook the teachers directed the children towards an awareness of the differences in lifestyles then and now. Here is an example of the introductory strategy adopted by one of the teachers:

a] Re-capped on Scotland 200 years ago (a previous class project).
b] Gave several general lessons on aspects of Scotland through the ages.
c] Focused on the period 100 years ago; invited a local historian who showed slides and photographs of late 19th century Scotland.
d] Gave lessons on how to use the disks and produced wall charts on use of the software.

The teachers introduced one group of children at a time to their character. It was recommended that

A Hundred Years Ago

---

JEAN MUIR                                                Storysheet 1a

Mrs Jean Muir is a poor 29 year old widow with no children. She was widowed when her husband was tragically killed at work, when a barrel from a dray-cart fell on top of him. Left alone with only 6d in her purse, Mrs Muir went to the Poor Relief Authorities who gave money to those in need. The poor relief offered her 10s 6d per month to live on, but Mrs Muir knew that this would not be enough. However, on asking for more she was told that this was all they could give her and, if she would not accept this then because she was a widow it was now up to her parents to look after her.

Therefore, with a pound borrowed from a kind neighbour, she sets off to travel to her parents' home in Campbeltown.

Figure 15.2   Specimen character storysheet.

---

at least a full week be spent on character building and the planning of routes to the stated destinations, before any work with the computer began. During this week the groups, with the help of the first storysheet for each character, enlarged upon their character's background through such activities as creative writing, role play, art and general class discussion. One of the character storysheets is shown in Figure 15.2. These were purposefully made brief, in order to leave most of the attributes of each character open to the fullest development by the group. Character background was built up by a variety of methods; in some of the classrooms life-size figures were produced by the children, giving their characters a immediate visual identity accessible to all. These were displayed on the walls along with a variety of written work giving details of the character's personality, work, home-life, family and friends. Each group tended to have an alloted section of wall space for their work. These character-building activities were seen to be extremely important to the initial buildup of the project activity. The teachers recognised the need for the children to identify with their character in order to capture their interest and to create a positive foundation on which to build.

Each group was issued with the first of the storysheets before they began any work on the computer. Thereafter, at specific destinations the groups each received further storysheets, which directed them to their next stopping point. In all there are four storysheets for each character, the final one giving each character a happy ending to their travels. "Killing-off" of characters en route is not possible.

Some of the teachers involved in the piloting of the project were fairly inexperienced with regard to using a computer as a major teaching aid. In these initial stages concern was expressed about this lack of experience. The simple question in most minds was 'will I be able to use it (the computer) effectively enough in order to generate confidence in my pupils?' Schools where the use of the computer was fairly new faced the further problem of it still being a novelty in the classroom:

> As the sound of the trolley rumbling along the corridor was heard by the eager ears of my class, the atmosphere around us changed to one of excitement. They had not yet managed to accept 'its' coming and going as normal.

It was in fact the teachers who were initially apprehensive about using the computer. The pupils on the other hand showed fewer reservations, and soon became completely familiar with the handling of the disks and the computer keyboard and printer controls.

As mentioned above, the project is suited to group work. However it is for the teacher to organise her class in the best possible way to suit each individual child's needs. One of the teachers worked in a semi-open plan school where co-operative teaching was common practice. She found that no difficulties arose through seating the children in mixed ability groups. However, she found it beneficial to place certain pupils in certain character groups as the character seemed to suit their personality.

Once organised into groups, and character building completed, the children were ready to begin their journeys on the computer. Class organisation was a key factor at this point. In the initial stages it was important to adhere to the normal daily timetable of tasks whilst incorporating the project into the curriculum. This allowed the teacher to spend time with a group on the computer explaining the steps required in using it. As the project progressed the children soon became more proficient in operating the computer, and the presence of the teacher was no longer required. This allowed her to spend more time with groups who were working on other project activities which were not computer based.

One major attribute of the project is that in its design it offers the teacher the opportunity to work with it as often as she wishes. The teacher may prefer to use the project as a secondary facility incorporated into her normal classroom timetable or, she may want to make it her whole centre of interest. One suggestion of how a teacher may integrate the package into her classroom timetable is that work on the project take place three days a week. A rota system could be established whereby each group, in a week, spends an allocated time during one day on the computer, "travelling" through Scotland and collecting relevant information from the databases. In the second day the database material can be used for research and study, and the third day could be given over to related aesthetic activities. The advantage of the rota system is that there is a continual flow of organised activity and during the initial stages the teacher can spend time with the group using the computer while the remainder of her class are involved in other project activities.

In the actual piloting of the package one class teacher decided to use it as a basis for her complete centre of interest. In this class the project work took place every day of the week. Once a week each group used the movement simulator to journey from one zone to another; the next two days were spent studying the information contained in the database passages, and with the help of the teacher, deciding which areas of interest to follow up. The two remaining days were spent carrying out aesthetic work related to the passages. The teacher's rota ensured that each group used the movement simulator once a week. Every area of the curriculum was drawn into the project work, allowing the class to learn something about every aspect of life in late nineteenth-century Scotland.

Teachers found that the pupils remained well-motivated throughout the project. Each child enjoyed being an active participant in a wide variety of activities. Over the course of the project, teachers noticed a gradual change in many of the pupils. Several commented on the way the children became more receptive to the needs of others and were more willing to partake in group activities. Many of the children showed an acute awareness of the difficulties their character was experiencing (e.g. lack of money and dealing with delicate situations such as evictions and industrial disputes). In one or two cases it was noted that attendance became more regular, and that school work 'took on a new meaning'. An out-of-school interest was also aroused, with parents, grandparents and local residents contributing their experiences and resources. Overall it was felt that many of the pupils matured as a result of having to make decisions democratically. It was found that some pupils became more tolerant, while others became more ready to share their ideas and opinions.

One aspect of difficulty which arose during piloting was that each group passed through different zones collecting a variety of information from the databases, and carrying out a variety of different activities. The problem was to ensure that the whole class derived benefit from each group's experiences, by learning of the places they visited and the situations in which their character was placed. Teachers tackled this problem in different ways: there were class discussions, panel sessions and question and answer periods, dramatisations of incidents which happened during the journeys, and the presentation of wall-displays and compilation of group-books of information and creative work.

Teachers had to bear in mind the need for some assessment of children's progress. It was a question of noting the area of activity into which each task involved in the project work fell, and also of achieving a correct balance between individual and group products. Teachers already familiar with groupwork found this easier, maintaining or extending their normal styles of assessment. The same was also true of the administration and organisation of the project work: teachers used to flexible grouped activities were able to direct their efforts to getting the most out of it; those with less groupwork experience found it more difficult.

The overall opinion of the teachers was that the package supported a situation in which they could allocate a specific piece of work to a certain child. This meant that the less able pupil could work at his/her own pace and still participate in project-related work. In this way, all members of the class could be fully involved in work on the project. Indeed, the positive classroom atmosphere was a noticeable feature of package use. We conclude this section with a comment made by one of the teachers:

> I feel that two of the most important features which have come from this project and which cannot be ignored are enjoyment and motivation on the part of both teachers and pupils alike.

## THE NEXT STEPS

The response from teachers who have used the package, and from educationists of all kinds who have looked at the materials or observed them in use has been encouraging. We have shown that Scotland 100 Years Ago can make a contribution to environmental studies in the upper primary school. However, the evaluation of the package is still proceeding. More primary schools will use it. It will also be used in some secondary school History classes, with pupils of up to 15 years old. As a result of feedback from the trials, minor modifications are constantly being made to the pack, so that it has not yet reached its final form, although the general shape is satisfactory.

During the first trials, possibilities for teacher modification of the software were not taken up, since teachers were concentrating on the utility of the package as it stood. Many teachers who use the package will prefer to use it unaltered, and therefore it was important to develop a form in which it would be satisfactory at this level. However, during current trials teachers are being encouraged to use the facilities for modifying the software, by replacing zones on the movement-simulator, and adding and removing items to the databases. Only when this stage is completed will the full value of the package be known.

Results from the evaluation of _Scotland 100 Years Ago_ are having and will continue to have a significant influence on the evolution of the Simulation-Database Project. "Scotland" was the first package produced by the project, and experiences with it have helped to shape the development of the "Do-it-yourself" simulation-database-creating package and the packages currently under production on first-century Palestine and a river system.(6)

Work with the package has also stimulated, among project team members, teachers and even pupils, a lot of hard but productive thinking about what computers can contribute to the classroom. We are all convinced that computers are powerful machines which have a valuable place in schools. However, care is needed to ensure that they are used appropriately, to do those jobs to which their power is suited

NOTES

1. _Primary Education in Scotland_ Edinburgh HMSO Page 126.

2. _Environmental Studies in the Primary School: the Development of a Policy_ Scottish Committee on Environmental Studies in the Primary School (SCES) 1981 Page 1.

3. Ibid., page 8.

4. The Simulation-Database Project is based at St. Andrew's College of Education, Glasgow, and is funded by the Scottish Education Deprtment.

5. The pilot studies described in this chapter were carried out using Apple II computers with double disk drives, running Terrapin LOGO, and Silentype or Epson FX or RX printers. Versions of the package are being developed for other computers and LOGO implementations.

6. For details of current progress on _Scotland 100 Years Ago_ or other elements of the project's work, contact the Project Director, Simulation-Database Project, St. Andrew's College of Education, Bearsden, Glasgow G61 4QA, Scotland.

Chapter 16

# THE FUTURE WITH LOGO

## AT THE FRONTIERS

The last three or four years has seen a massive change in the relationship of LOGO to education. In the early '80s LOGO was still largely an experiment, its potential only perceived in a few schools or research institutions. It has now entered a phase of acceptance, although on a partial basis. Turtle graphics, either on the screen or with a floor turtle, is an facility which is now becoming well-known, and is being incorporated into the normal curriculum in many schools. Other features still hover on the experimental fringes, although interest in them is constantly increasing.

The rapid adoption of turtle graphics is not without possible dangers, especially if this one feature of LOGO is taken out of the context of how LOGO was conceived and the full range of features which it can offer. If teachers who are not happy with the sort of learning environment which LOGO is intended to foster are obliged to use LOGO because it is on the curriculum by order of some higher authority, then a LOGO may be taught which lacks the essential features of LOGO. Exercises in turtle graphics may be set and marked in the same way as sums or spelling tests. This is not to say that such a practice is necessarily entirely useless, although some will consider it to be. But it is certainly using a powerful engine to achieve a minor or even trivial objective. "Turtle texts", whether in the form of books or sets of work cards, require to be treated with care, so that work with LOGO does not become a slog through cards 1 to 18, creating odd shapes for no apparent reason, with marks at the end for how many have been done and how neat they are.

Again, this is not to say that structure is unnecessary; but that any structure adopted should give plenty of room for the spontaneity and the excitement which exploration with LOGO can generate.

Another possible danger is that LOGO becomes identified with primary schools or with the "less able" or those with learning difficulties. This misapprehension is linked to the ideas that LOGO is only turtle graphics, and that turtle graphics are only for the handicapped or the very young. (There is also possibly an element of the view that learning, particularly at the secondary level, should be stern and hard rather than enjoyable and stimulating.) The notion that, for instance, average and above average students in secondary schools should study computer programming through BASIC or COMAL, whilst the "poorer" students may use LOGO because they can make pictures easily, displays a sad and fundamental ignorance about LOGO.

A serious possible outcome, should such views become widespread is that the current discontinuity between computer activities in primary and secondary schools may continue, with LOGO classed in popular educational belief as a primary school activity. In fact LOGO offers a major element of continuity across the age ranges. Its particular application and use will change from the infants through to the upper levels of the secondary school (and beyond), but the principles of its operation remain the same. LOGO could become a major factor in removing the disparity of computer experience which frequently exists between primary and secondary schools.

LOGO's acceptance is so far only partial, and many LOGO possibilities have still to emerge from the stage of experimentation and development. Control technology and music are those areas nearest to this emergence into general use. LOGO is beginning to be adopted as a language in which to teach good programming practice. However, other facilities such as language-processing and simulation still have some way to go, and more problems to overcome.

Problems with language-processing and the whole area of developing software in LOGO draws attention to a basic limitation on current LOGO progress: the capabilities of the machinery. With the current generation of microcomputers encountered in schools, any attempt to construct something beyond a fairly small-scale list-processing system leads to the designer becoming increasingly concerned with memory conservation and worried about the declining speed of execution. The conclusion to be drawn is that some LOGO facilities will not realise their full potential until hardware development has reached a stage which allows them to do so.

The current rate of hardware evolution suggests that this is not a long term problem and that within a few years the type of computers entering schools will be able to support comfortably the full range of LOGO facilities. New facilities will then of course be appearing on the horizon and entering the experimental phase. The next section will consider some of the possibilities which the future holds.

## NEW HORIZONS

The context for a view of future developments is the evolution of computing machinery. The current generation of school microcomputers is of the 8-bit variety, with a total addressable memory of 64K bytes. The earliest computers to appear in schools offered very limited amounts of user-available RAM (Random Access Memory, where current programs and information are held): 4, 8 or at most 16K. Now all the RAM that an 8-bit computer can give the user is being offered.

However, the sophistication and power which educators require from computer-based learning material has advanced as rapidly, if not more so. Colourful drill-and-practice exercises are no longer satisfactory as the novelty of the computer wears off, and serious questions are asked about what sort of productive learning environments computers can support. The potentialities of genuinely diagnostic programs, which do more than just count right and wrong answers, extensive simulations, which allow a high level of decision-making, and some of the learning environments supported by LOGO are realised, but the current generation of school microcomputers severely limits their practical implementation.

The next generation of school microcomputers will remove much of this limitation. They are based on 16-bit or even 32-bit chips, which makes them much faster than 8-bit computers, and gives them the ability to address much larger memories.

They will have bigger on-board memories, and memory will be easily expandable. The development of single chips with large memory capacities (64K and plus) makes this feature simple to implement. Ongoing reductions in the number of chips needed (as integration continues to increase) and in the price of computer memory per unit mean that this new generation of computers will remain within the price range which schools and school systems can afford.

These computers will be able to support improved facilities. They will be able to run larger programs without frequent disk-access to load small pieces of program. They will be able to support higher resolution graphics. They may offer parallel processing, the ability to carry out two or more processes simultaneously. They will have a wide array of communications links with the outside world and built-in interfaces. They will have enhanced sound-processing capacities.

How will LOGOs develop to take advantage of such improved facilities? Higher resolution graphics will mean that drawings with LOGO can become more detailed and more realistic, and can move into three dimensions. More complex list-processing systems will be supported, and therefore new command and control structures will emerge to make development of such systems as straightforward as possible. Examples might be new file-operating commands and array-handling. LOGO compilers will be offered so that large systems can be run as efficiently as possible after they have been developed. Links with the external environment will depend to some extent on developments in peripherals. Connections with synthesizers will produce powerful music processing capacities. Connections with lasers may lead to the creation of three-dimensional holographic turtle worlds filling whole rooms. In fact, none of these suggestions is based on speculation: all are available on computers still too expensive for the average school, or are well on the course of development.

An implication of the enhanced facilities which LOGOs will offer is that LOGO will move beyond its current largely educational context. The ability to model complex systems will have applications in business, administration, and systems planning and simulation in many areas. Graphics possibilities will have applications for design of all types. Music generation will have implications for the professional music world.

By some future stage it may well be that LOGO is no longer called LOGO. Its essential features may be incorporated in a computing environment which will supersede it. Recently-develped computer languages like Smalltalk and Boxer enable whole classes of objects with user-defined properties to be created: they could come to offer in this way the characteristics of a number of current computer environments. Those who see the value of what LOGO can offer will not mourn the eventual passing of LOGO if its successor makes available all that LOGO can, plus more, whilst retaining the accessibility and the creative and constructive potential which LOGO offers.

Looking specifically at education, we can ask what features LOGOs on the emerging generation of school computers will put at the disposal of teachers and pupils? Enhanced turtle graphics is clearly one such feature: one aspect of it will be greater clarity and detail; another may be the ability to view three-dimensional drawings from different positions; and more lifelike pictures and better animation could be further possibilities. An enhanced music facility, offering many simultaneous channels and a large variety of instrumental tones could have a significant impact on educational practice. Control and robotics applications are becoming a central part of computer education; these will become closely linked to command systems in LOGO, which permit easy and understandable use of all sorts of devices. Finally, a major area of expansion may well be in applications programs written in LOGO: complex simulations of mechanical, social, historical, linguistic and other types of system; interactive tutorial programs, which learn from interaction with the user as well as systematically diagnosing his/her errors; and databases which can be built up and queried through almost conversational processes.

## THE HUMAN CONTEXT

Because the future is the future, nothing can be predicted with certainty. But it does seem to most observers that LOGO has a very important place in the educational computer-use of tomorrow.

We mentioned right at the beginning of this book LOGO's roots in artificial intelligence. As the computer's power to support software which displays features of "intelligent" behaviour increases, the influence of artificial intelligence work upon thinking and development work in education will increase, and computing environments which arise from activity in artificial intelligence will become more important.

It would be wrong however to end on an image suggestive of computers aping the behaviour of humans (or at least notional intelligent humans), for it is imperative that the overpowering image of the omnicompetent machine does not blind us to the priority of human beings and human values. Education is above all a humanistic concern, an endeavour to help develop good human beings, people with the characteristics of people. Moral decisions about the desirable characteristics of human beings, whether made positively or by default, will guide the application of computer technology, just like other products created by man. LOGO carries moral implications, since it can encourage responsibility and initiative, co-operation and interaction, creativity and experiment, action and reflection. But it will only realise these moral potentialities if used positively and sensitively by teachers who share the moral goals.

Moral and social implications are closely linked, since moral goals represent desirable behavioural characteristics, and human behaviour is inescapably and fundamentally social in nature. History also shows us that man's use of his tools, and his relationships with other men are intimately connected. The computer, like the railway or the nuclear reactor, will in its usage reflect people's relationships with each other.

As it is currently used, LOGO is a vehicle for interaction between people. It is a frequent observation of LOGO-using teachers and observers in their classrooms that LOGO activity stimulates and supports discussion, debate, collective reasoning (i.e. thinking out something as a group), and co-operation. Underpinning this activity lies the relationship between the user and the computer. As an educational environment, LOGO places the decision-making responsibility squarely on the user and anyone who can help him. The user controls the computer, and having to make the decisions means having to think things out and if necessary calling in more advice and opinion to help reach a conclusion. Contrast this with the situation where the child at the computer is a passive receptor of information and a slavish obeyer of commands issued peremptorily and with no concern for his individuality (children are not fooled by programs which ask for their first names and gratuitously insert them at intervals throughout the run).

In LOGO then, there is a powerful vehicle for constructive and creative learning. Along with other teaching and learning tools and strategies promoting the same type of learning environment, LOGO can be part of an educational experience which promotes thinking, responsibility, and humane values. In this educational experience we must all, whether teachers, parents or children, take on the role of learners, and keep to our quest for understanding and wisdom.

# Chapter 17

# LOGO RESOURCES

This chapter presents a selection of items which the LOGO-user or potential LOGO-user may find useful. LOGO materials are beginning to appear in large numbers, and a list of resources cannot therefore hope to include everything or be completely up to date. Some comment has been made on most of the items listed; these comments are however offered as personal opinions only. Readers may find their own judgements different.

Contents of this chapter are as follows:

## A. BOOKS

For ease of reference, this section has been divided into a number of parts, and books placed in the part which seemed most appropriate. However, several of the books included could easily have been listed in more than one part; the placement of a book in one part does not indicate that it has no relevance to other parts. Within each part, books have been arranged as much as possible in order of publication date. After the ISBN, (P) indicates a paperback edition, (H) a hardback edition.

### i. Artificial Intelligence and LISP

For those who wish to look at the general context in which LOGO has appeared, some reading on artificial intelligence is a must. The following have been found particularly useful.

Joseph Weizenbaum,
Computer Power and Human Reason
San Francisco W.H. Freeman 1976
ISBN 0 7167 0463 3 (P) 0 7167 0464 1 (H)
A powerful warning that computers and their activities are human products with awesome implications for humanity.

P.H. Winston, Artificial Intelligence
Reading, MA./London Addison Wesley 1977
ISBN 0 201 08454 6 (H)
A comprehensive and readable college textbook which gives a good summary of the artificial intelligence field, and includes a good introduction to LISP.

Margaret Boden,
Artificial Intelligence and Natural Man
Brighton Harvester Press 1977
ISBN 0 85527 700 9 (P) 0 85527 435 2 (H)
A comprehensive university textbook.

Pamela McCorduck, Machines who Think
San Francisco W.H. Freeman 1979
ISBN 0 7167 1135 4 (P) 0 7167 1072 2 (H)
A very readable and stimulating account of the development of A.I. including some lively pen-portraits of the key figures.

Alan Bundy (ed.),
Artificial Intelligence: An Introductory Course
Edinburgh University Press 1980
ISBN 0 85224 410 X (P)
A university textbook for a first course in Artificial Intelligence. Programs are given in LISP and in LOGO.

John Haugeland (ed.) Mind Design
Cambridge, MA./London MIT Press 1981
ISBN 0 262 58052 7 (P) 0 262 08110 5 (H)
A collection of papers by important A.I. figures. Difficult, but worthwhile material to dip into for study purposes.

Elaine Rich, Artificial Intelligence
London McGraw-Hill 1983 ISBN 0 07 052261 8 (P)
A fairly comprehensive college textbook.

Tim O'Shea & John Self,
Learning and Teaching with Computers
Brighton Harvester Press 1983
ISBN 0 7108 0665 5 (P)
An interesting and readable consideration some of the applications of artificial intelligence to education and training.

Donald Michie & Rory Johnston,
The Creative Computer
London Viking 1984 ISBN 0 670 80060 0 (H)
London Penguin 1985 ISBN 0 14 022465 3 (P)
A wide-ranging and fascinating survey of the many areas in which "intelligent" computers may be employed.

Sherry Turkle, The Second Self
London Granada 1984
ISBN 0 246 12568 3 (P) 0 246 12216 1 (H)
A detailed and concerned analysis of "computer culture" and its effects on the way in which people think and behave. Not a short book or an easy read, but compelling and thought-producing.

BYTE magazine, Vol. 10, No. 4, April, 1985
Peterborough, NH. BYTE Publications
(Special Issue on Artificial Intelligence.)
An collection of useful articles by key figures.

There are several introductions to LISP available, most of them of very recent publication. Here are some of them.

W.D. Maurer,
<u>The Programmer's Introduction to LISP</u>
London Macdonald and Jane's 1975
ISBN 0 356 03980 3 (H)
New York American Elsevier 1975
ISBN 0 444 19572 6 (H)

P.H. Winston & B.K.P. Horn, <u>LISP</u>
Reading, MA./London Addison-Wesley 1981
ISBN 0 201 08329 9 (P)

I. Danicic, <u>Lisp Programming</u>
Oxford Blackwell 1983 ISBN 0 632 01181 5 (P)

Tony Hasemer, <u>A Beginners Guide to LISP</u>
Reading, MA./London Addison-Wesley 1984
ISBN 0 201 14634 7 (P)

Steve Oakley, <u>LISP for Micros</u>
London Newnes 1984 ISBN 0 408 01442 3 (P)

Christian Queinnec, <u>LISP</u>
London Macmillan 1984 ISBN 0 333 36795 2 (P)

David S. Touretzky, <u>LISP</u>
New York Harper & Row 1984 ISBN 0 06 046657 X (P)

Robert Wilensky, <u>LISPcraft</u>
New York/London Norton 1984 ISBN 0 393 95442 0 (P)

## ii. The Philosophy of LOGO

This section includes works which concentrate on thinking about LOGO, its underlying assumptions and its wider implications.

Seymour Papert, <u>Mindstorms</u>
Brighton Harvester Press 1980
ISBN 0 71080 472 5 (P) 0 85527 163 9 (H)
The original LOGO classic, and a compulsive read, which discusses the philosophy of LOGO and its implications for children, schools and society.

Robert P. Taylor (editor),
<u>The Computer in the School: Tutor, Tool, Tutee</u>
New York Teachers College Press 1980
ISBN 0 8077 2611 7 (P)
A collection of articles on computers in learning by Alfred Bork, Thomas Dwyer, Arthur Luehrmann, Seymour Papert and Patrick Suppes. Different approaches are well contrasted.

Horacio Reggini,
<u>Alas para la Mente</u> (in Spanish)
Buenos Aires Ediciones Galapago 1982
ISBN 950 562 058 6 (P)
<u>LOGO, des Ailes pour l'Esprit</u> (in French)
Paris CEDIC/Fernand Nathan 1983
ISBN 2 712 0514 5 (P)
This excellent and readable consideration of LOGO and its cultural implications is not available in English, but ought to be. References are given so that those who can read Spanish or French may have access to it. Worth getting hold of even if your Spanish/French is not too good, as it includes many stimulating LOGO ideas and programs.

John Allen, Ruth Davis, & John Johnson
<u>Thinking About [TLC] LOGO</u>
New York Holt, Reinhart & Winston 1984
ISBN 0 03 064116 0 (P)
Holt-Saunders International Edition
ISBN 4 8337 0188 X (P)
A thoughtful and entertaining discussion with numerous examples of the ideas which lie behind LOGO programming. Well illustrated!

<u>iii. LOGO tutorials</u>

There are now plenty of LOGO textbooks on the market. We consider here those we think are of particular value.

Harold Abelson, <u>LOGO for the Apple II</u>
Peterborough, NH. BYTE/McGraw-Hill 1982
ISBN 0 07 000426 9 (P)
(Red cover - deals with Terrapin LOGO)
Harold Abelson, <u>Apple LOGO</u>
Peterborough, NH. BYTE/McGraw-Hill 1982
ISBN 0 07 000425 0 (P)
(Blue Cover - deals with Apple/LCSI LOGO)
An excellent introduction to LOGO, whatever implementation you have, by one of those at the centre of its development.

David Thornburg, <u>Discovering Apple Logo</u>
Reading, MA./London Addison-Wesley 1983
ISBN 0 201 07769 8 (P)
An imaginative and stimulating introduction to the possibilities of turtle graphics, with plenty of good examples.

## Logo Resources


Peter Ross, *LOGO Programming*
London Addison-Wesley 1983
ISBN 0 201 14637 1 (P)
An excellent book by one of the Edinburgh LOGO group; not a book for the absolute beginner, but a collection of powerful techniques and ideas. Be prepared to think hard as you use it; you'll find it's worth the effort.

Gary Bitter & Nancy Ralph Watson,
*Apple Logo Primer*
Reston, VA Reston Publishing Co. 1983
ISBN 0 8359 0314 1 (P)
Systematic, but not as attractive or inspiring than the introductions already mentioned.

Anne McDougall, Tony Adams and Pauline Adams,
*Learning LOGO on the Apple II*
Sydney Prentice Hall of Australia 1983
ISBN 0 7248 0732 2 (P)
*Learning LOGO on the Commodore 64*
London/Melbourne Pitman 1984
ISBN 0 85896 162 8 (P)
Good introductions, giving plenty of help to the beginner in both turtle graphics and list-processing.

David Thornburg, *Computer Art and Animation*
Reading, MA./London Addison-Wesley 1984
ISBN 0 201 07958 5 (P) Different versions available for different computers - the ISBN given is for the Texas Instruments TI99/4A.
Takes a lot longer to cover less ground than the same author's *Discovering Apple Logo* .

Roger Haigh & Loren Radford,
*LOGO for Apple Computers*
New York Wiley 1984 ISBN 0 471 88023 X (P)
An attractive introduction.

Richard Lambert,
*LOGO (and more) for the Commodore 64*
Beaverton, OR Dilithium Press 1984
ISBN 0 88056 348 6 (P)
Inviting, but disappointingly thin introduction.

Donald Martin, Stephen Prata & Marijane Paulsen
*Apple Logo Programming Primer*
Indianapolis Sams 1984 ISBN 0 672 22342 2 (P)
A detailed account, with plenty sample programs.

Boris Allan, Introducing LOGO
London Granada 1984 ISBN 0 246 12323 0 (P)
An enthusiastic and stimulating work, which covers a lot of interesting ground in a short space. Well worth acquiring.

Boris Allan,
Building with LOGO on the Commodore 64
London Sunshine Books 1984
ISBN 0 946408 48 3 (P)
More of the same variety as the same author's Introducing LOGO . Good ideas on most pages.

Anne Sparrowhawk, LOGO
London Pan Books 1984 ISBN 0 330 28676 5 (P)
Contains some useful material.

Graham Field, LOGO on the Sinclair Spectrum
London Macmillan 1985 ISBN 0 33 38376 1 (P)
A concise introduction which manages to convey the power of LOGO and its wide range of applications. Written for Sinclair LOGO, but since this is a standard LCSI implementation, the programs presented are easily translated into other LOGOs.

Martin Lesser, Logo for Micros
London Newnes 1985 ISBN 0 408 01510 1 (P)
Written it would seem for scientists and engineers, but contains plenty of interesting material which would be of value to anyone wanting to see what LOGO can do. It includes a simulation of BASIC in LOGO which could form a useful conversation-piece.

Peter Ross, Logo Programming for the IBM PC
Wokingham, UK. Addison-Wesley 1985
ISBN 0 201 15028 X (P)
A version for the IBM PC of Ross's excellent LOGO Programming , mentioned above. Includes commands and procedures for IBM PC LOGO, Dr LOGO, and Waterloo LOGO.

## iv. LOGO for teachers

It is not always easy to tell what sort of audience some books are aimed at. Those in this section seem to be directed towards interesting teachers in learning and then using LOGO.

BYTE magazine, Vol. 7, No. 8, August, 1982
Peterborough, NH. BYTE Publications

(Special Issue on LOGO.)
An excellent collection of articles on LOGO by major figures in the LOGO community which ought to be published as a book.

J. Dale Burnett, LOGO: An Introduction
Morris Plains, NJ. Creative Computing Press 1982
ISBN 0 916688 39 9 (P)
Printed in very big type under the apparent impression that all teachers are short-sighted, and running to only 67 pages, this is nevertheless a thought-provoking and open-ended LOGO taster.

A. Martin, D. Radburn, R. Keeling, & J. Lane (eds)
Microscope LOGO Special
London Heinemann/Ginn 1983
ISBN 0 602 22692 9 (P)
A collection of accounts of research and teaching with LOGO, largely by teachers. A slim volume, but well worth tracking down.

Carolyn Green & Christi Jaeger,
Teacher, Kids, and Logo
Irvine, CA. Educomp 1983 (2nd ed. 1984)
ISBN 0 9612226 1 1 (P)
Attempts to develop a turtle graphics curriculum through most of the primary school age range (Grades K - 6). Supplies a host of teaching ideas, and even lesson plans, although many teachers will prefer to develop the ideas in their own style.

Donna Bearden, Kathleen Martin, & Jim Muller,
The Turtle's Sourcebook
Reston, VA. Reston Publishing Co. 1983
ISBN 0 8359 7890 7 (P)
Largely consists of a collection of copiable worksheets, notices and diagrams for use in teaching with turtle graphics. For teachers to dip into at their discretion.

Ray Hammond, Forward 100
London Viking 1984 ISBN 0 670 80039 2 (H)
A comprehensive "background and resources" book, which covers, readably and in considerable detail, many of the questions surrounding LOGO and its use. An extremely useful LOGO resource in itself.

Peter Goodyear,
LOGO: a guide to learning through programming
Chichester, UK Ellis Horwood 1984
ISBN 0 85312 711 5 (P) 0 85312 608 9 (H)

Adopts the interesting strategy of offering a programming course in a notional LOGO so that everybody will have the same difficulty translating the examples into real LOGOs. Nevertheless, a useful introduction for students, with background information, a sound introduction to the language, and a long bibliography.

Anne Moller,
LOGO Programming; a practical guide for parents and teachers
London Century Communications 1984
ISBN 0 7126 0220 8 (P)
Contains some useful material.

Serafim Gascoigne
Microchild: Learning through LOGO
London Macmillan 1984 ISBN 0 333 37450 9 (P)
An disappointingly thin introduction.

v. LOGO for children

These books are all aimed at introducing beginners, particularly children, gradually to LOGO.

Daniel Watt, Learning with LOGO
New York McGraw-Hill 1982 ISBN 0 07 068570 3 (P)
(Terrapin Logo for the Apple II edition)
Daniel Watt, Learning with Apple LOGO
New York McGraw-Hill 1984 ISBN 0 07 068571 1 (P)
(Apple Logo (LCSI) version)
A weighty but readable introduction, aimed at children of secondary school age, but very useful to any LOGO learner. Lots of useful material and good ideas.

Donna Bearden, 1 2 3 My Computer and Me
Reston, VA Reston Publishing Co. 1983
ISBN 0 8359 5228 2 (P)
Nicely produced but very expensive workbook for young children.

John Cunliffe, Play LOGO
London Andre Deutsch 1984
ISBN 0 233 977 18 X (P)
Designed for use by parents and children together, this book manages to be exciting and stimulating, without becoming too directive. Good for whetting the appetite.

As LOGO is adopted by more school systems, a number of what one could describe as "turtle graphics textbooks" are appearing. Some teachers may find them useful; for others, they may be too directive, with too much instruction and not enough exploration. Look carefully before you buy. Here are some examples:

Pamela Sharp, Turtlesteps
Bowie, MD. Brady 1984 ISBN 0 89303 906 3 (P)

Harold Bailey, Kathleen Brautigan & Trudy Doran,
Apple LOGO: Activities for Exploring Turtle Graphics
Bowie, MD. Brady 1984 ISBN 0 89303 312 X (P)

Joan Webb, Peter von Mertens & Maggie Holmes,
Explorer's Guide to Apple LOGO
Hasbrouck Heights, NJ. Hayden 1984
ISBN 0 8104 6227 3 (P)

LOGO teaching packages for children are also beginning to appear. These may include sets of work cards, games, puppets, badges, handbooks, and software. Compare the contents and the price with your exact requirements, as some of these can be very expensive.

A teacher-training pack entitled "Posing and Solving Problems with LOGO" has been produced by the MEP (Microelectronics Education Programme) Primary Project. It is a collection of discrete items, some of which may be found more useful than others. To be dipped into and used as it suits your objectives. The address is: MEP Primary Project, St. James' Hall, King Alfred's College, Winchester, Hampshire SO22 4NR.

## vi. Specialised LOGO work

This section includes some books focusing on particular areas of LOGO use.

Paul Goldenberg,
Special Technology for Special Children
Baltimore University Park Press 1979
ISBN 0 839 11441 9 (P)
Considers the way in which intelligent technology (including turtles) can help children with learning difficulties due to physical handicaps or other problems.

Harold Abelson & Andrea diSessa, Turtle Geometry
Cambridge, MA./London MIT Press 1981
ISBN 0 262 01063 1 (H)
Develops mathematical thinking, through the medium of turtle geometry, from introductory to graduate level.

Donald Martin & Jennifer Ann Martin,
88 Apple Logo Programs
Indianapolis Sams 1984 ISBN 0 672 22343 0 (P)
A collection of utilities and other programs, including games, graphic designs, a database, and a flying machine microworld. It can, with care, be profitably dipped into, but not a book to be used as an introduction to LOGO or to be put in front of a beginner.

Andre Myx, Plus loin avec LOGO
Paris CEDIC/Nathan 1984 ISBN 2 7124 0572 2 (P)
If you can read French, this book presents a good introduction to list-processing with LOGO. French versions of LOGO are referred to, but the primitives are fairly obvious in meaning, and procedures can be translated without too much difficulty.

## vii. Research on LOGO

As was indicated in Chapter 1, there is a lot of research on LOGO in progress. Notes at the end of Chapter 1 included addresses of some centres of LOGO research from which publications can be obtained. However, reports on work with LOGO are appearing in a wide variety of journals and other publications.

There are a few LOGO periodicals. The newsletters of the National Logo Exchange and the Young People's Logo Association contain some accounts of research. National Logo Exchange also maintains a register of LOGO research, which is sent to members. Addresses of these organisations are given in Section C of this chapter. LOGO Almanack , published by the British LOGO User Group, contains accounts of LOGO research and experience, and is not restricted to British material. An important source of current LOGO research is the proceedings of the annual LOGO conferences at MIT; the first of these was held in 1984. LOGO articles are encountered in The Computing Teacher and Classroom Computer Learning in the U.S., and Microscope and

Computers in Schools in the U.K., as well as specialist journals in particular areas such as Artificial Intelligence, Mathematics Education, and so on.

LOGO Almanack
Volume 1 (1983) contains papers from the 1983 conference of BLUG; Volume 2 (1984) contains papers from the 1984 BLUG conference, as well as other research reports and discussions. Gives a good idea of current LOGO activity in the U.K. Details about subscription and purchase of back issues from: Allan Martin, Co-ordinating Editor, LOGO Almanack , Department of Learning Resources, St. Andrew's College of Education, Bearsden, Glasgow G61 4QA, Scotland.

Renata J. Sorkin (ed.),
Pre-proceedings of the 1984 National LOGO Conference
Laboratory for Computer Science
Massachusetts Institute of Technology 1984
A good indication of the current state of thinking about LOGO in North America. A large collection of short papers, together with abstracts of current LOGO activities and an up-to-date bibliography make this a very useful resource which provides plenty of food for thought.

The Computing Teacher
ICCE, University of Oregon, 1787 Agate Street, Eugene, OR 97403-1923, U.S.A.

Classroom Computer Learning
5615 West Cermak Road, Cicero, IL 60650, U.S.A.

Microscope
is the journal of MAPE (Micros and Primary Education), whose address is:
c/o Mrs G. Jones, 76 Sudbrooke Holme Drive, Sudbrooke, Lincolnshire, England.

Computers in schools
is the journal of MUSE (Microcomputer USers in Education), whose address is:
P.O. Box 43, Hull HU1 2HD, England.

## B. SOFTWARE AND HARDWARE

### i. LOGO implementations

LOGO implementations are now available for most popular microcomputers. A process of constant upgrading of LOGO implementations is going on which means that comments below may be quickly overtaken by events.

ACT APRICOT: Two LOGOs are available for the Apricot F1, Dr LOGO or Logotron LOGO.

AMSTRAD: A version of Dr LOGO is available for the CPC 464 with disk system.

APPLE: There are two versions of LOGO for the Apple II, Apple LOGO and Terrapin LOGO; these are fairly similar, except that the Terrapin version includes music generation and permits machine code routines to be included in LOGO programs. Krell LOGO is almost identical to Terrapin LOGO. A "Sprite LOGO" developed by LCSI is available which offers turtle graphics with sprites. MacLOGO is available for the Mackintosh, as is ExperLogo, a compiled LOGO which includes array handling and three-dimensional "Bunny Graphics".

ATARI: Atari LOGO was prepared by LCSI and is similar to Apple LOGO, but offering in addition music, sprites (the Atari has "hardware sprites" which do not require large amounts of computer memory to support them), and a very useful WHEN construction. With their current low prices, Atari computers are well worth consideration as dedicated LOGO machines, particularly with such a good LOGO available for them.

BBC (ACORN): There are currently four versions of LOGO available for the BBC (Acorn) microcomputer. Logotron LOGO is close to the LCSI standard found on other computers, whilst LSL Logo is closer to the Edinburgh LOGO available on the RML computers. The other versions are Open LOGO, developed at the Open University and included in some of its distance learning packages, and Acornsoft LOGO. Add-on Sprite Boards are being developed to give sprite facilities to some of these implementations. The full range of the BBC micro's music facilities and operating system calls are available through LOGO.

COMMODORE: CBM LOGO for the Commodore 64 is virtually identical to Terrapin LOGO for the Apple; however it also supports sprites (although these are software sprites which do consume memory).

IBM: The development of LOGO for the IBM PC may seem irrelevant to schools now; however it does indicate that a major computer manufacturer sees LOGO as perhaps having significance beyond the educational. It will also enable the possibilities of LOGO on a 16-bit computer, with much greater memory addressable than on currently-used educational computers, to be demonstrated. There are currently several LOGOs available for the IBM PC, the most notable being IBM PC LOGO, an LCSI version, Dr LOGO, and Waterloo LOGO.

KAYPRO: TLC LOGO is available for Kaypro computers, and an additional colour graphics board allows sprites to be supported.

RESEARCH MACHINES: RML LOGO for the 380Z and 480Z has been developed at Edinburgh and varies slightly in terms of commands used from the others. A LOGO is available for the RML Nimbus computer which offers parallel processing, with up to 8 processes running simultaneously and capable of passing information and messages to each other.

SINCLAIR: An LCSI LOGO is available for the Sinclair Spectrum, and a version of Terrapin LOGO for the QL computer.

TANDY: Tandy Color LOGO is something of a disappointment, offering only turtle graphics. It offers a good turtle graphics package, but does not offer the range and flexibility of other possibilities which full LOGOs possess. Whether it should be termed a real LOGO is open to dispute.

TEXAS INSTRUMENTS: One of the earliest microcomputer LOGOs was implemented on the Texas Instruments TI99. It included a sprite capability.

## ii. Turtles

The "Edinburgh Turtle", for a long time the only

British turtle available, is offered in two forms, the "attached" version with a long umbilical cord familiar to British turtle-using teachers, and a new "unattached" radio-controlled version. It has a simple dome-shape, and can therefore be easily given an identity as hedgehog, beetle, space-invader or whatever is desired. It is available from: Jessop Microelectronics Ltd., Unit 5, 7 Long Street, London E2 8HN

The Valiant Turtle is of the unattached variety, control being maintained via an infra-red beam. Long battery-charging periods are necessary before use, but these can take place overnight. It has a deliberate turtle shape, which makes it easy to see which way it is going, but makes it difficult to see it as anything but a turtle. Available from: E.J. Arnold & Son Ltd., Parkside Lane, Dewsbury Road, Leeds LS11 5TD.

The Zero 2 robot is a turtle of the attached variety, at lower cost than the Edinburgh or Valiant types. It is extremely accurate, and can also follow a black line. Expansion modules will allow collision-detection, speech and /or sound generation, hole- and edge-detection, attachment of a pickup arm, and an infra-red remote control link. Available from: Intergalactic Robots Ltd., Unit 208, Highbury Workshops, 22 Highbury Grove, London N5 2EE.

The Terrapin Turtle II, developed at MIT, possesses touch-sensing abilities as well as movement. It is available from: Terrapin Inc., 380 Green Street, Cambridge, MA 02139, U.S.A.

The BBC Buggy can be used as a turtle, and includes a bar-code reader, light-sensor, and touch-sensors. Available from: Economatics Ltd., 4 Orgreave Crescent, Dore House Industrial Estate, Handsworth, Sheffield S13 9NQ.

## C. CONTACTS

LOGO groups are now being established in many countries. The following list therefore only represents some, and is now probably out of date. Contact BLUG, NLX or your nearest group to find contacts in countries not included here.

Logo Resources

U.K.: BLUG
c/o London New Technology Centre, 86-100 St. Pancras Way, London NW1 9ES
BLUG (British LOGO Users Group) was founded towards the end of 1982. It publishes a quarterly newsletter Logos, a children's magazine Turtle Tracks and an annual journal, LOGO Almanack, and organises regional meetings and an annual LOGO conference. Being the first LOGO group in Europe, BLUG has attracted members from throughout Western Europe, and also from Australia and New Zealand. Its annual conference is the major British LOGO gathering.

U.S.A.: The major U.S. LOGO groups are:
National Logo Exchange
P.O. Box 5341, Charlottesville, VA 22905
NLX produces a monthly newsletter and maintains an index of LOGO research.

Young Peoples Logo Association
1208 Hillsdale Drive, Richardson, TX 75081
YPLA produces two newsletters, Turtle News (for the under-18's) and Logo Newsletter, and maintains an on-line bulletin board.

FOLLK (Friends of LISP/Logo and Kids)
436 Arballo Drive, San Francisco, CA 94132
FOLLK publishes a quarterly magazine, FOLLK-Lore and maintains a LOGO bulletin board, "FOLLK-Net".

Canada: ECOO/SIGLOGO (Special Interest Group on LOGO of the Educational Computing Organisation of Ontario), c/o Faculty of Education, Queen's University, Kingston, Ontario K71 3N6, Canada
Produces a newsletter Logophile.

France:
Association Francaise des Utilisateurs de Logo
12 rue de la Montagne Ste Genevieve, 75005 Paris
AFUL was set up on the model of BLUG, and produces a very lively magazine LOG on which appears every two months.

GREPACIFIC
51 Boulevard des Batignolles, 75008 Paris
GREPACIFIC was founded by French LOGO researchers, and publishes reports of research in schools with LOGO.

Netherlands: LOGO Centrum Nederland
Postbus 1408, 6501 BK Nijmegen, The Netherlands

West Germany: German LOGO Group
c/o Stephen Molyneux, Innosoft GmbH, Innocentiastr. 31, 2000 Hamburg 13, West Germany.
South America: Asociacion Amigos de LOGO
Salguero 2969, Buenos Aires, 1425 Argentina.
Organises conferences, maintains liaison between LOGO interest groups throughout latin America, and produces a regular bulletin.

Japan: Two LOGO magazines are available.
Logosome Z's appears twice a year, mostly in Japanese but with some material in English. Available from: Setsuko Abe, Logosome Z's, Geodesic Inc., Parkheight 402, 1091 Kumagawa, Fussa-Shi, Tokyo, Japan.
LOGO is a monthly, all in Japanese, Available from: Hiroyoshi Goto, Bynas Division, Uny Co. Ltd., 3F Dainagoya Building, 28-123 Chome Meieki, Nakamura-Ku, Nagoya, 450 Japan.

# INDEX

Index